Women of the Constitution

WIVES OF THE SIGNERS

Janice E. McKenney

A Project of the District of Columbia Daughters of the
American Revolution

ROWMAN & LITTLEFIELD
Lanham • Boulder • New York • London

Published by Rowman & Littlefield
A wholly owned subsidiary of The Rowman & Littlefield Publishing Group, Inc.
4501 Forbes Boulevard, Suite 200, Lanham, Maryland 20706
www.rowman.com

16 Carlisle Street, London W1D 3 BT, United Kingdom

British Library Cataloguing in Publication Information Available

Library of Congress Cataloging-in-Publication Data
The hardback edition of this book was previously cataloged by the Library of Congress as
follows:
McKenney, Janice E., 1942–
    Women of the Constitution : wives of the signers / Janice E. McKenney.
        p. cm.
    "A Project of the District of Columbia Daughters of the American Revolution."
    Includes bibliographical references and index.
    1. United States. Constitution—Signers—Biography. 2. Statesmen's spouses—United
States—Biography. 3. United States—History—1783–1815—Biography. 4. United
States. Constitutional Convention (1787). 5. Founding Fathers of the United States. I.
Daughters of the American Revolution. District of Columbia. II. Title.
    E302.5.M35 2013
    973.09'9—dc23
    [B]   2012024619

ISBN 978-0-8108-8498-4 (cloth : alk. paper)
ISBN 978-1-4422-4439-9 (pbk. : alk. paper
ISBN 978-0-8108-8499-1 (ebook)

Printed in the United States of America

Contents

Illustrations

Preface

Thirty-nine men signed the Constitution in 1787. At the time, twenty-six of them were married. Four were widowed, and six had yet to marry for the first time. Abraham Baldwin of Georgia, Daniel of St. Thomas Jenifer from Maryland, and Nicholas Gilman of New Hampshire never married at all. Several of the signers married more than once, as did at least five of their wives. In all, the stories of forty-three wives are related here.

This book consists of essays on each of the wives, as well as "vital statistics," where known: name, birth, parents' names, marriages, children, and death. A brief documented biography follows, after which a bibliography is given. If the subject of the essay left any letters or other papers, the location is noted at the beginning of the bibliography. The bibliographies generally refer to published works, although dissertations are sometimes cited; the endnotes, however, often include archival material containing some reference to the individual.

An appendix lists the residences associated with the wives of the signers, including references to websites containing photographs and additional information.

The biggest difficulty in preparing this publication was source material. For some wives, such as Dolley Madison and Martha Washington, many biographies have been published, creating problems in reducing the essays to a size comparable to other entries. And for some—Elizabeth Garnett Bassett and Rebecca Call Gorham, for example—there are almost no extant sources. Perhaps future researchers will uncover unexplored papers hidden in libraries or archives that will shed further light on the lives of these women.

The lives of these women spanned about 150 years, from the turn of the eighteenth century and the birth of Deborah Read Rogers Franklin to the middle of the nineteenth century and the death of Elizabeth Schuyler Hamilton. Management of their homes and families was the mainstay of their existence. Most had middle- or upper-class backgrounds, were fairly well educated for the time, and fulfilled their roles admirably. In an age when girls often married young, the average age of first marriage for these women was twenty-three. The youngest bride, Mary Alsop King, was only sixteen, but at least six were over thirty.

Only four wives were childless, and three of those women were older, second wives. Susannah French Livingston bore the most children—thirteen—but the average number of offspring per wife was a little over five.[1] However, only about two-thirds of these children survived to adulthood. Indeed, two of the women—Elizabeth Higbee Brearley and Martha Dandridge Custis Washington—outlived all of their offspring. Death from childbirth was far from uncommon, affecting at least six of the forty-three wives and perhaps shortening the lives of others. Despite deaths in childbirth, the average age at death of these women was about fifty-nine. The youngest to die were Maria Apthorp Williamson at twenty-three and Mary Laurens Pinckney at twenty-four, both in childbirth. The last survivor of these wives, Eliza Hamilton, was the longest-lived; she died at ninety-seven, almost a hundred years after the death of Elizabeth Hartwell Sherman.

In an age when women were subject to their husbands, what, if anything, did these women contribute? As previously stated, management of the home and family was paramount and even more important to the signers because of the many separations necessitated by war and public service. To cite a popular example, without the management of the family finances and business ventures by Debby Franklin, it is unlikely that her husband, Benjamin, would have been able to spend so much time in public pursuits. Mary Middleton Butler, Mary Norris Dickinson, Sarah Middleton Pinckney, and Martha Washington all brought considerable wealth to their husbands and families. Ann Ennals Bassett brought religion, in the form of Methodism, influencing her husband to give up strong drink and free his slaves. George Clymer, Thomas Fitzsimons, and Rufus King all inherited much of the family businesses from their fathers-in-law. And a few—King, William Few, and Hugh Williamson—changed their residences to that of their wives. For the most part, given the available records, the marriages appear to have been solid. Even Eliza Hamilton never lost faith in her husband, who was not always faithful to her.

Note

1. Mary Beth Norton, *Liberty's Daughters: The Revolutionary Experience of American Women, 1750–1800* (Cornell, N.Y.: Cornell University Press, 1996); page 72 states that white women could expect to bear five to seven live children.

Acknowledgments

This project, which languished for many years, was originally begun by the District of Columbia Daughters of the American Revolution (D.C. DAR) during the administration of 1988–1990 state regent Damitra Meeds to commemorate the bicentennial of the signing of the Constitution. Much appreciation is given to Mrs. Meeds for her great interest and support in promoting the project despite the passage of so many years.

I would like to express my gratitude to Shari K. Thorne-Sulima, 2010–2012 state regent, whose state regent's project assisted with the publication of this book. Thanks also to each of our D.C. DAR honorary state regents who have nurtured its production through the years: Damitra Meeds, Bertha Clark, Doris French, Margaret Brewer, Veronica Miller, Martha Hilton, June Miller, Barbara Taylor, Margaret MacKenzie, Marlene Taggart, Adele Bowyer, and Priscilla Baker.

Julia Miller Rogers, 2012–2014 state regent, would like to express her appreciation to the many members whose love, dedication, and research brought this book to publication. The following D.C. Daughters made a dream become a reality: Catherine Ball, Mary Ann Barnes, Cornelia Bates, Emily Bennett, Marie Biereau, Ruth Browne, Myra Clark, Geraldean J. Colevas, Marian H. Cooley, Jean Crosby, Marcia Driesbach, Janet Earle, Ardis W. Finamore, Mildred Galloway, Margaret Gentges, Marcia Guzauskas, Amy Gilreath, Margaret Grieve, Eunice Haden, Diana Hale, Mildred Hand, Gayle Harris, Nancy Harris, Cindy Hays, Gladys Jackson, Betty Jane Jordan, Mary Kennedy, Doris Lequin, Helen Livingstone, June McCubbin, Dorothy Mercy, Emily Pardue, Alva Phelps, Ann Pippin, May Rose Robertson, Ann Schaeffer, Merva Schweikart, Doris Schulten, Ruth Stultz, Gladys Taylor, Claudine Thomas, Valerie H. Tompkins, Judith Vars, Elizabeth Vondersmith, Dorothy J. Werner, Lloyce West, Grace Whitson, and Adele Worthington. Incomplete record keeping during the many years of preparing this book may have resulted in names being omitted from this list, but appreciation is extended to all D.C. Daughters for making this publication possible.

In addition to the District Daughters, I would also like to express my appreciation to Martin Gordon, a longtime colleague, who now serves as a consultant to Scarecrow Press. A chance meeting at a military history luncheon led to his introducing me to Bennett Graff, senior acquisitions editor at Scarecrow Press, who enthusiastically accepted the manuscript. At the publisher, Jin Yu and Kellie Hagan ushered the manuscript through production, making many valuable suggestions and recommendations along the way.

There were many who assisted me in obtaining the illustrations for the book, but two deserve special mention. Jeff Joeckel, archivist for the National Register of Historic Places (National Park Service), was instrumental in obtaining many of the photographs of the residences pictured in the book, and Susan Grinols at the De Young Museum in San Francisco led me to the owner of the Mary Alsop King portrait. To these and all the other gallery and museum personnel who helped me illustrate the book, I am truly grateful.

Although this book has been the combined effort of a countless number of people, I alone am responsible for its content, including any errors that may be found.

* * *

The National Society Daughters of the American Revolution (NSDAR), founded in 1890, incorporated by an Act of Congress, and headquartered in Washington, D.C., is a nonprofit, nonpolitical volunteer women's hereditary service organization united in its mission of historic preservation, education, and patriotism. The District of Columbia State Society (D.C. DAR) was organized as one of the state societies of the NSDAR in 1901. In honor of the bicentennial of the Constitution in 1989, the D.C. DAR undertook to create a publication celebrating the wives of the signers of the Constitution of the USA. *Women of the Constitution: Wives of the Signers* is the fruit of many years of research, writing, and editing by countless dedicated members of the D.C. State Society.

Ann (Nancy) Ennals Bassett

Birth: c. 1752, Dorchester County, Maryland
Parents: Henry Ennals Jr. and Mary Nevitt
Marriage: 22 December 1774, Richard Bassett (1745–1815)
Children: Richard Ennals (1775–1776); Ann (Nancy) (1777–1854); Mary
             (c. 1780–1807)
Death: 20 March 1784

Ann Ennals was born about 1752 in Dorchester County, Maryland, to Mary and Henry Ennals Jr. The Ennals, a wealthy, old Maryland family, included Ann's uncle, Joseph, who was a judge. Ann, known as Nancy in the family, was one of five children: brothers Thomas and Henry (Harry) and sisters Catherine (Kitty) and Mary (Polly).[1] Their father died in 1760, when Ann was about eight years old.[2] Richard Bassett, who came from Cecil County, Maryland, read law in the office of Robert Goldsborough, a prominent attorney in Cambridge, Maryland, whose mother was an Ennals. It is likely that Ann met her future husband during his studies there. She and Richard Bassett were married on 22 December 1774 by the Reverend Samuel Keene, when Bassett was twenty-nine and Ann was about twenty-two.[3] At the time Bassett was an attorney, expert in property, libel, and inheritance law, practicing in Dover, Kent County, Delaware. Bassett was also a property owner at Bohemia Manor, Maryland, where he had inherited one thousand acres in 1765. In the year of his marriage, Bassett was appointed to the Kent County Committee of Correspondence, where he represented the conservative wing of the revolutionary movement against Great Britain. He was also the captain of a cavalry militia troop in Dover and served on the Delaware Council of Safety.[4] On 22 September 1775 the Bassetts became the parents of a son, Richard Ennals Bassett, who died the following February. On 20 August 1777 they had a daughter, named Ann after her mother and great-grandmother. Another daughter called Mary, after Ann Ennals's mother and sister, followed.[5]

In October 1776 Bassett was elected to the Legislative Council of Delaware (upper house), where he served until 1780.[6] In the meantime, Freeborn Garrettson, one of the early founders of Methodism in America, had met Ann's sister Kitty. Kitty fell in with the then schismatic evangelical faith and soon thereafter converted both her sisters, Nancy and Polly, and also their brother Henry. Ann's husband, Richard, was at first unimpressed. He even thought of picking up stakes and moving far away because of the "noisy Methodists."[7] In spite of these feelings, however, he became a good friend of Francis Asbury, the great Methodist itinerant preacher (later bishop), whom he met in 1778.[8] In 1780 Asbury reported that Ann Ennals Bassett, "a bright example of holiness," was in great distress but was soon comforted by her husband's conversion after a vision.[9] In January 1783 Garrettson reported he had visited "Sister Bassett, who in her affliction, is one of the happiest women I have met with a living witness of sanctification, whose soul seems to be continually wrapped in the flame of love."[10] Asbury and other prominent Methodists were frequent visitors, and in 1784 Bassett contributed $2,000 to the building of Wesley Chapel in Dover. The Bassetts, despite their wealth and prominence, lived simply. Their house and table were reported to be very plain, with no distilled liquor being served.[11] Nancy Bassett and her sisters were distinguished for their piety and zeal. Yet another Methodist minister, Thomas Ware, said that "the lady of Counselor Bassett, and her two sisters Mrs. Jones and Mrs. Ward, possessed an uncommon degree of the true missionary spirit, and greatly aided the young preachers."[12]

Ann Ennals Bassett died on 20 March 1784 when she was about thirty-two years of age. Garrettson, who was with her during her last illness, reported that she seemed "filled with the perfect love of God . . . and left the world praising God."[13] She left behind her husband and two young daughters. Her elder daughter, Ann Bassett, married on 11 February 1795 James Asheton Bayard (1767–1815), a prominent attorney, who also served in the U.S. Congress, both as a representative and a senator from Delaware.[14] The Bassetts' younger daughter, Mary, died unmarried in 1807, eight years before her father.[15]

Bassett was a slave-holder, but through his wife's influence he turned to Methodism and came to believe in the injustice of slavery. While serving in the Delaware House of the Assembly, Bassett introduced an act, which was adopted in 1787, making it easier to manumit slaves. He also manumitted his own slaves and joined an abolition society.[16]

Notes

1. Mary Nevitt and Henry Ennals Jr. were married in 1751. According to Benjamin F. Cummings, *The Ennals Family of Maryland* (Salt Lake City, 1916), Ann was the eldest child, making her birth most likely in 1752. Also see Dorchester County Land Records, Abstracts by James McAllister Jr., Maryland State Archives. William S. Muse, *Memoranda of the Leeds, Bozmans, Kerrs, Ennals . . .* (Chestertown, Md.: Hope H. Barroll, 1917), states that Ann's mother's name was Margaret Nevitt, but all other records show her name as Mary.

2. The will of Henry Ennals Jr. is dated 8 September 1760 and was probated 20 October of the same year. The original is in the Maryland State Archives, and a copy is in the NSDAR Library, Washington, D.C.

3. "Richard Bassett," *Maryland Genealogical Bulletin* 18 (April 1947): 21.

4. Gaspare J. Saladino, "Richard Bassett," *American National Biography* (New York: Oxford University Press, 1999), 2: 319–20.

5. Bassett-Freeman Collection, Manuscript Collection No. 75, family papers collected by Mrs. David O. Hamrick, 1986, Troup County Archives, LaGrange, Georgia. The papers do not include Mary's birth, but other records show that he had a daughter Mary who died in 1807. *Genealogical Record of the Bayard Family in America . . .* (Wilmington: Delaware Historical Society); "Richard Bassett," *Maryland Genealogical Bulletin*, 21.

6. John Lednum, *A History of the Rise of Methodism in America . . .* (Philadelphia: privately printed, 1859), 272.

7. Nathan Bangs, *The Life of the Rev. Freeborn Garrettson . . .* (New York: J. Emory and B. Waugh, 1830), 104–5; Lednum, *A History of the Rise of Methodism in America . . .*, 167, 249–50, 257, 261.

8. Elmer T. Clark et al., eds., *The Journal and Letters of Francis Asbury*, 3 vols. (Nashville: Abingdon Press, 1958), 1: 313.

9. Clark et al., *The Journal and Letters of Francis Asbury*, 1: 337–38; Bangs, *The Life of Rev. Freeborn Garrettson*, 105.

10. Bangs, *The Life of Rev. Freeborn Garrettson*, 224.

11. Bangs, *The Life of Rev. Freeborn Garrettson*, 246.

12. Lednum, *A History of the Rise of Methodism in America . . .*, 276.

13. Bangs, *The Life of Rev. Freeborn Garrettson*, 106; Clark et al., *The Journal and Letters of Francis Asbury*, 1: 656 (entry of 9 November 1790). "Richard Bassett," *Maryland Genealogical Bulletin*, 21, states that Ann Bassett died on 20 March 1784.

14. Leon deValinger Jr. and Virginia E. Shaw, eds., *A Calendar of Ridgely Family Letters, 1741–1899 . . .*, 3 vols. (Dover: privately printed, 1948), 1: 299.

15. deValinger and Shaw, *A Calendar of Ridgely Family Letters*, 1: 277. Newspaper records in the Maryland State Archives show that Mary Bassett died on 27 August 1807.

16. Saladino, "Richard Bassett," 2: 320.

Bibliography

Bangs, Nathan. *The Life of the Rev. Freeborn Garrettson . . .* , 2nd ed. New York: J. Emory and B. Waugh, 1830.

Clark, Elmer T., et al., eds. *The Journal and Letters of Francis Asbury*. 3 vols. Nashville: Abingdon Press, 1958.

Conrad, Henry C. *History of the State of Delaware*. 3 vols. Wilmington: privately printed, 1908.

Cummings, Benjamin F. *The Ennals Family of Maryland*. Salt Lake City, 1916 (typescript in the Library of Congress).

deValinger, Leon Jr., and Virginia E. Shaw, eds. *A Calendar of Ridgely Family Letters, 1742–1899*. 3 vols. Dover: privately printed, 1948.

Donnan, Elizabeth, ed. *Papers of James A. Bayard, 1796–1815*. New York: Da Capo Press, 1971.

Johnston, George. *History of Cecil County, Maryland, and the Early Settlements around the Head of the Chesapeake Bay and on the Delaware River, with Sketches of Some of the Old Families in Cecil County*. Elkton: privately printed, 1881.

Lednum, John. *A History of the Rise of Methodism in America*. Philadelphia: privately printed, 1859.

Mallery, Charles P. *Ancient Families of Bohemia Manor, Their Homes and Their Graves*. Wilmington: Historical Society of Delaware, 1900.

Martin, Roger A. *A History of Delaware through Its Governors, 1776–1984*. Wilmington: McClafferty Printing, 1984, 80–89.

Muse, William S. *Memoranda of the Leeds, Bozmans, Kerrs, Ennals . . .* Chestertown, Md.: Hope H. Barroll, 1917.

Pattison, Robert E. "The Life and Character of Richard Bassett." *Papers of the Historical Society of Delaware*, No. 29. Wilmington: Delaware Historical Society, 1900.

"Richard Bassett," *Maryland Genealogical Bulletin* 18 (April 1947): 21.

Saladino, Gaspare J. "Richard Bassett." *American National Biography*. New York: Oxford University Press, 1999, 2: 319–20.

Scharf, John Thomas. *History of Delaware, 1690–1888*. 2 vols. Philadelphia: L. J. Richards & Co., 1888.

Simpson, Matthew. *Cyclopedia of Methodism*. Philadelphia: Everts and Stewart, 1878.

———. *A Hundred Years of Methodism*. n.p., 1876.

Tipple, Ezra Squier. *Francis Asbury, The Prophet of the Long Road*. New York: Methodist Book Concern, 1916.

———. *The Heart of Asbury's Journal*. New York: Eaton & Mains, 1904.

Williams, William Henry. *The Garden of American Methodism: The Delmarva Peninsula, 1769–1820*. Wilmington: Scholarly Resources (Peninsula Conference of the United Methodist Church), 1984.

Elizabeth (Betsy)
Garnett Bassett

Birth:	c. 1760, Maryland
Parents:	George Garnett and Elizabeth Harris
Marriage:	1796, Richard Bassett (1745–1815)
Children:	None
Death:	c. 1819, Bohemia Manor, Maryland

Elizabeth Garnett, known in the family as Betsy, came from Maryland and married Richard Bassett in 1796, making their home at Bassett's Dover house.[1] The couple had evidently known one another for several years, and Elizabeth's niece, Ann Garnett, was a contemporary and friend of Richard Bassett's daughters, Ann and Mary.[2] Like Bassett's first wife, Ann, Betsy Garnett was an ardent Methodist and "a pious woman."[3] In 1792 Bassett had inherited more of the Bohemia Manor estate, including the mansion, and the following year he purchased additional manor land, bringing his holdings to six thousand acres, about one-third of the entire manor. In addition to the house at Bohemia Manor, Bassett owned a house in Dover and about 1813 purchased another house in Wilmington.[4] Until his retirement, however, the mansion at Bohemia Manor was usually let, while the Bassetts lived either in Dover or Wilmington.[5]

From 1793 to 1799 Bassett held the chief justiceship of the Court of Common Pleas in Delaware. As a Federalist he served as a presidential elector for John Adams in 1797. Two years later Bassett was elected as the governor of Delaware and continued that post until 1801, when he resigned to become one of Adams's "midnight" appointments as a judge of the U.S. Circuit Court. Bassett's son-in-law James Asheton Bayard had actively lobbied for Bassett's appointment, but he did not long hold the office, for the Jeffersonian Republicans abolished his judgeship in 1802.[6]

The Bassetts spent the rest of their lives in retirement at Bohemia Manor, devoting much of their time to Methodism. They participated in several religious camp meetings. At one in 1802 there were about seven thousand attendees, and it was necessary to have three preachers engaged at the same time. In 1805 at a camp meeting near Smyrna, Betsy Garnett Bassett was seen "shouting, full of the love of God, as she often was, [and] she would as soon embrace a pious daughter of Africa, in her rejoicing, as a white sister."[7] While the Bassetts lived at Bohemia Manor, he held two camp meetings in 1808 and 1809 in a beautiful grove on his land, each followed by a great revival and reformation. Kitty Bruff and Polly Ward, the sisters of Bassett's first wife, also attended the camp meetings.[8] In addition, church leaders were often welcomed in the family home.

Nancy Bassett's husband, James Asheton Bayard, described Betsy as having, in addition to her pious nature, "so much kindness and goodness in her character than [he] could discover in the actions of anybody else, that no one . . . could know her, without esteeming her and loving her."[9]

In 1814 Richard Bassett suffered a stroke and was thereafter paralyzed. After a second stroke in 1815, he died in August and was buried in the family vault at Bohemia Manor.[10] Betsy Bassett died about four years later.[11] During her lifetime, however, prominent Methodist clergymen continued to visit at the mansion. Unfortunately, it burned down not long after the Bassetts' deaths, and many old and valuable paintings were destroyed, including family portraits.[12]

Notes

1. Leon deValinger Jr. and Virginia E. Shaw, eds., *A Calendar of Ridgely Family Letters, 1741–1899* . . . , 3 vols. (Dover: privately printed, 1948), 1: 155–56; John Lednum, *A History of the Rise of Methodism in America* . . . (Philadelphia: privately printed, 1859), 274.

2. deValinger and Shaw, *Ridgely Family Letters,* 1: 201, 299. Ann Garnett at times evidently lived with the Bassetts, for she is referred to in letters from Bassett's son-in-law, James A. Bayard. She was born in 1787 and died unmarried in 1822. Also, Bassett was assisting Ann in obtaining a legacy from the death of her father, Benjamin Garnett, a Revolutionary War veteran.

3. Nathan Bangs, *The Life of the Rev. Freeborn Garrettson* . . . (New York: J. Emory and B. Waugh, 1830), 106.

4. Gaspare J. Saladino, "Richard Bassett," *American National Biography* (New York: Oxford University Press, 1999), 2: 320.

5. deValinger and Shaw, *A Calendar of Ridgely Family Letters*, 1: 156.

6. Saladino, "Richard Bassett," 2: 320.

7. Lednum, *A History of the Rise of Methodism in America* . . . , 274–75.

8. Bangs, *The Life of Rev. Freeborn Garretson* . . . , 253.

9. James A. Bayard to Richard Bassett, 30 December 1797, "Papers of James A. Bayard, 1796–1815," ed. Elizabeth Donnan, *Annual Report of the American Historical Association for the Year 1913* (Washington: Government Printing Office, 1915), 2: 47.

10. Richard Bassett's body and those of his daughters and son-in-law were moved in 1865 to the Wilmington-Brandywine Cemetery in Wilmington, Delaware. It is not known where his wives are now buried.

11. Chancery Court Records in the Maryland State Archives show that the property of Elizabeth Bassett was being transferred in 1819, which implies that she had died. The property was left to Ann Bassett Bayard, who in turn left it to her children. RG 3555.06, Chancery Court Records, Delaware State Archives, Richard Bassett vs. Richard Harrington, 1818, show that Elizabeth Bassett died sometime between the start of the case in 1818 and its conclusion in 1820.

12. Lednum, *A History of the Rise of Methodism in America . . .*, 277.

Bibliography

Bangs, Nathan. *The Life of the Rev. Freeborn Garrettson . . .*, 2nd ed. New York: J. Emory and B. Waugh, 1830.

Clark, Elmer T., et al., eds. *The Journal and Letters of Francis Asbury.* 3 vols. Nashville: Abingdon Press, 1958.

Conrad, Henry C. *History of the State of Delaware.* 3 vols. Wilmington: privately printed, 1908.

deValinger, Leon Jr., and Virginia E. Shaw, eds. *A Calendar of Ridgely Family Letters, 1742–1899.* 3 vols. Dover: privately printed, 1948.

Donnan, Elizabeth, ed. *Papers of James A. Bayard, 1796–1815.* New York: Da Capo Press, 1971.

Johnston, George. *History of Cecil County, Maryland, and the Early Settlements around the Head of the Chesapeake Bay and on the Delaware River, with Sketches of Some of the Old Families in Cecil County.* Elkton: privately printed, 1881.

Lednum, John. *A History of the Rise of Methodism in America.* Philadelphia: privately printed, 1859.

Mallery, Charles P. *Ancient Families of Bohemia Manor, Their Homes and Their Graves.* Wilmington: Historical Society of Delaware, 1900.

Martin, Roger A. *A History of Delaware through Its Governors, 1776–1984.* Wilmington: McClafferty Printing, 1984, 80–89.

Pattison, Robert E. "The Life and Character of Richard Bassett." *Papers of the Historical Society of Delaware*, No. 29. Wilmington: Delaware Historical Society, 1900.

"Richard Bassett." *Maryland Genealogical Bulletin* 18 (April 1947): 21.

Saladino, Gaspare J. "Richard Bassett." *American National Biography.* New York: Oxford University Press, 1999, 2: 319–20.

Scharf, John Thomas. *History of Delaware, 1690–1888.* 2 vols. Philadelphia: L. J. Richards & Co., 1888.

Simpson, Matthew. *Cyclopedia of Methodism*. Philadelphia: Everts and Stewart, 1878.
———. *A Hundred Years of Methodism*. n.p., 1876.
Tipple, Ezra Squier. *Francis Asbury, The Prophet of the Long Road*. New York: Methodist Book Concern, 1916.
———. *The Heart of Asbury's Journal*. New York: Eaton & Mains, 1904.
Williams, William Henry. *The Garden of American Methodism: The Delmarva Peninsula, 1769–1820*. Wilmington: Scholarly Resources (Peninsula Conference of the United Methodist Church), 1984.

Jane (Jenny) Ballareau
Parker Bedford

Birth:	13 June 1746, Woodbridge, New Jersey
Parents:	James Parker and Marie Ballareau
Marriage:	c. 1773, Gunning Bedford Jr. (1747–1812)
Children:	Juliana (b. 1773, died in infancy); Anna Maria (1775–1835); Susanna (b. 1778, died in childhood); Gunning James (1782–1842); Henrietta Jane (1788–1871)
Death:	26 July 1831, Brandywine Hundred, Delaware

Jane Ballareau Parker, born in Woodbridge, New Jersey, on 13 June 1746, was the daughter of James Parker, a prominent printer and journalist, and Marie Ballareau Parker.[1] James Parker, with the assistance of his friend Benjamin Franklin, to whom Jane was known as "Jenky," had set up a press in New York City, and from 1744 to 1752 Parker was the public printer for New York. In 1753 Parker's partner took over the New York press, and the family returned to Woodbridge, New Jersey. The following year Parker established the first permanent press in New Jersey, and in 1758 he started New Jersey's first magazine, becoming the government printer for New Jersey and the king's printer until 1770. Samuel Franklin Parker, Jane's older brother, born in 1745 and named for Franklin, also became a printer. On 24 June 1770, while visiting in Burlington, New Jersey, James Parker died and was buried the following day in Woodbridge.[2] He died in debt, and for many years thereafter the family tried diligently to sort out his financial affairs.[3]

Jane Parker, known as Jenny within her family, was a very accomplished young woman. From her Huguenot mother she learned to speak French fluently, and she assisted her father in editing his newspaper, *The Post Boy of New York*.[4] Her father's friend and patron Franklin had encouraged him to give his daughter a classical education.[5] It was said that her grace, intellect, and conversational powers naturally gave her a leading place in cultured society.[6]

In late 1772 or early 1773 Jane married Gunning Bedford Jr., who had graduated as valedictorian in September 1771 at the College of New Jersey (now Princeton University).[7] The member of a family that could trace its history back to the founding of Jamestown, Virginia, Bedford was described as a large, stout, bony man who never adopted trousers, but who adhered to knee britches and buckled shoes and who wore a queue with powdered hair.[8] On 14 October 1773, Juliana, the Bedfords' first child, was born. The following year Gunning Bedford was awarded a master's degree from the College of New Jersey. There is a story that Jane took Juliana with her when she attended the graduation, leaving the baby with Mrs. Witherspoon, wife of John Witherspoon, president of the college, during the ceremony.[9]

Bedford was then licensed to practice law in Chester County, Pennsylvania, later gaining admission to the Sussex County, Delaware, bar. In 1779 Bedford opened a law practice in Dover, Delaware, and then in Wilmington in 1783. Juliana died in infancy, but their second daughter, Anna Maria, born 8 December 1775, lived until 1835. Susanna, their third daughter, who was born on 10 December 1778, also died in childhood. Their only son, Gunning James, called "feeble-minded" in the vernacular of the day, was born in 1782 and died in 1842. The Bedfords' youngest child, Henrietta Jane, was born 8 December 1788 and died in 1871. Like her mother, Henrietta Jane learned to speak fluent French. She also became proficient at the piano, harp, and guitar. None of the Bedford children ever married.[10]

Samuel Franklin Parker, Jane's brother, died in December 1779 after a long illness. As a major in the New Jersey militia during the Revolutionary War, he was buried with full military honors. Jane's husband, Gunning Bedford Jr., represented Delaware in the Continental Congress (1783–1785) and became the state's attorney general in 1784. Resigning in 1789, Bedford was appointed federal district judge for Delaware, a position he held until his death on 30 March 1812. At the time of his death, the Bedfords lived at Lombardy Hall, a large gray stone mansion on a farm of 250 acres in Brandywine Hundred, to which they had moved in 1793.

Jane Bedford lived a long life and was blind for several years before her death. Her youngest daughter, Henrietta Jane, is said to have devoted herself to caring for her mother and afflicted brother. Jane lived at Lombardy Hall until 1817, when she moved back into Wilmington. She died at her home on 26 July 1831, aged 85, and was buried beside her husband in the graveyard of the First Presbyterian Church in Wilmington.[11] In 1921 the graves of Jane and her husband and children were moved to the grounds of the Masonic Home Cemetery in Wilmington.[12] Her tombstone relates that she was "by nature endowed with rare personal attractions and intellect of the highest order to which were added the refinements of culture; benevolent in feeling as an angel of mercy to the poor and afflicted, beloved and valued as a neighbor and friend."

Notes

1. *Genealogies of Pennsylvania Families* (Baltimore: Genealogical Publishing Co., Inc., 1982), 1: 32–33; paper written by Samuel Eugene Parker, April 1899, Parker family folder, Historical Society of Delaware, Wilmington, Delaware. The date is also shown on one paper as 1748, but most sources report that she was 85 at her death, making the date 1746.

2. Chris Tami, *New York City Wills, 1766–1771*, 267. Online database via Ancestry .com.

3. See Alan Dyer, *A Biography of James Parker, Colonial Printer, 1715–1770* (Troy, N.Y.: Whitston Publishing Co., 1982).

4. John P. Nields, *Gunning Bedford, Jr . . .* (Wilmington: Historical Society of Delaware, 1907), 1. The newspaper also went by other names during its publication.

5. William Thompson Read, *Life and Correspondence of George Read* (Philadelphia: J. B. Lippincott, 1870), 510.

6. Samuel Eugene Parker, "Gunning Bedford, Jr., Signer of the Constitution," *The New York Genealogical and Biographical Record* 31 (January 1900): 2.

7. *Genealogies of New Jersey Families* (Baltimore: Genealogical Publishing Co., Inc., 1996), 1: 687. In the Gunning Bedford Jr. file at the Historical Society of Delaware is a letter dated 9 April 1773 from Benjamin Franklin in London, addressing Jane as "Dear Jenky" and congratulating her on her marriage (published in *The Writings of Benjamin*

Franklin [New York: The Macmillan Co., 1906] 6: 36–38). Some biographies state that the Bedfords married as early as 1770, but this letter makes it appear that the marriage took place later than is generally thought.

    8. Harold J. Littleton, "Gunning Bedford, Jr., and his Home Lombardy Hall," *Delaware Heritage Commission* (Winter 1985): 45.

    9. Bedford File, Historical Society of Delaware, Wilmington, Delaware.

    10. *Genealogies of New Jersey Families,* 1: 687; Gunning Bedford Jr. file, Historical Society of Delaware. The birth and death records are taken from the Parker family Bible, donated to the society by Henrietta Jane Bedford in her will. Mention is made in the Bedford family file, Historical Society of Delaware, that Gunning James Bedford was "feeble-minded," which might account for none of the children marrying.

    11. *Genealogies of New Jersey Families,* 1: 687; obituary in *Delaware Free Press,* copy in Parker family file, Delaware Historical Society.

    12. Charles R. Green, *Delaware Heritage: The Story of the Diamond State in the Revolution* (Wilmington: William N. Cann, 1975), 205–6.

Bibliography

The papers of the Bedford family are among the holdings of the Delaware Historical Society. In addition, the following publications were used in preparing this essay:

Conrad, Henry C. "Gunning Bedford, Junior." *Historical and Biographical Papers,* Vol. 3. Wilmington: Historical Society of Delaware, 1900.

Dyer, Alan. *A Biography of James Parker, Colonial Printer, 1715–1770.* Troy, N.Y.: Whitston Publishing Co., 1982.

Genealogies of New Jersey Families. Baltimore: Genealogical Publishing Co., Inc., 1982.

Genealogies of Pennsylvania Families. Baltimore: Genealogical Publishing Co., Inc., 1996.

Green, Charles R. *Delaware Heritage: The Story of the Diamond State in the Revolution.* Wilmington: William N. Cann, 1975.

Littleton, Harold J. "Gunning Bedford, Jr., and his Home Lombardy Hall." *Delaware Heritage Commission* (Winter 1985): 45.

Myers, Patty. *Ancestors and Descendants of Lewis Ross Freeman.* Camden, Maine: Penobscott Press, 1995.

Nields, John Percy. *Gunning Bedford, Jr . . . 1789–1812.* Paper read at presentation of Bedford's portrait, 18 November 1907.

Parker, Samuel Eugene. "Gunning Bedford, Jr., Signer of the Constitution." *The New York Genealogical and Biographical Record* 31 (January 1900): 1–3.

Parker, Theodore. *Genealogy and Biographical Notes of John Parker of Lexington and His Descendants.* Worcester, Mass.: C. Hamilton, 1893.

Jean Blair Blair

Birth:	26 October 1736, Edinburgh, Scotland
Parents:	Archibald Blair and Helen Hamilton
Marriage:	26 December 1756, John Blair (1732-1800)
Children:	John (born c. 1757, died in infancy); Mary (1758-1820); Helen (Nelly) (1759-1773); Jane (Jenny) (1760-1800); Christian (born and died 1765); James (Jemmy) (1770-1791)
Death:	22 November 1792, Williamsburg, Virginia

John Blair, born in Williamsburg in 1732, came from a prominent Virginia family. He was the son of John Blair, a colonial official, and the nephew of James Blair, founder and first president of the College of William and Mary. After graduating from that institution, he studied law at the Middle Temple in London. On 26 December 1756 in Edinburgh, Scotland, he married his cousin, twenty-year-old Jean Blair, whose father Archibald Blair (1690–1767) was described as a writer.[1]

Jean had two brothers: John Blair, who remained in Scotland, and James Blair, who made his home in Williamsburg. One of James's sons, John Blair, was killed in action during the Revolutionary War, while another, Archibald, succeeded his cousin John Blair in 1776 as clerk of the Virginia Council.[2]

After returning to Virginia, John Blair and his wife, Jean, made their home in Williamsburg where John took up the practice of law and became active in political affairs. From 1766 to 1770 he sat in the Virginia House of Burgesses as the representative of William and Mary, and from 1770 to 1775 he held the position of clerk of the Virginia Council. John Blair took part in the Virginia constitutional convention in 1776 and sat on the committee that framed a declaration of rights and the plan for a new government. He then served on the Privy Council from 1776 to 1778. In 1778 the legislature elected him as a judge of the General Court, and he soon became the chief justice. In 1780 he was elected to the high chancery court of Virginia. He attended the Constitutional Convention and assisted in the ratification. Blair was named an associate justice of the U.S. Supreme Court in 1789, a position he held for seven years until his retirement in 1796.[3]

Jean and John Blair had six children, two of whom died in infancy. Their daughter Nelly died in her early teens, and their son James at the age of twenty-one. Mary Blair married Robert Andrews of the College of William and Mary, and Jenny Blair married James Henderson. Mary had no children, and all four of Jenny's died before reaching adulthood. Thus, there are no descendants of Jean Blair and her husband.[4]

Jean died in 1792 in Williamsburg after a long illness. Her tombstone reads that "Her conduct through life was truly exemplary and amiable in discharging all the duties of her station as a wife, a mother and a friend; and her piety shone forth with peculiar luster during a protracted, painful, and distressing illness, which she sustained without a murmur . . ." Her husband, John, returned to Williamsburg after his retirement and lived there quietly until his death in 1800. Both were buried in the graveyard of Bruton Parish Church in Williamsburg.[5]

Notes

1. *Midlothian (Edinburgh), Scotland: Parish and Probate Records. Vol. V: The Register of Marriages of the City of Edinburgh, 1751–1800*, database online, Ancestry.com, 2001

(also published in Francis J. Grant, ed., *Register of Marriages of the City of Edinburgh, 1751–1800* [Edinburgh, Scotland: J. Skinner, 1922], 65); *Bruton Parish Churchyard and Church: A Guide to the Tombstones, Monuments, and Mural Tablets* (Williamsburg, Va.: Bruton Parish Church, 1976), 51, 52; *The Scots Magazine* 29 (1767): 334.

2. Daphne Gentry and Brent Tartar, "The Blair Family of Colonial Williamsburg: A Research Note," *Virginia Genealogical Society Quarterly* 32 (May 1994): 111.

3. Maeva Marcus, "John Blair, Jr.," *American National Biography* (New York: Oxford University Press, 1999), 2: 914–15.

4. Gentry and Tarter, "The Blair Family of Colonial Williamsburg," 109; Bernard M. Caperton, "Three Williamsburg Wills: The Honorable John Blair, Jr.; The Reverend James Henderson; Mary Blair Andrews," *The Virginia Genealogist* 29 (July–September 1985): 205–6; Daphne Gentry, "Robert Andrews," *Dictionary of Virginia Biography* (Richmond: The Library of Virginia, 1998) 1: 167–68; Robert K. Headley Jr., *Genealogical Abstracts from 18th-Century Virginia Newspapers* (Baltimore: Genealogical Publishing Co., Inc., 1987), 30 (death of Nelly Blair).

5. *Bruton Parish Churchyard and Church*, 51.

Bibliography

Two letters of Jean Blair (and references to her in others) are among the Blair, Bannister, Braxton, Horner Whiting Papers located in the Special Collections Research Center, Earl Gregg Swem Library, College of William and Mary, in Williamsburg. No other collection of papers is known to exist. In addition, there are the following sources of information:

Caperton, Bernard M. "Three Williamsburg Wills: The Honorable John Blair, Jr.; The Reverend James Henderson; Mary Blair Andrews." *The Virginia Genealogist* 29 (July–September 1985): 205–12; (October–December 1985): 252–58.

Drinard, J. Elliott, "John Blair, Jr." *Proceedings of the Thirty-Eighth Annual Meeting of the Virginia State Bar Association* (1927): 436–49.

Gentry, Daphne. "Robert Andrews." *Dictionary of Virginia Biography*. Richmond: The Library of Virginia, 1998, 1: 167–68.

Gentry, Daphne, and Brent Tarter. "The Blair Family of Colonial Williamsburg: A Research Note." *Virginia Genealogical Society Quarterly* 32 (May 1994): 103–12.

Horner, Frederick. *The History of the Blair, Banister, and Braxton Families*. Philadelphia: J. B. Lippincott, 1898.

Marcus, Maeva. "John Blair, Jr." *American National Biography* (New York: Oxford University Press, 1999), 2: 915–16.

Mary (Molsey) Grainger Blount

Birth:	1761, Wilmington, North Carolina
Parents:	Caleb Grainger and Mary Walters
Marriage:	12 February 1778, William Blount (1749–1800)
Children:	Cornelius (born c. 1779, died in infancy); Ann (Nancy) (1780–1832); Mary Louisa (1782–1847); William (Billy) Grainger (1784–1827); Blount (1787–1790); Richard Blackledge (1789–1858); Jacob (1791–1809); Barbara (1792–1836); Elizabeth (Eliza) Indiana (1794–1835)
Death:	7 October 1802, Knoxville, Tennessee

Mary Grainger, known as Molsey within the family, was born in 1761 in Wilmington, North Carolina, to Caleb Grainger and his wife, Mary Walters.[1] She was the granddaughter of Joshua Grainger, one of the founders of Wilmington, and the Grainger family was prominent in land ownership and political affairs in the New Hanover County area.[2] She had four brothers: Caleb Jr., Cornelius Harnett, William, and John.[3] Although there appears to be no documented information on her childhood or young adulthood, based on the position of her father, it is assumed that Mary Grainger had a life of refinement and social gentility related to his obvious financial success. Her father died in 1765, leaving her "two Negro wenches and what Children they have, or may hereafter have . . . being Little Hager and Venice. Also, was one Lott of Land in Wilmington, Containing Thirty feet front upon the Street, and Common Depth of Lotts . . . one Good Bed and Furniture, two Mahogany Tables, Six Mahogany Chairs, one Large Mahogany framed Looking Glass, and Such of my Plate as I shall leave a List . . . shall be delivered to her at the Age of Seventeen Years, or day of Marriage."[4]

William Blount, the son of a landholding family in North Carolina, often visited the Grainger home, providing Caleb Grainger's widow with financial advice for settling her husband's estate.[5] Blount was an active member of the Church of England and a vestryman in Craven County, North Carolina.[6] He was also a paymaster in the North Carolina forces for the Revolutionary War. Mary's brother, Caleb, also served in the war, first as a captain and then major in the 1st North Carolina Regiment.[7]

On 12 February 1778, William Blount married Mary, and they began life together at his plantation, Piney Grove, a comfortable farm acquired from the estate of his grandfather, Thomas Blount, near the present city of Greenville, North Carolina. By 1783 he had acquired an estate of approximately six thousand acres. The Blounts had at least nine children, six of whom reached adulthood. Their first, Cornelius, was born about a year after their marriage and died in infancy. In October 1780 they had a daughter Ann, called Nancy, and two years later another daughter, Mary Louisa. Nancy married Henry I. Toole of eastern North Carolina and secondly Weeks Hadley. Mary Louisa married Pleasant Moorman Miller, who served in Congress as a representative from Tennessee. William and Mary Blount's son William Grainger, who also served in the U.S. Congress from 1815 to 1819, was born in 1784. Another son called Blount, who was born three years later, died in 1790 of "ague and fever."[8] Richard Blackledge, named for the man who married William Blount's sister Louisa, was born in 1789, and Jacob, named for Blount's father and brother, was born in 1791. Jacob Blount died at eighteen while attending William and Mary College in Virginia. Two more daughters were born to the Blounts: Barbara born in 1792 and Elizabeth Indiana born in 1794.[9] Barbara married, as his second wife, General Edmund Pendleton Gaines, while Elizabeth Indiana married Dr. Edwin Wiatt, who served in the War of 1812 as a surgeon.

The Blounts' marriage was marked by many separations, for Mary generally remained at home in North Carolina with the children while her husband engaged in politics or business. Mary's mother, Mary Walters Grainger, lived with them, keeping her daughter company during her son-in-law's absences. There were amusements, however—dances, musicals, and theater in New Bern; drives to visit friends and relatives; and races in Washington.[10]

William Blount and his brothers established a company engaged in merchandizing and commerce and also became land speculators in what is now Tennessee and Alabama. In addition to his service as Craven County's representative to the General Assembly of North Carolina, William Blount represented North Carolina in the Continental Congress (1782–1783 and 1786–1787) and at the Federal Convention at Philadelphia in 1787.[11]

In 1790 President George Washington appointed Blount as governor of "the territory south of the Ohio River," and he and his family prepared to move to Tennessee. It has been said that Mary cried for days at the thought of moving away from comfort and into the wilderness. Mary, William, and their two sons arrived in October of that year, while their two daughters remained with an aunt in North Carolina. Until their house was finished in 1792, the Blounts stayed with their friends, the family of William Cobb. In the exposed cabin Mary lived in fear that Indians would kill or kidnap her children. But more people were moving west, and Blount was one of the founders of Knoxville, Tennessee, where he built a new house befitting his position. There, with the family reunited, Mary created a place of family warmth and gaiety. She also planted a garden on the grounds of the house, and her social life revived.[12] One writer has described Mary as "a gentle, lovable woman . . . [who] so won the hearts of even the Cherokee chieftains, that when carrying firewood and tomahawk to the settlements . . . they passed by the town where she had her dwelling."[13]

In the meantime, William Blount was president of the convention that formed the constitution of the new state in 1796. In the same year he was elected to represent Tennessee in the U.S. Senate but was expelled for participating in a plan to incite a military movement on the part of southern Indians against Spanish possessions in the Mississippi Valley for the benefit of Great Britain. Blount was soon elected to the Tennessee state senate, later becoming speaker of that body. Prior to his expulsion from the Senate, however, Mary, along with other family members, joined William in Philadelphia, where they were considered an attractive couple. They took pleasure in attending plays, balls, dinners, and receptions in the capital city and watched the inaugurations of John Adams and Thomas Jefferson. Mary left Philadelphia for North Carolina in March 1797. While staying in Raleigh, she fell from her carriage, badly shattering her arm. After leaving Philadelphia and staying for two months in Raleigh with his wife,

William Blount returned to Tennessee. In late 1799 Mary, her mother, and her children joined him in Knoxville and began a new round of balls and banquets.[14]

In March of the following year, Mrs. Grainger fell ill with malaria, and soon Mary and two of the children also became ill. Mrs. Grainger died. Then William Grainger fell ill, and his father took care of him. It was too much for William Blount, who died suddenly at age fifty-one on 21 March 1800. The children, ranging in age from six to twenty, and Mary were left in the care of William Blount's half-brother Willie Blount, who had acted as his brother's secretary. Mary lived only two years longer, succumbing to jaundice in October 1802.[15] William and Mary Blount are buried in the graveyard of the First Presbyterian Church in Knoxville, Tennessee. In their honor, the county of Blount and town of Blountville in Tennessee are named for William Blount, and the town of Maryville and county of Grainger are named for Mary Grainger, his wife.

Notes

1. Eugene C. Hicks, ed., *Sir Ellis Hicks (1315) Captain John Ward (1598) John Wright (1500) Philip le Yonge (1295) and 7,812 Descendants* (Wilmington, N.C.: Wilmington Printing Co., c. 1982), 428. Mary Blount's gravestone in the graveyard of the First Presbyterian Church, Knoxville, Tennessee, states that she was forty-one years old at her death in 1802.

2. Elizabeth Francenia McKoy, *Early Wilmington Block by Block from 1733 On* (Wilmington, N.C.: s.n., 1967), 110–11.

3. McKoy, *Early Wilmington Block by Block from 1733 On*, 110; J. Bryan Grimes, *North Carolina Wills and Inventories* (Baltimore: Genealogical Publishing Co., 1967), 159.

4. Grimes, *North Carolina Wills and Inventories*, 202–5.

5. William Henry Masterson, *William Blount* (Baton Rouge: Louisiana State University Press, 1954), 37.

6. William S. Powell, ed., *Dictionary of North Carolina Biography* (Chapel Hill: University of North Carolina Press, 1979), 1: 178.

7. Francis B. Heitman, *Historical Register of Officers of the Continental Army during the War of the Revolution, April 1775 to December 1783* (Baltimore: The Genealogical Publishing Co., 1973), 256.

8. Alice Barnwell Keith et al., *The John Gray Blount Papers* (Raleigh: North Carolina State Department of Archives, 1952–1982), 2: 119–20.

9. There may have been another Cornelius born in 1793 who died in infancy. Also, Mary was evidently pregnant during her visit to Philadelphia in 1797.

10. Masterson, *William Blount*, 44, 134, 156.

11. Thomas H. Winn, "William Blount," *American National Biography* (New York: Oxford University Press, 1999), 3: 59–61.

12. Masterson, *William Blount*, 212–13, 220, 255, 281–82.

13. Edmund Kirke, "Knoxville in the Olden Time," *Harper's New Monthly Magazine* 71 (June–November 1885): 73.

14. Masterson, *William Blount*, 310–11, 324–26, 343.

15. Masterson, *William Blount* , 345.

Bibliography

"The Blount Mansion," *Tennessee Historical Quarterly* (June 1963): 25–27, 103–122.

Burns, Inez E., rev. *History of Blount County, Tennessee, From War Trail to Landing Strip, 1795–1955.* Tennessee Historical Commission, sponsored by Mary Blount Chapter, NSDAR, 1957. Evansville, Ind.: Whipporwill Publications, 1988.

Folmsby, Stanley J. "William Blount," *Dictionary of North Carolina Biography.* Chapel Hill: University of North Carolina Press, 1979, 1: 183.

Goodpasture, Albert V. "William Blount and the Old Southwest Territory." *American Historical Magazine and Tennessee Historical Quarterly* 8 (January 1903): 1–13.

Keith, Alice Barnwell. "Three North Carolina Blount Brothers in Business and Politics, 1783–1812." Ph.D. dissertation, University of North Carolina, 1940.

———. "William Blount in North Carolina Politics." In Joseph C. Sitterson, ed., *Studies in Southern History.* Chapel Hill: University of North Carolina Press, 1957, 47–61.

Keith, Alice Barnwell, et al. *The John Gray Blount Papers.* 4 vols. Raleigh: North Carolina State Department of Archives, 1952–1982.

Kirke, Edmund. "Knoxville in the Olden Time." *Harper's New Monthly Magazine* 71 (June–November 1885): 68–77.

Masterson, William Henry. *William Blount.* Baton Rouge: Louisiana State University Press, 1954.

Mitchell, Memory F. *North Carolina's Signers.* Raleigh: North Carolina Division of Archives and History, 1964.

Walker, Nancy Wooten. *Out of a Clear Blue Sky: Tennessee's First Ladies and Their Husbands.* Cleveland, Tenn.: n.p., 1971.

Wheeler, John J. *Reminiscences and Memoirs of North Carolina and Eminent North Carolinians.* Baltimore: Genealogical Publishing Co., 1966.

William Blount, the Man and His Mansion. Knoxville, Tenn.: Blount Mansion Association, c. 1977.

Winn, Thomas H. "William Blount." *American National Biography.* New York: Oxford University Press, 1999, 3: 59–61.

Wright, Marcus Joseph. *Some Account of the Life and Services of William Blount . . .* Washington, D.C.: E. J. Gray, 1884.

Elizabeth (Betsy) Higbee Brearley

Birth:	c. 1751, near Trenton, New Jersey
Parents:	Joseph Higbee and Rachel Wright
Marriage:	17 April 1783, David Brearley (1745-1790)
Children:	Joseph Higbee (1785-1805); David Higbee (1786-1820); George (1791-1792)
Death:	20 August 1832, Trenton, New Jersey

In 1779 David Brearley was elected chief justice of the New Jersey Supreme Court, which required that he spend more time in Trenton, where he became acquainted with the Higbee family. The Higbees, Joseph and Rachel, lived on King Street and were the parents of Joseph, Catherine, and Elizabeth. (Four sons had died in infancy.) On 17 April 1783 their daughter Elizabeth, at age thirty-two, became the second Mrs. David Brearley. The Brearley family then moved from Allentown to Trenton.

Elizabeth's father, Joseph Higbee, had for many years been most active in the affairs of Trenton's St. Michael's Episcopal Church, and David and Elizabeth had delayed their wedding until its reopening. The Anglican church had been closed from 1776 to 1783 because its parishioners had included so many Loyalists, and it was used as a military hospital during the war.[1]

David began to assume a goodly share of lay duties of the church. He was first elected to the vestry and between 1785 and 1790 served as warden. In 1786 he was a delegate to the Episcopal General Conference and assisted in writing the new Book of Common Prayer. In the same year the New Jersey legislature appointed him to attend the federal Constitutional Convention in Philadelphia, and David later presided over the New Jersey state convention that ratified the Constitution. In 1789 he served as a presidential elector, and President George Washington appointed him to the position of federal district judge.

In the meantime, three sons were born to the family: Joseph, David, and George. They were very little boys when, on 16 August 1790, their father, after having been ailing for many months, died. David left his wife, Elizabeth, and her sons, as well as William, Elizabeth, and Esther from his first family, reasonably well cared for, although there were debts. David's wife received half the estate, the six children received the other half, and special provisions in his will specified that Joseph was to receive his "small sword" and David his "Scotch pistols, inlaid with silver."[2] Elizabeth and the children moved in with her father, while their own house was let. David's extensive library was sold to raise money. Elizabeth outlived her three sons, George dying in 1792, Joseph in 1805, and David in 1820. None of the three left any descendants. Elizabeth was eighty-one years old when she died on 20 August 1832. She was buried beside her husband in St. Michael's churchyard.[3]

Notes

1. Hamilton Schuyler, *A History of St. Michael's Church, Trenton* . . . (Princeton, N.J.: Princeton University Press, 1926), passim.

2. "Calendar of Wills, 1786–1790," *Documents Relating to the Colonial, Revolutionary, and Post-Revolutionary History of the State of New Jersey*, First Series (Trenton, N.J.: MacCrellish and Quigley Co., 1941), 36: 29. By this time both Harriet and Polly were married. Harriet was still receiving support from her natural father, and presumably Polly had been taken care of upon her marriage. See chapter on Elizabeth Mullen Brearley.

3. Schuyler, *A History of St. Michael's Church, Trenton*, 366.

Bibliography

Brearley, William. *Genealogical Chart of the American Branch of the Brearley Family*. Detroit, privately printed, 1886.

Cooley, Eli Field. *Genealogy of Early Settlers of Trenton and Ewing, "Old Hunterdon County," New Jersey*. Trenton: The W. S. Sharp Printing Co., 1883.

Lee, Francis Bazley. *History of Trenton, New Jersey. The Record of Its Early Settlement and Corporate Progress*. Trenton: F. T. Smiley & Co., 1895.

Schuyler, Hamilton. *A History of St. Michael's Church, Trenton* . . . Princeton, N.J.: Princeton University Press, 1926.

The Society of Cincinnati in the State of New Jersey. Bethlehem, Pa.: Times Publishing Co., 1960.

Elizabeth Mullen Brearley

Birth:	c. 1741, Amwell, New Jersey
Parents:	John Mullen and Elizabeth Edwards
Marriage:	c. 1767, David Brearley (1745–1790)
Children:	Harriet Luttrell (c. 1760–1819) (by Henry Lawes Luttrell, 2nd Earl Carhampton [1743–1821]); William Brearley (c. 1768–after 1790); Mary (Polly) Brearley (c. 1770–after 1790); Elizabeth (Betsey) Brearley (c. 1773–1800); Esther (Hetty) Brearley (1777–1819)
Death:	3 August 1777, Allentown, New Jersey

Elizabeth Mullen was born about 1741 in Amwell, New Jersey, to John and Elizabeth Mullen. Her father was a merchant of Irish descent who died in 1749 when Elizabeth and her siblings (William, Rebecca, Sarah, and Mary) were still children. Her mother later married a man whose last name was Stevenson, and the family moved to a large house in Trenton. Elizabeth's sister Rebecca married Colonel George Reading, son of Governor John Reading, and had several children. Sarah Mullen married Thomas Biles and had children but was widowed at an early age. William, who died in 1765, and Mary appear to have remained single.[1]

At about eighteen years of age, Elizabeth, who was reputed to have been quite beautiful, fell in love with Henry Lawes Luttrell, elder son of the Earl of Carhampton, then serving as an ensign with the 48th Regiment of Foot, temporarily stationed in Trenton during the French and Indian War. A crisis occurred when the earl procured for his son a commission as a captain in the 16th Regiment of Light Dragoons, which required the young man to leave for England. The couple decided to elope. Although a marriage ceremony was purported to have been performed by the regimental chaplain, no evidence of any such marriage has been found. In addition, any such contract would not have been legal as both parties were under age. Henry and Elizabeth had already embarked on a ship to take them from New York to England when her mother arrived to take her back to Trenton. Luttrell returned to England alone. The affair had been consummated, however, and Elizabeth gave birth to a daughter, Harriet, at the Mullens' former home in Amwell.[2]

David Brearley was admitted to the New Jersey Bar on 15 May 1767 and established his home and law practice in Allentown, around the same time he and Elizabeth married.[3] Meanwhile, Luttrell was serving with his regiment in Portugal. He did not forget his daughter, however, as he periodically sent funds for her maintenance and education.[4]

The Brearley house was next door to Isaac and Hannah Rogers, whose son James married Harriet in 1779. The family had lived in the house less than four years when, on 26 February 1771, a fire totally destroyed it. The *Pennsylvania Gazette* reported: "On Tuesday Night, the 26th, ult., the House of David Brailow [sic], Esq., Attorney at Law, at Allentown in New Jersey, was entirely consumed by Fire, together with all his Books and Furniture; the Family with Difficulty escaped with their lives."[5] The Brearleys soon built a new house on the site.

In 1776 David joined the New Jersey Militia as a captain and quickly advanced through the rank of lieutenant colonel to colonel of the 2nd Regiment. In command less than two months, David received word in June 1777 that his wife was gravely ill, and on 3 August Elizabeth died. The notice of her death, which appeared in the *Pennsylvania Gazette*, bespeaks of her husband's love:

> On the 3rd instant died at Allentown in New Jersey, Elizabeth Brearley, wife of Colonel David Brearley, after a long and painful illness, which she bore with great fortitude, it may with truth be said of this Lady, that her external form (for she was eminently beautiful) was but a fair copy of her mind; and it would be doing injustice to her memory not to say, that she possessed all the qualities that adorn human nature.[6]

The Brearleys had four children: William, Mary (Polly), Elizabeth (Betsey), and Esther (Hetty). William was quite young when he went to sea and left no further trace. Polly married Ebenezer Hopkins and had two sons, David and Edward. Betsey married John Potts and had three sons, David, John, and Edward. Hetty never married. Harriet Luttrell and James Rogers had seven children. After her husband's death in 1791 Harriet moved from Allentown to Bordentown and later married Dr. Henry Gale, who outlived her.[7]

Notes

1. *Calendar of New Jersey Wills* (Trenton: New Jersey Historical Society, 1918), 30: 351–52; Josiah Granville Leach, *Genealogical and Biographical Memorials of the Reading,*

Howell, Yerkes, Watts, Latham, and Elkins Families (New York: privately printed by J. B. Lippincott, 1898), 48–51.

2. George S. L. Ward and Louis Rogers, *A Sketch of Some of the Descendants of Samuel Rogers of Monmouth County* (Philadelphia: Collins Printing House, 1888), 13–14; Donald Scarinci, *David Brearley and the Making of the United States Constitution* (Trenton: New Jersey Heritage Press, 2005), 47–48.

3. Robert G. Ferris and James H. Charleton, *The Signers of the Constitution* (Arlington, Va.: Interpretive Publications, 1986), 148.

4. Ward and Rogers, *A Sketch of Some of the Descendants*, 15; Scarinci, *David Brearley*, 49.

5. *Pennsylvania Gazette*, No. 2202, 7 March 1771, as quoted in Scarinci, *David Brearley*, 51.

6. *Pennsylvania Gazette*, 13 August 1777, as quoted in *Documents Relating to the Revolutionary History of the State of New Jersey*, Second Series (Trenton, N.J.: John L. Murphy), 1: 446.

7. Ward and Rogers, *A Sketch of Some of the Descendants*, 15–16; Scarinci, *David Brearley*, 122, 247.

Bibliography

Brearley, William. *Genealogical Chart of the American Branch of the Brearley Family.* Detroit: privately printed, 1886.

Cooley, Eli Field. *Genealogy of Early Settlers of Trenton and Ewing, "Old Hunterdon County," New Jersey.* Trenton: The W. S. Sharp Printing Co., 1883.

Lee, Francis Bazley. *History of Trenton, New Jersey. The Record of Its Early Settlement and Corporate Progress.* Trenton: F. T. Smiley & Co., 1895.

Scarinci, Donald. *David Brearley and the Making of the United States Constitution.* Morristown, N.J.: New Jersey Heritage Press, 2005.

Ward, George S. L., and Louis Richards. *A Sketch of Some of the Descendants of Samuel Rogers of Monmouth County, New Jersey.* Philadelphia: Collins Printing House, 1888.

Rachel Pierce Broom

Birth: 17 February 1752, Greenville, New Castle, Delaware
Parents: Robert Pierce and Elizabeth
Marriage: 14 December 1773, Jacob Broom (1752–1810)
Children: Ann (Nancy) (1775–1824); James Madison (1776–1850); Eliza-
            beth (1777–before 1784); Esther (Hetty) Willis (1779–before
            1822); Rachel (born 1781, died in infancy); Sarah (Sally)
            (1783–after 1822); Elizabeth Pierce (1784–1807); Jacob Pierce
            (1786–1842); Rachel Maria (1788–1864); Lavinia (1790–before
            1826); Nicholas Way (born 1793–before 1810)
Death: 16 June 1823, Philadelphia, Pennsylvania

Rachel Pierce, daughter of Robert and Elizabeth Pierce of Greenville, New Castle, Delaware, was born 17 February 1752 and christened on 30 March 1752 at Old Swedes (later Holy Trinity) Church in Wilmington. Rachel was one of four children; she had a brother, Robert Jr., and two sisters, Ann and Sarah. The Pierces were ardent patriots of the Revolutionary War. It is said that her father was a soldier in the Continental Army much sought after by the British. While on furlough at his home, he managed to escape a British contingent of soldiers by leaping out of a window, running into a nearby cornfield, and hiding himself until the contingent passed out of town.[1]

On 14 December 1773 Rachel, described by Broom's biographer as "an estimable woman,"[2] married Jacob Broom at the same church in which she was christened. The Reverend Lawrence Gerelius, a friend of the groom, performed the ceremony. Broom was the son of a blacksmith, who later became a prosperous farmer. Broom himself became in turn a farmer, surveyor, and businessman. It was his prominence in the thriving Wilmington business community that thrust him into politics. He was a strong patriot, but the influence of his Quaker friends and relatives kept him from fighting in the Revolutionary War. Broom provided his family with a wealthy home, the Nicholas Way mansion at Third and Shipley Streets in Wilmington.[3]

Rachel bore eleven children, eight of whom survived childhood, all christened in the Old Swedes Church.[4] The Broom's oldest son, James Madison, graduated from the College of New Jersey (Princeton) in 1794 and was a member of the Delaware congress for one term (1805–1807); his son, Jacob Pierce Broom (1808–1864), was the candidate of the National American Party for the presidency of the United States in 1852.[5] The Brooms' younger son Jacob Pierce established himself in Philadelphia. Their six surviving daughters, Ann, Elizabeth, Rachel, Sarah, Lavinia, and Esther Willis, all married and left descendants.

After serving at the Constitutional Convention in Philadelphia, Jacob Broom returned to Delaware and local politics, becoming Wilmington's first postmaster in 1790. He also built a substantial house in 1795 near his cotton mill where he lived with his family until 1802 when his mill burned down. He then sold the property to E. I. DuPont, founder of a gunpowder factory, in whose family it still remains.

After Jacob Broom's death in 1810, it took six years to settle his estate. His wife received their home in Wilmington, stables, gardens, and furniture, including many sterling silver pieces. Broom left an extensive estate, including money, bonds, shipping interests, stocks, animals, and conveyances, all of which was divided among his children and grandchildren. Rachel died 16 June 1823 in Philadelphia and was buried in Christ Church Cemetery.[6]

Notes

1. William W. Campbell, *The Life and Character of Jacob Broom* (Wilmington: Historical Society of Delaware, 1909), 13.
2. Campbell, *Life and Character of Jacob Broom*; Delaware Marriage Records, 36:26, Delaware State Archives.
3. Betty C. Homan, "The Elusive Jacob Broom—Signer," *Daughters of the American Revolution Magazine* 121 (December 1987): 860.
4. *The Records of Holy Trinity (Old Swedes) Church* (Wilmington: Historical Society of Delaware, 1890), 740.
5. Campbell, *Life and Character of Jacob Broom*, 5, 13–14.
6. Philadelphia City Death Certificate, original filed in the Philadelphia City Archives; Will of Rachel Broom, 25 Jul 1823, RG 2545.001, Delaware State Archives, Dover, Delaware. Jacob Broom is also buried in Christ Church Cemetery in Philadelphia.

Bibliography

Campbell, William W. *Life and Character of Jacob Broom*. Wilmington: Delaware Historical Society, No. 51, 1909.

Curtis, Charles M., and Charles Lee Reese, Jr. *History of Old Swedes Church*. Wilmington: Delaware Tercentenary Commission, 1938.

Homan, Betty C. "The Elusive Jacob Broom—Signer." *Daughters of the American Revolution Magazine* 21 (December 1987): 860, 897.

Martin, John Hill. *Chester and its Vicinity, Delaware County, Pa. . . .* Philadelphia: William H. Pile and Sons, 1877.

The Records of Holy Trinity (Old Swedes) Church. Wilmington: Historical Society of Delaware, 1890. Reprint, Baltimore: Genealogical Publishing Co., Inc., 1999.

Wright, Edward. *Early Church Records of New Castle County, Delaware*. Westminster, Md.: Willow Bend Books, 2000.

Mary (Polly) Middleton Butler

Birth:	1750, Charleston, South Carolina
Parents:	Thomas Middleton and Mary Bull
Marriage:	10 January 1771, Pierce Butler (1744–1822)
Children:	Sarah (Sally) (1772–1831); Anne Elizabeth (Eliza) (1774–1854); Frances (1774–1836); Harriot Percy (1775–1815); Pierce (1777–1780); Thomas (1778–1838); two additional sons died in infancy
Death:	13 November 1790, New York, New York

Mary (Polly) Middleton was born about 1750 in Charleston, South Carolina, to parents who were both members of socially prominent and wealthy families in South Carolina. Her parents, Thomas Middleton (1719–1766) and Mary Bull (1723–1760), also had two other children, William (1744–1768) and Sarah (1746–1775). The Middleton family members were perhaps the greatest landholders in colonial South Carolina, but it was from the Bull side of the family that Mary received the bulk of her inheritance. The Middletons were also very active in politics and government. Her father was in the state legislature, as well as a colonel in the militia, and one of Mary's first cousins—Arthur Middleton—signed the Declaration of Independence. Mary's mother died in February 1760, and in August of the same year her father married Anne Barnwell, with whom he had four more children—two boys named Henry who died in infancy, Elizabeth, and Anne. Thomas Middleton died in 1766, and his son and Mary's brother, William, died two years later.

At the time of her marriage to Pierce Butler on 10 January 1771, Mary Middleton was a wealthy heiress. Her father, mother, maternal grandfather, and brother, William, were all dead, and her sister, Sarah, died a few years later. Her mother had been the daughter of Captain John Bull and his second wife, also called Mary. It was this grandmother, who died the same year as the Butlers' marriage, who was Mary's benefactor. Even after Mary Butler's death, more of the Bull estate would come to the Butler family. This included several large plantations, lands, slaves, and lots in lower South Carolina.

Although fully aware of his aristocratic Irish lineage, Major Butler was also very aware of the financial and social opportunities afforded by his marriage to Mary Middleton. Through the marriage he gained entry into several of the most prestigious and wealthy families of colonial South Carolina. From this beginning, Butler became one of the wealthiest planters in the United States.

During the Revolutionary War, Butler managed to escape before the fall of Charleston, but Mary and their children were stranded in the enemy-occupied city. It was not until December 1781 that the family was reunited in Philadelphia, and it was late in 1782 when they were able to return to Charleston.

Butler's political and business endeavors caused Mary to move with him to Philadelphia and New York City, but she remained a true product of Charleston's aristocracy and requested of her husband that should she die her remains would be returned to her native city. She had been bed-ridden in excruciating pain for more than six months prior to her death in New York on 13 November 1790. Her wish was honored, and she was buried near the wall of St. Michael's Church in Charleston, close by the Butler pew. She left behind five surviving children, four young daughters and a son at school in London.

In his later years, Pierce Butler moved to Philadelphia to live near his daughter Sally and her family. Sally had married James Mease, a Philadelphia physician and scientist. Two of their three sons changed their surname to Butler (one of the terms of their grandfather's will) and one of them, also called Pierce Butler, married the actress Fanny Kemble, who wrote about slavery and her life in the South. Twins Eliza and Frances never married, nor did their sister Harriot Percy. The Butlers' older son Pierce had died at three in January 1780 from burns suffered in a fire. Their younger son Thomas, educated in Europe, married Eliza de Mallevault of Martinique and, for the most part, made his home in France.

Bibliography

The information in this essay is based on a section of the book *Major Butler's Legacy: Five Generations of a Slaveholding Family* (Athens: University of Georgia Press, 1987) by Malcolm Bell Jr. Papers of the Butler family are among the collections of the Historical Society of Pennsylvania. Other sources include:

Edgar, Walter B., et al., comps. *Biographical Directory of the South Carolina House of Representatives.* Columbia: University of South Carolina Press, 1974–.

Engel, Beth Bland. *The Middleton Family.* Jesup: Jesup Sentinel, 1972. 257.

Lipscomb, Terry W., ed. *The Letters of Pierce Butler, 1790-1794: Nation Building and Enterprise in the New American Republic.* Columbia: University of South Carolina Press, 2007.

St. Michael's Episcopal Church. Charleston: Nelson's Printing Co. (Vestry of St. Michael's Church), 1979.

Eleanor Carroll Carroll

Birth:	5 April 1732, Maryland
Parents:	Daniel Carroll and Ann Rozier
Marriage:	1750, Daniel Carroll (1730–1796)
Children:	Daniel (1752–1790); Mary (1754–1784)
Death:	13 April 1763, Maryland

Eleanor Carroll was the daughter of a Daniel Carroll, wife of a Daniel Carroll, and mother of a Daniel Carroll. Her father, Daniel Carroll (1707–1734), was a member of that illustrious Roman Catholic family of Maryland, which originated in Litterluna, King's County, Ireland. He was the son of Charles Carroll, called "The Immigrant," and the uncle of the famous Charles Carroll of Carollton, signer of the Declaration of Independence. Daniel married a great heiress, Ann Rozier (1710–1764), and they became the parents of three children: Charles Carroll of Duddington (1729–1773); Mary Carroll (1733–1825), who married Ignatius Digges; and Eleanor Carroll, who married Daniel Carroll II, signer of the Constitution.

Eleanor was born in 1732 in Maryland. Her father, who died two years later, left Eleanor and her sister, Mary, five hundred acres of land. When Eleanor was three years old, her widowed mother married Colonel Benjamin Young, a commissioner of Crown Lands, who had come to Maryland from England. They had several children, one of whom, Notley Rozier Young, married Daniel Carroll's sister Mary as his second wife.

Nothing is known of Eleanor's education, but no doubt like other girls of the period and class, she was educated at home and learned to read, write, do fine sewing and embroidery, and run a house and plantation. She married in 1750, at the age of eighteen, her second cousin Daniel Carroll II, bringing him a large dowry of 3,000 pounds. Daniel Carroll II had been born in 1730, son of Eleanor Darnall and Daniel Carroll of Upper Marlboro, a wealthy merchant and landowner. Young Daniel had been sent to Flanders in 1742 for his education and remained there for six years. His brother was the distinguished archbishop of Baltimore, John Carroll. Besides his father's prosperous merchant business, which he inherited, Daniel Carroll purchased large landholdings in Maryland.

Daniel Carroll II and Eleanor became the parents of two children: Daniel Carroll III and Mary. About 1755 Eleanor Carroll's portrait was painted with her son. Against a dark background, she is shown sitting on a green chair and wearing a dress of lustrous golden brown, probably made of satin. The cuffs and neckpiece are made of a delicate white fabric, trimmed with wide lace. The fingers are long and delicate. One hand is shown clasping her son; the other is holding the loosened rose-colored sash of his little white gown. Her hair is auburn, and her eyes are brown. She is not beautiful but has a lively, pleasant, alert look. The child's eyes are brown, like his mother's, and on his head he wears a jaunty blue cap, trimmed with a large white feather. He holds a rattle with a red handle and bells that resemble small sleigh bells.

It is unfortunate that, like so many other women of the time, Eleanor's tastes, habits, and interests are unknown. She probably spent her days like other women of her age and class, managing a large and prosperous household, supervising the rearing of her children, entertaining family and her husband's friends, and, as a member of a prominent Roman Catholic family, attending to her religious duties.

Eleanor Carroll died at thirty-one, on 13 April 1763, long before her husband became a public figure. The *Maryland Gazette* for 28 April 1763 stated:

> On Tuesday last died here, universally regretted, Mrs. Eleanor Carroll, Consort of Mr. Daniel Carroll of this Place, after a long illness, which she bore with that Patience, Fortitude, and Resignation to the Divine Will, which denote a sincere Christian. She was blessed with all the Qualifications that make a good Wife, tender Mother, Kind Mistress, and affectionate Friend. Her benevolent Disposition, affability of Manners, and great Sense, procured her the Friendship and Esteem of all her acquaintance.

Eleanor and Daniel Carroll's son, Daniel Carroll III, was born in 1752. He married Elizabeth Digges, daughter of William Digges of Warburton Manor. Elizabeth was a niece of Ignatius Digges, whose second wife was Mary Carroll, sister of Eleanor Carroll. Elizabeth Digges Carroll survived her husband many years, dying in 1843. Daniel Carroll III was a merchant and owned considerable property but evidently died in debt in 1790, six years before the death of his father. Eleanor Carroll and her husband, Daniel, are today represented by numerous descendants through their son. The Carrolls' daughter, Mary, was born in 1754 and married Patrick Sim in 1777. Mary and Patrick Sim had four children, none of whom had any issue.

Eleanor's widowed husband, Daniel Carroll II, never remarried. He was not a public figure until the Revolutionary War, when Maryland granted Catholics the right to vote and hold political office. From then until his death, Daniel Carroll was an active public servant. In 1777 he was elected to the Governor's Council, which controlled the executive department in Maryland and during the war had charge of the state's military forces. In 1781 he became a state senator and was also elected a delegate to the Continental Congress, where he signed the Articles of Confederation. Carroll was again selected to represent Maryland at the Constitutional Convention in 1787. He served as a representative of Maryland in the First Congress and voted for the bill to locate the District of Columbia on the Potomac River. In 1791 he was named one of the commissioners to survey and limit a part of the territory of the ten-mile square. He served as a commissioner until May 1795, when he resigned because of age and feeble health. He died at his home in Rock Creek in May 1796.

In his will, made 4 May and probated 21 May 1796, he devised all of his estate, both real and personal, to his brother, Archbishop John Carroll, and his friends and relatives by marriage Notley Young and Robert Brent in trust for the maintenance and education of his three grandchildren, his children having predeceased him.

Bibliography

This essay is based on M. Virginia Geiger's *Daniel Carroll, One Man and His Descendants* (Baltimore: College of Notre Dame of Maryland, 1979). Other sources are as follows:

Barnes, Robert, comp. *Marriages and Deaths from The Maryland Gazette, 1727–1839*. Baltimore: Genealogical Publishing Co., Inc., 1973.

Bowie, Effie Gwynn. *Across the Years in Prince George's County*. Richmond: Garrett and Massie, Inc., 1947, 116–17, 274–77.

Dictionary of American Biography. New York: Charles Scribner's Sons, 1929, 2: 523–24.

Downing, Margaret Brent. "The Earliest Proprietors of Capitol Hill," excerpt from *The Records of the Columbia Historical Society* 21 (1918).

Farquhar, Roger B. *Historic Montgomery County, Maryland: Old Homes and History*. Silver Spring, Md., 1952, 197–98.

Geiger, M. Virginia. "Anywhere so long as there be Freedom, Genealogy of the Family of Charles Carroll of Carrollton, 1737–1998." Baltimore: College of Notre Dame, 1998.

———. "Daniel Carroll, a Framer of the Constitution." Ph.D. dissertation, Catholic University of America, 1943.

A Grateful Remembrance: The Story of Montgomery County, Maryland. Rockville, Md.: Montgomery County Government and Montgomery County Historical Society, 1976, 44, 67, 75–78, 152.

Papenfuse, Edward C., et al. *A Biographical Dictionary of the Maryland Legislature*. Baltimore: Johns Hopkins University Press, 1979, 1: 199–200.

Purcell, Richard. "Daniel Carroll, Framer of the Constitution." *Records of the American Catholic Historical Society* 52 (1941): 65–87, 137–60.

Elizabeth Meredith Clymer

Birth:	c. 1743, Philadelphia, Pennsylvania
Parents:	Reese Meredith and Martha Carpenter
Marriage:	18 March 1765, George Clymer (1739–1813)
Children:	William Coleman (1766–1774); Henry (1767–1830); John Meredith (c. 1769–1794); Julian (born and died 1770); Margaret (Peggy) (1772–1799); Son (born and died 1773); Elizabeth (born c. 1775, died in infancy); Ann (Nancy) (c. 1780–1810); George (1783–1848)
Death:	24 February 1815, Northumberland County, Pennsylvania

Elizabeth Meredith was the elder daughter of Reese Meredith and his wife, Martha Carpenter, a distant relative of George Clymer's mother. Elizabeth's siblings included her brother Samuel and sister Ann. Reese Meredith was a native of England, born at Leominster in 1708. He was educated at Oxford and came to America in 1729, landing in Philadelphia, where he soon entered the counting house of merchant John Carpenter, his future father-in-law.[1] Reese was said to have had a generous and elevated mind. While George Washington was visiting Philadelphia in 1755, he entered a coffeehouse where he knew no one and was thus entirely unnoticed. Meredith came in and, noting that Washington was in an awkward situation, introduced himself and invited him home with him. He behaved with so much kindness and hospitality that Washington remained at the Meredith house the remainder of his visit to the city and made it his home on each visit thereafter to Philadelphia.[2]

Elizabeth's mother, Martha, the daughter of Philadelphia merchant John Carpenter and Ann Hoskins, died in 1769. Her grandfather Samuel Carpenter had established the first "coffee house" in Philadelphia, in the neighborhood of Front and Walnut Streets. He also had a wharf, crane, and bakery.

On 18 March 1765 at Christ Church, Philadelphia, Elizabeth married George Clymer, who had come to work for her father the previous year. Descended from a respectable family from Bristol, England, he was the only child of Christopher Clymer and Deborah Fitzwater. His parents died while he was a child, and the family of his mother's sister raised him. Clymer's uncle, William Coleman, was a prosperous merchant, one of Pennsylvania's provincial judges of the supreme court, and a friend of Benjamin Franklin.[3] In 1772 Reese Meredith made Clymer a partner, along with his son Samuel. The firm became Meredith and Sons, continuing to operate under that name until Meredith's death in November 1778, whereupon it became Meredith and Clymer.[4]

George Clymer became very public spirited, taking an active political role during protests against the Stamp Act in 1773. He headed a vigilance committee and was later a member of the Committee of Safety. Elizabeth accompanied her husband on a visit to New York and Boston for several weeks in 1774. In his diary, John Adams wrote that he had met her at a dinner, describing her as a "very facetious and social lady."[5]

After the battle of Brandywine in September 1777, the British began advancing on Philadelphia, and Clymer moved his family to a house in Chester County, about twenty-five miles outside the city. The British invasion on Pennsylvania impelled the family to move once more, further into the interior near York and Lancaster. British soldiers sought out the Clymers' house in Chester County, ransacking it, destroying much of the household furniture, and raiding the wine cellar. The family did not return to their home in Philadelphia until the spring of 1779.[6]

Elizabeth Clymer's brother Samuel Meredith (also her husband's business partner) was also active in the war. As a soldier Meredith served with distinction at Trenton, Princeton, Brandywine, and Germantown. He was made a brigadier general in the Pennsylvania militia but resigned in 1778 to return to the family business. Later, Samuel Meredith became the first treasurer of the United States, serving from 1789 to 1801. The Clymers were also close to Elizabeth's sister Ann who married Henry Hill, a prosperous wine merchant in Philadelphia. He was an original member of the Philadelphia City Troop and became colonel of the 4th Pennsylvania Regiment during the Revolutionary War. Hill later became a member of the Pennsylvania legislature and died of yellow fever in 1798. Ann had died in December 1787.[7]

Elizabeth and George Clymer had nine children, three of whom died in infancy. Elizabeth outlived all but two. William Coleman, the eldest, was born in 1766 and died in 1774 when he was eight years old. Henry, who married Mary Willing, was born a year after William Coleman and graduated from the College of New Jersey (Princeton) in 1786. He read law with James Wilson, also a signer of the Declaration of Independence and Constitution, and was admitted to the bar. John Meredith, always called by his second name, graduated from Princeton in 1787. He joined the First Philadelphia City Troop in September 1794, dying of tetanus just two months later when his unit was engaged in the Whiskey Rebellion at Parkinson Ferry.[8] Margaret (Peggy), born in late 1772, married George McCall, a merchant, in March 1794. She and her husband died within a few days of each other in 1799 of yellow fever, leaving two sons in the care of their grandparents. Julian, born in 1770, and Elizabeth, born about 1775, both died in infancy. Ann (Nancy) was born about 1780, married Charles Lewis in 1807, and died three years later. George Clymer Jr. was born in 1783 and died in 1848. His only child, Dr. Meredith Clymer, was Assistant Surgeon General during the Civil War and a noted specialist in mental diseases.[9]

In the fall of 1782, the family moved to Princeton, New Jersey. They returned to Philadelphia in the fall of 1784, although their sons Meredith and Henry remained at Princeton to attend the College of New Jersey (Princeton).[10] Yellow fever struck in 1793, and both Elizabeth and her brother became ill. The children were sent away from the city, while George Clymer devoted himself to caring for his wife and brother-in-law. The following year began on a happier note with the weddings of Henry and Peggy but ended tragically with the death of Meredith.[11]

In 1796 George Clymer was appointed with two others to negotiate a treaty with the Cherokee and Creek Indians in Georgia. In April Elizabeth traveled with her husband from Philadelphia to Savannah in a vessel that proved somewhat unsafe and unfit for the voyage. After a stormy passage, the ship made harbor in Charleston and changed crews. The Clymers continued on to Savannah, making their destination some twenty-nine days after they set out from home.[12]

Following this trip, George Clymer retired from political life. He later became the first president of the Philadelphia Bank and a sponsor of the Academy of Fine Arts, also in Philadelphia. In 1798 the Clymers bought an estate with magnificent gardens in Bucks County, Pennsylvania. The house, which had been previously owned by Robert Morris, became known as Summerseat and is located in Morrisville, opposite Trenton, New Jersey. In 1799 it was given to Henry Clymer, whose family made it their home. George Clymer died there on 24 July 1813. After his death, Elizabeth moved, along with her son Henry and his family, to Northumberland County, Pennsylvania, where she died two years later.[13]

Notes

1. James R. MacFarlane, *George Clymer: His Family and Descendants* (Sewickley, Pa.: Sewickley Printing-Shop, 1927), 12.

2. Harry Clinton Green and Mary Walcott Green, *Wives of the Signers* (Aledo, Tex.: WallBuilder Press, 1997), 280. The date of the marriage is shown as 22 March 1765 in *Pennsylvania Archives*, Second Series (Harrisburg, Pa.: E. K. Meyers, 1876), 2: 60. The records of Christ Church, Philadelphia, in *Pennsylvania Archives*, Second Series, 8: 175, show the date as 18 March 1765.

3. Green and Green, *Wives of the Signers*, 5.

4. Jerry Grundfest, "George Clymer: Philadelphia Revolutionary, 1739–1813," Ph.D. dissertation, Columbia University, 1973, 35.

5. Charles Francis Adams, *The Works of John Adams . . .* (Boston: Little Brown & Co., 1865), 2: 348.

6. Robert K. Wright Jr. and Morris J. MacGregor Jr., *Soldier-Statesmen of the Constitution* (Washington, D.C.: Government Printing Office, 1987), 153; Grundfest, "George Clymer," 131–32, 145.

7. Edward Carpenter, *Samuel Carpenter and His Descendants* (Philadelphia: J. B. Lippincott Co., 1912), 256.

8. Grundfest, "George Clymer," 32, 422–23. Grundfest states (32, 529) that according to papers at the Historical Society of Pennsylvania, Meredith died of tetanus rather than exposure.

9. Carpenter, *Samuel Carpenter and His Descendants*, 257–58, 261–62; Valeria E. Clymer Hill and Emily Elsworth Clymer, *A Record and Genealogy of the Clymer Family* (1949), 15 (Ancestry.com).

10. Grundfest, "George Clymer," 169.

11. Grundfest, "George Clymer," 426–27.

12. Grundfest, "George Clymer," 427–29.

13. MacFarlane, *George Clymer*, 9; Hill and Clymer, *A Record and Genealogy of the Clymer Family*, 11.

Bibliography

Bell, Whitfield Jenks. *Patriot-Improvers: Biographical Sketches of Members of the American Philosophical Society.* Philadelphia: American Philosophical Society, 1999, 1: 237–47.

Carpenter, Edward. *Samuel Carpenter and His Descendants.* Philadelphia: J. B. Lippincott, 1912.

Green, Harry Clinton, and Mary Wolcott Green. *Wives of the Signers.* Aledo, Tex.: WallBuilder Press, 1997.

Grundfest, Jerry. "George Clymer: Philadelphia Revolutionary, 1739–1813." Ph.D. dissertation, Columbia University, 1973 (typescript printed New York: Arno Press, 1982).

Hill, Valeria E. Clymer, and Emily Elsworth Clymer. *A Record and Genealogy of the Clymer Family.* 1949.

MacFarlane, James R. *George Clymer: His Family and Descendants.* Sewickley, Pa.: Sewickley Printing-Shop, 1927.

Nevin, David Robert Bruce. *Continental Sketches of Distinguished Pennsylvanians.* Philadelphia: Porter & Coates, 1875, 51–59.

Susan Williamson Dayton

Birth:	1758, Elizabeth, New Jersey
Parents:	Matthias Williamson and Susannah Halstead
Marriage:	28 March 1779, Jonathan Dayton (1760–1824)
Children:	Elias (1780–1824); Susan Williamson (1782–1804); Mary Lydia (Molly) (1784–1822); Hannah Rolfe (1790–1878)
Death:	after 1843, Elizabeth, New Jersey

Susan Williamson was the daughter of Matthias Williamson (1716–1807) and Susannah Halstead (1730–1793) of Elizabethtown, New Jersey.[1] She had five brothers—William, Matthias, Jacob, Benjamin, and Isaac Halstead—and two sisters, Jane and Margaretta. Matthias Williamson was a well-to-do harness and saddle maker who lived in a large mansion across from the courthouse at the intersection of Broad Street and the King's Highway, facing the parade ground during this most exciting period of the colonists' history. The inhabitants of Elizabethtown lived in houses, some of stone or brick, situated on plots of four to six acres. Each premise was surrounded by a wooden fence to keep out wandering fowl or pigs, as well as cattle as they were driven along the streets to and from the town range. In back of the houses were gardens, orchards, and numerous outbuildings.[2] While not attending church, visiting neighbors, and watching parades, Susan and her siblings could play in the orchards.

In 1774 Matthias Williamson was elected to serve on the Committee of Correspondence for Elizabethtown, and the following year he accepted a commission as colonel of a regiment of light horse. In 1776 he was designated as a brigadier general in the New Jersey militia, eventually becoming the quartermaster general for that state. In 1780 he was taken prisoner and, until exchanged, held on Long Island. Two of Susan's brothers, Matthias and William, also served in the war. Her brother Matthias eventually became a lawyer, and her brother Isaac became the governor of New Jersey (1817–1829).[3] Sister Margaretta married Jonathan Dayton's brother William but died young in 1794.

Jonathan Dayton had joined his father's regiment in 1776 after graduating from the College of New Jersey (Princeton) and saw extensive action. While the New Jersey Brigade was in Elizabeth, Jonathan married Susan Williamson on 28 March 1779 at Connecticut Farms, New Jersey. The Reverend W. Hoyt, a Presbyterian clergyman, performed the ceremony.[4] The following year Dayton was captured by a Tory band in New Jersey and detained as a prisoner of war on Staten Island but was quickly exchanged. He then once again served with his father, participating in the siege of Yorktown.[5]

In 1783 Jonathan returned home, studied law, and established a practice. He also operated a retail and wholesale mercantile firm with his father and served in the New Jersey Assembly in 1786–1787 and 1790. When his father declined to be a delegate to the Constitutional Convention, Jonathan Dayton took his place. In 1791 he was elected as a representative in Congress and was the Speaker of the House from 1795 to 1799. He then served as a senator from 1799 to 1805. Jonathan Dayton's public reputation had begun to suffer in 1800 when some of his dealings showed a conflict of interest, and he was later implicated in Aaron Burr's western conspiracy. Although indicted, Dayton's case was dismissed on the grounds that there was no proof of an overt act of treason.[6]

Jonathan and Susan Dayton had four children. Susan Williamson Dayton, born in 1782, married the Reverend Frederick Beasley on 23 August 1803, just as he was moving to a pastorate in Albany, New York. It was while he was rector of St. John's in Elizabethtown that they became well acquainted. Susan died on 27 November 1804 after giving birth to a daughter.[7] Molly, the Daytons' second daughter, married Thomas Heyward Gibbons, the son of a wealthy Georgia planter whose father had been a Tory and had moved to New Jersey after the war. Their third daughter, Hannah, married Dr. Oliver Hatfield Spencer in 1813 and after his death, Dr. George Ross Chetwood. In 1824 Elias Dayton, Susan and Jonathan's only son, went to Ohio on business for his father but died on the journey home. He never married.

In 1805 Jonathan Dayton retired to his home, Boxwood Hall, in Elizabethtown, which he bought in 1795, and gave some attention to farming. He also served two terms in the New Jersey Assembly from 1814 to 1815. In his later years, he is said to have been a contented and happy man, still active in New Jersey and Elizabethtown affairs, which reflects very much to the credit of his wife, Susan. When the Marquis de Lafayette returned to America in 1824 for a tour and visit with his many friends, the Daytons were his hosts and entertained him in their home. The visit took place just one week before Dayton's death on 9 October.[8]

In 1836 Susan transferred her house to her daughter Hannah and son-in-law, the same year she was granted a pension as a Revolutionary War widow. She died about 1843 in Elizabeth, New Jersey.[9]

Notes

1. File for Susan Dayton, Revolutionary War Pension and Bounty-Land Warrant Application Files, National Archives and Records Service, Washington, D.C., M804, states that she was seventy-six years old (born 22 July 1760) when her claim was made in 1836, but New Jersey records show that she was christened 20 August 1758 at Saint John's Episcopal Church in Elizabeth, making her seventy-eight; Esther M. Graham, *Signers of the United States Constitution from New Jersey* (Washington, D.C.: NSDAR Library, 1953), 8–9.

2. Edwin F. Hatfield, *The History of Elizabeth, New Jersey* (New York: Carlton & Lanahan, 1868), 664.

3. William Nelson, *New Jersey Biographical and Genealogical Notes from the Collections of the New Jersey Historical Society* (Newark: New Jersey Historical Society, 1916), 9: 211.

4. File for Susan Dayton, Revolutionary War Pension and Bounty-Land Warrant Application Files, National Archives and Records Service, Washington, D.C., M804.

5. Harry M. Ward, "Jonathan Dayton," *American National Biography* (New York: Oxford University Press, 1999), 6: 278–80.

6. Ward, "Jonathan Dayton," 6: 278–80.

7. Hatfield, *The History of Elizabeth, New Jersey,* 618.

8. Robert G. Ferris and James H. Charleton, *The Signers of the Constitution* (Arlington, Va.: Interpretive, 1986), 157; William H. Shaw, comp., *History of Essex and Hudson Counties, New Jersey* (Philadelphia: Everts and Peck, 1884), 1: 623.

9. File for Susan Dayton, Revolutionary War Pension and Bounty-Land Warrant Application Files, National Archives and Records Service, Washington, D.C., M804. The pension was increased in 1843, and she received back payments. There is no record, however, that the pension continued past 1843.

Bibliography

Graham, Esther M. *Signers of the Constitution from New Jersey.* Washington, D.C.: NSDAR Library, 1953.

Halstead, William Leon. *The Story of the Halsteads of the United States.* Privately published, 1934.

Hatfield, Edwin F. *History of Elizabeth, New Jersey.* New York: Carlton & Lanahan, 1868.

Murray, Nicholas. *Notes, Historical and Biographical, Concerning Elizabethtown, Its Eminent Men, Churches, and Ministers.* Elizabethtown, N.J.: E. Sanderson, 1844.

Schuyler, Hamilton. *History of St. Michael's Church in Trenton, New Jersey.* Princeton, N.J.: Princeton University Press, 1926.

Thayer, Theodore. *As We Were—The Story of Old Elizabethtown.* Newark, N.J.: New Jersey Historical Society, 1964.

Mary (Polly) Norris Dickinson

Birth:	10 July 1740, Philadelphia, Pennsylvania
Parents:	Isaac Norris II and Sarah Logan
Marriage:	19 July 1770, John Dickinson (1732–1808)
Children:	Sarah (Sally) Norris (1771–1835); Isaac Norris (1773–1777); Mary (1774–1775); John (born and died 1778); Maria (1783–1854)
Death:	23 July 1803, Wilmington, Delaware

Mary Norris, known as Polly to her friends and relatives, was one of the most amiable and desirable heiresses in the Quaker city of Philadelphia in 1769. She was the sole surviving child of Sarah Logan, daughter of colonial statesman James Logan, and Isaac Norris II, a wealthy merchant, leader of the Quaker party, and speaker of the Pennsylvania Assembly for many years. Mary was also the granddaughter of Mary Lloyd and the first Isaac Norris, a respectable merchant from Jamaica, who became mayor of Philadelphia and an official of the province of Pennsylvania. During a visit to London in the years 1706–1708, he helped rescue William Penn from debtors' prison.

Polly was mistress of Fair Hill, a handsome Jacobean-style mansion overlooking the Delaware River, built by her grandfather Norris on 530 acres in the Northern Liberties. She was born on 10 July 1740[1] in Philadelphia in the "Slate Roof House," famous as the residence of William Penn on his second visit to the city. It was also owned by her grandfather, but after his death on 4 June 1735, her family moved to Fair Hill, where Polly and her sister, Sarah, known as Sally to the family, grew up under the strict and loving care of their father. Their mother had died on 13 October 1744, following Sally's birth.

Although education was not considered important for girls in those days, the sisters had the advantage of the large, well-selected Norris library begun by their scholarly grandfather. They were very likely tutored in the Quaker religion, history, literature, horticulture, and possibly Latin and music by their father, who was also a scholar.

Fair Hill was a center of hospitality, and Polly learned to be a gracious hostess. She enjoyed a wide acquaintance with leaders of the colonial period, including Benjamin Franklin and John Dickinson. She was attracted to the latter charming young lawyer and revolutionary. He had been a delegate to the Stamp Act Congress in New York, and while he strongly advocated repeal of the act, he was opposed to any violent resistance. Polly heartily endorsed his position on this issue, and they soon became friends. Polly's cousin Deborah Logan wrote that Mary "had a very sweet and benevolent expression of countenance, a solid judgment, good sense, a most affectionate disposition, the tenderest sensibility of heart, and elevated piety."[2]

Dickinson was already a good friend of Polly's father, and when Speaker Norris died unexpectedly on 13 July 1766 without making a will, Dickinson endeavored to assist his two daughters in settling the estate in accordance with the wish and intention of their father that it be preserved as long as possible in the male line of the family. Isaac Norris left considerable property and three estates in the Liberties: Sepviva of 155 acres, Fair Hill of 530 acres, and Somerville of about 200 acres. The last tract he intended to reserve for his two daughters upon his death.[3] The legal work went slowly.

In 1769 Polly suffered the loss of her sister, Sally, to smallpox and thereafter relied more and more on John Dickinson for companionship and counsel. Their friendship grew into love so that when Dickinson proposed to her, Polly was most pleased to accept. However, she was very disturbed when he expressed his desire that their marriage be a civil one "out of meeting" and secret. He explained that he had religious reservations about the Society of Friends and organized religion. As for the secrecy, Dickinson divulged his disgust at the vulgarity conspicuous at weddings in those days. He "disliked the house of the parents filled with company remaining to tea and to supper, punch dealt out with profusion for two days, the gentlemen escorting the groom to his chamber, where they sometimes a hundred, claimed the privilege of 'kissing the bride.'"[4] Polly respected John's reservations and propriety, and the day of the wedding was set.

In anticipation of their marriage, Polly and John considered it their sacred obligation to honor what Polly was convinced had been her father's intention in conveying the estates of Fair Hill and Sepviva to the son of Charles Norris, the brother of the Speaker, and in 1790 Joseph Parker Norris became the owner of the estates. Polly and John further advised the Friends of their desire to establish a trust in the care of the Society for the proper education of poor orphan children and continued their philanthropic efforts throughout their lives.

The marriage of Mary Norris and John Dickinson took place on Thursday evening, 19 July 1770, at the home of her Aunt Norris. The wedding was kept as secret as possible. Dickinson even wrote the publishers of every newspaper requesting them not to insert any other account of his marriage than this: "Last Thursday, John Dickinson, esquire, was married to Miss Mary Norris." George Bryan, Dickinson's friend from Assembly days, who was a justice of the peace and justice of the Court of Common Pleas in Philadelphia, performed the ceremony.[5] Polly was in her thirtieth year, and John was thirty-eight.

Needless to say, the Norris family, their friends, and the Quaker Society were appalled by the secret civil marriage of Polly and John. William Logan, of "Stenton," wrote to his brother-in-law, "I am greatly concerned for the example Polly has set by this her outgoing in marriage. I fear that she has slipped from the Top of the Hill of the reputation she has gained in the society and among her friends. It will be a long time before she gains it again if ever."[6] He reported that there were very few present, namely, John's mother, his brother Philemon, Dr. Cadwalader, his wife and son Lambert, Mary's cousin Hannah Harrison, some of Samuel Norris's children, and the Norris household.

John MacPherson, serving in Dickinson's law office, wrote a friend, "the . . . amiable Miss Polly . . . is a young lady endowed with every qualification to make the marriage state happy, with a fortune of £50,000 (some say £80,000)."[7] As it turned out, no marriage proved a truer union through the vicissitudes of life. Some old friends and some new ones sent congratulations, but Mary Norris Dickinson had to satisfy her conscience. She made an apology to the Philadelphia Monthly Meeting for the breach of discipline in the conduct of her marriage. She was excused and never again departed from the Society's rules.

Polly enjoyed a delightful, though rigorous, post-wedding journey with her husband and four friends by horse and carriage into the western counties of Pennsylvania, as far as Carlisle by way of Reading. The bridal couple's companions were Polly's cousin Hannah Harrison, Charles Thompson, and Thomas Mifflin and his wife. They looked forward to visiting old friends, and Dickinson, now having a determining voice in the Norris estate, wanted to look over the landholdings and other investments in the areas visited. Dickinson reported to Aunt Mary Norris that his bride was an excellent traveler: "With her every disagreeable thing in travelling is tolerable and everything not disagreeable is pleasing."[8]

The Dickinsons made their home at Fair Hill for the next six years. With their shared wealth, they began an ambitious building program to remodel their mansion from its Jacobean aspect to a more classic Georgian style. As originally built by the first Isaac Norris, it was sixty feet square and had an English basement, one main floor, and a hip roof broken by dormer windows. The entrance doors were recessed and opened into transverse halls, which divided four large rooms. No extravagance was displayed in its interior furnishings. Its charm lay in its highly polished oak and cedar wainscoting and the spacious, livable quality of the rooms. Polly's father had constructed two dependencies, one of which was for his library, considered second in the colony only to that of James Logan.[9] Dickinson rebuilt chimneys, reframed the front and back doors with arches, added seventeen new windowsills and trusses, constructed a new staircase, and trimmed the interior with mahogany. He imported twenty-one mahogany logs, some of which he used for a new townhouse he was building in Philadelphia. Polly, however, refused to live there. At Fair Hill, they improved the library-study and added a bathing house, fishpond, and grotto.

For the gardens Polly's grandfather had sought many specimens of plants from Europe and the southern colonies. It had the first willow trees, a sprout of which had been presented to Norris's granddaughter, Debby Fields, by Benjamin Franklin. It also had the first catalpa trees in the province, which were brought from the South. Remembering the beautiful gardens he visited during his years in England, Dickinson delighted Polly by redesigning the setting for their classic Georgian mansion. The gardens were laid out in the old English style of square parterres and beds, regularly intersected by graveled walks and grass walks with clipped hedges. Several kinds of French fruit trees were imported, together with selected plants, shrubs, and herbs, at considerable cost. The credit for the elegance and final beauty of the gardens and the greenhouse was given to the ladies of the family, who were great lovers of nature and enthusiastic gardeners.

John Adams recorded in his diary that he dined at Fair Hill when he was a delegate to Philadelphia in 1774. He was greatly impressed by its imposing appearance and beautiful prospect of the city, the river, its fine gardens, and the "very grand library," which was collected by Speaker Norris and the father of Mrs. Dickinson.[10]

To make their happiness complete, the Dickinsons were blessed with the birth of a daughter, whom they named Sarah, on 10 December 1771. The happy father wrote his friend James Wilson that their little girl was "as hearty as if she had been born in the Highlands of Scotland. I hope in a few months you will know much more truth there is than you ever thought in the expression *in est sua gratis parvis* [small things have their reward]."[11]

While Polly was happily engaged in nurturing their adored baby, her loving husband was attending the Pennsylvania legislature. Dickinson opposed the Declaration of Independence in 1776. Becoming dissatisfied with the leadership in Pennsylvania, he moved his family to his plantation, Poplar Hall, in Kent County, Delaware, on 16 December 1776.[12]

The Dickinsons had departed none too soon from Philadelphia. The Continental Congress had to flee to Baltimore, and a detachment of the British Army under the command of Colonel Thomas Twisleton burned Fair Hill in the belief that it was owned by "rebel Dickinson."[13] Although Polly found Dickinson's boyhood home comfortable, she missed Fair Hill and her friends and relatives in Philadelphia. While her husband managed the farm, read books, and studied movements of the British Army anxiously, Polly raised their family and managed the household duties of the mansion. The family now included Isaac Norris, born in 1773, and John, born in 1776, as well as Sarah, then five years old. Unfortunately the two younger children died in 1778, Isaac at four and John at one. Another daughter, Mary, had also died as an infant in 1775. In 1783 the Dickinsons had their last child, a daughter called Maria.

In May 1779 Dickinson accepted appointment as a delegate to Congress from Delaware. He pushed for ratification of the Articles of Confederation on both the state level in Delaware and in Congress. While in Congress he moved his family back to a rebuilt Fair Hill, which made Polly very happy.

By the 1790s Dickinson had again moved his family to Delaware. Family life was relaxed and happy in Wilmington, and Polly encouraged visits from friends and kinsmen. The best of all guests were Deborah Norris Logan and her family. Debby was the wife of Dickinson's excellent friend and physician Dr. George Logan. They lived at Stenton, which Dr. Logan had inherited from his father, and they had three sons, one of whom eventually married Maria Dickinson.

Polly Norris was a good correspondent. She preferred the quiet life as she had long periods of ill health after 1790 until her death. She asked Isaac Norris III, who through her had inherited Fair Hill, to visit them as often as possible. She assured him that "we live in a very easy way, and if you can be satisfied with simplicity it will do—the rule here is for everybody to do as they please—eat, fast—ride or walk—read or converse—sleep or wake without the least constraint—do come and try."[14] Her letters were often filled with piety.

His quiet and gentle wife grew dearer to Dickinson with the passing years. He expressed his love and tenderness for her in a brief note that he sent from Dover: "My Love, I have but one moment to thank you for thy letter, to express my happiness in hearing of thy being better and of our children being well, to assure thee that I am very hearty; and that thou art dearer if possible to thy own."[15] With the consent of his wife, Dickinson bequeathed the Norris library, to which he had added selected books, to the college that bears his name in Carlisle, Pennsylvania, founded in 1773.[16] In 1801 he edited a two-volume edition of his own works.

On 23 July 1803 his beloved wife, Mary Norris Dickinson, who had been in ill health a long time, died in Wilmington, Delaware. She was laid to rest by her grieving family in the Friends Burial Ground in Wilmington. Dickinson greatly missed his loyal and devoted companion of thirty-three years. Affliction increased his sympathy for those suffering and in need. His elder daughter, Sarah, now ran the household smoothly and acted as her father's amanuensis. It was she with whom he discussed the charities and good works he supported, and Sally brought him back to the Quaker faith.

In the spring of 1807 Dickinson's younger daughter, Maria, and her second cousin Albanus Logan decided to marry. The marriage was planned in accordance with the Society of Friends, which was "the most earnest wish" of Maria's sister, Sally. The couple announced their intention before the Friends' monthly meeting on 4 February 1808. On 8 February Dickinson felt abnormally weary and went upstairs in the early evening, with the assistance of a servant. The next day his fever was high. Dr. Logan, Debby, and their son Albanus were summoned. John Dickinson died on 14 February 1808 and was buried beside his wife in the Friends Burial Ground in Wilmington.

Notes

1. Several dates have been given for the birth of Mary Norris. The date of 10 July 1740 is used in the finding aid to the Logan Papers in the Historical Society of Pennsylvania.

2. As quoted in Charles Janeway Stiller, *The Life and Times of John Dickinson, 1732–1738* (Philadelphia: J. B. Lippincott Co., 1891), 313.

3. Stiller, *Life and Times of John Dickinson*, 331–32.

4. Stiller, *Life and Times of John Dickinson*, 318.

5. Milton Embick Flower, *John Dickinson, Conservative Revolutionary* (Charlottesville: University of Virginia, 1983), 82–83.

6. Stiller, *Life and Times of John Dickinson*, 317.

7. Flower, *John Dickinson, Conservative Revolutionary*, 83.

8. John Dickinson to Mary Norris, 20 September 1770, quoted in Stiller, *Life and Times of John Dickinson*, 320–21.

9. Flower, *John Dickinson, Conservative Revolutionary*, 85–86.

10. Henry Simpson, *The Lives of Eminent Philadelphians, Now Deceased* (Philadelphia: William Brotherhead, 1859), 748.

11. Flower, *John Dickinson, Conservative Revolutionary*, 91.

12. David Lewis Jacobson, *John Dickinson and the Revolution in Pennsylvania, 1764–1776* (Berkeley: University of California Press, 1965), 121.

13. Simpson, *The Lives of Eminent Philadelphians, Now Deceased*, 748.

14. Jacobson, *John Dickinson and the Revolution in Pennsylvania*, 272.

15. Jacobson, *John Dickinson and the Revolution in Pennsylvania*, 273.

16. Simpson, *The Lives of Eminent Philadelphians, Now Deceased*, 753.

Bibliography

Two volumes of papers of Mary Norris Dickinson are contained in the collections of the Library Company of Philadelphia. The first volume consists of letters, written mostly prior to her marriage to John Dickinson. The second consists of poems, reflections, and other writings, both written and copied by Mary Norris and her sister Sarah. There are also letters and papers of Mary Norris Dickinson in the R. R. Logan collection at the Historical Society of Pennsylvania, and her letters to her Ridgely family friends are contained in *A Calendar of Ridgely Family Letters, 1742–1899*, edited by Leon de Valinger and Virginia E. Shaw in three volumes (Dover, 1948). Published sources include the following:

Colburn, Howard T. "The Historical Perspective of John Dickinson," in *Dickinson College, Early Dickinsonia*. Carlisle, n.p., 1961, 3–37.

———. "John Dickinson, Historical Revolutionary," *Pennsylvania Magazine of History and Biography* 83 (July 1959): 271–92.

Conrad, Henry C. *History of the State of Delaware*. 3 vols. Wilmington: privately printed, 1908.

Cook, Frank G. "John Dickinson," *Atlantic Monthly* 65 (January 1890): 70–83.

Curley, Ann Conser. "Mary Dickinson: A Quiet Woman of Substance," *Dickinson Magazine* (October 1990).

Flower, Milton Embick. *John Dickinson: Conservative Revolutionary*. Charlottesville: University of Virginia, 1983.

Fredman, Lionel C. *John Dickinson, American Revolutionary Statesman*. Charlotteville, New York, 1974.

Jacobson, David Lewis. *John Dickinson and the Revolution in Pennsylvania, 1764–1776.* Berkeley: University of California Press, 1965.

Nevin, David Robert Bruce. *Continental Sketches of Distinguished Pennsylvanians.* Philadelphia: Porter & Coates, 1875, 202–8.

Richards, Robert Haven. *The Life and Character of John Dickinson.* Wilmington: Historical Society of Delaware, 1891.

Scull, Florence D. *John Dickinson Sounds the Alarm.* Philadelphia: Auerbach Publishers, 1972.

Simpson, Henry. *The Lives of Eminent Philadelphians Now Deceased.* Philadelphia: William Brotherhead, 1859.

Stiller, Charles Janeway. *The Life and Times of John Dickinson, 1732–1808.* Philadelphia: J. B. Lippincott Co., 1891.

Tolles, Frederick B. "John Dickinson and the Quakers," in *Dickinson College, John and Mary's College.* Westwood, New Jersey: Revell, 1956, 67–88.

Wolf, Edwin. *John Dickinson, Forgotten Patriot.* Wilmington: n.p., 1967.

Catherine (Kitty) Nicholson Few

Birth:	7 August 1764, New York, New York
Parents:	James Nicholson and Frances Witter
Marriage:	8 July 1788, William Few Jr. (1748–1828)
Children:	Frances (1789–1885); Mary (1790–1872); Matilda (1794–1878); Albert (1797–1810)
Death:	7 August 1854, New York, New York

Catherine Nicholson, eldest daughter of the eight children (two of whom died in infancy) of Commodore James Nicholson (c.1736–1804) and his wife, Frances (1744–1832), was born in New York City on 7 August 1764.[1] The family had moved to the eastern shore of Maryland by 1775, where her father, formerly in the Royal Navy, offered his services to Maryland. In recognition of those services, he was appointed as a captain in the new Continental Navy the following year. Two of Catherine's uncles, Samuel and John Nicholson, also served as captains in the Continental Navy. After the war James Nicholson and his family returned to New York, where his house became a meeting place for Republican politicians of New York City, including the followers of Thomas Jefferson and Aaron Burr.

William Few, who represented Georgia, had served in the Continental Congress from 1780 to 1788 and had lived in New York intermittently when Congress met there. It was also there that he met Catherine, known informally as Kitty. On the occasion of her marriage, the Few Bible recorded "Catherine—married William Few, Ga., married in New York by Rev. Docr. Livingston the 8th July 1788."[2] Thomas Paine greatly admired Catherine, and he wrote her several letters. Upon her marriage he wrote her a long one: "I very affectionately congratulate Mr. and Mrs. Few on their happy marriage, every branch of the families allied by that connection; and I request my fair correspondent to present me to her partner, and to say for me, that he has obtained one of the highest Prizes on the wheel . . . [signed] Thomas Paine—or if you better like it, 'Common Sense.'"[3] Unfortunately, the two were estranged after Thomas Paine criticized formal religion. In later years, Catherine Few often told her great-granddaughter about her visit to Thomas Paine on his deathbed. Paine expressed a wish to see her, and she, reluctant to go, was urged by her family to answer his dying wish. William Few and his wife visited Paine, but when she spoke some words of Christian hope to the dying man, he turned his face to the wall and kept silent.[4]

Three of Kitty's sisters also married into political families. Hannah married Albert Gallatin, diplomat and secretary of the Treasury under Presidents Jefferson and Madison; Frances (Fanny) married Joshua Seney, a representative in Congress from Maryland; and Maria married John Montgomery, who also represented Maryland in Congress and was later mayor of Baltimore. Kitty Few and her husband had four children: Frances, Mary, Matilda, and Albert. Albert died in 1810 at the age of thirteen, but his sisters all grew to adulthood. Frances married her cousin Albert Chrystie, a New York banker, and her sister Matilda married John C. Tillotson. Mary Few remained single.

William Few became one of Georgia's first U.S. senators (1789–1793) and afterward served in the state assembly, having returned to Georgia in 1793.[5] In 1799 he decided to move to New York, stating, "My health was greatly impaired, and the health of my family was also declining. I then determined on visiting New York, May 1799. I set out with my family from Savannah, where we embarked for New York and arrived ten days later."[6] Yellow fever was then prevalent in New York, but his father-in-law took a spacious house on the eastern bank of the East River for both families, where they spent an agreeable summer, more healthy and pleasant than Georgia. William began thinking of moving permanently to New York, detesting both the scorching heat and the slavery of the South. He subsequently bought a five-acre farm in the Washington Square section of Manhattan.[7]

By 1801 William Few was into the political life of New York and served in that state's legislature from 1802 to 1804. He was also a successful banker. In 1816, at the age of sixty-eight, he retired and made his home with his daughter Frances and son-in-law Albert Chrystie at Fishkill, Beacon, New York. William Few died there on 16 July 1828. Catherine Few survived her husband by many years, living with her daughter Mary in New York. When she died in 1854, the following account appeared in the family Bible: "Not withstanding her great age, she died or rather calmly fell asleep in full and clear possession of her mind, and a bright hope of immortality in the kingdom of God and Christ and was buried in the family vault, Trinity Churchyard."[8]

Notes

1. Florence Knight Fruth, *Some Descendants of Richard Few of Chester County, Pennsylvania, and Allied Lines, 1682–1976* (Beaver Falls, Pa.: McClain Printing, 1977), 91. Much of the information was taken from the "Family Records of William Few and Wife, Catherine Few," William Few Collection, Georgia Department of Archives and History, which included original Bible records loaned by Katherine B. Clark, New York, 1958.

2. Fruth, *Some Descendants of Richard Few*, 92.

3. Fruth, *Some Descendants of Richard Few*, 92.

4. Fruth, *Some Descendants of Richard Few*, 92.

5. Charles C. Jones Jr., "William Few Lieutenant-Colonel Georgia Militia in the Revolutionary Service with Autobiography of Col. William Few of Georgia," *Magazine of American History with Notes and Queries* 7 (November 1881): 354.

6. Jones, "William Few," 356; Fruth, *Some Descendants of Richard Few*, 91.

7. Jones, "William Few," 356; Fruth, *Some Descendants of Richard Few*, 93.

8. Fruth, *Some Descendants of Richard Few*, 93.

Bibliography

Letters of Catherine Nicholson Few are included in the papers of William and Catherine Nicholson Few in the Hargrett Rare Book and Manuscript Library, University of Georgia, and in the papers of her brother James Witter Nicholson in the Hesburgh Library, University of Notre Dame, Indiana, and the Columbia University Library in New York. Other sources are as follows:

Ferris, Robert G., and James H. Charleton. *The Signers of the Constitution*. Arlington, Va.: Interpretive, 1986.

Fruth, Florence Knight. *Some Descendants of Richard Few of Chester County, Penn. and Allied Lines, 1682–1976.* Beaver Falls, Pa.: McClain Printing, 1977.

Jones, Charles C., Jr. "William Few, Lieutenant-Colonel Georgia Militia in the Revolutionary Service, with Autobiography of Col. William Few of Georgia." *Magazine of American History with Notes and Queries* 7 (November 1881): 339–58.

Lechter, Marion. "William Few, Jr." In *Men of Mark in Georgia*, ed. William J. Northen. 6 vols. Atlanta: A. B. Caldwell, 1907–1912. Spartanburg, S.C.: Reprint Co., 1974.

Catharine Meade Fitzsimons

Birth: c. 1740, Philadelphia, Pennsylvania (possibly Barbados)
Parents: Robert Meade and Mary Stretch
Marriage: 23 November 1761, Thomas Fitzsimons (1741–1811)
Children: None
Death: 20 June 1810, Philadelphia, Pennsylvania

Catharine Meade was the middle child of three born to Robert Meade (c. 1685–1754) and Mary Stretch. Robert Meade was an Irish refugee from Limerick and is known to have resided in Philadelphia as early as 1732. He also had extensive commercial enterprises in Barbados. He was prominent among Roman Catholics and helped to build St. Mary's Church in Philadelphia where he was buried in 1754.[1]

Catharine had an older brother, Garrett, and a younger brother, George, whose grandson was General George G. Meade of Civil War fame.[2] It appears that the children were in Barbados with their uncle, George Stretch, when their father died (their mother had evidently died earlier). At Robert Meade's death, his children inherited the vast fortune he had amassed in both Philadelphia and Barbados. Catharine's brothers became partners in Garrett and George Meade and Company, Inc., which operated out of Philadelphia, then the largest port in America. When Garrett retired from the company in 1772, it became known as George Meade and Company.[3]

Thomas Fitzsimons was born in County Wicklow, Ireland, in 1741 and immigrated to America about 1760. He joined the firm of George Meade and Company, and on 23 November 1761 he married Catharine. Thomas Fitzsimons became a partner in the company after Garrett Meade's departure. Although the Fitzsimons had no children of their own, they were godparents for three of George Meade's children: Henrietta, George, and Robert.[4]

Thomas Fitzsimons became a leading Philadelphian merchant of considerable talents, who had large and varied interests, and he owned his own shipping vessels. During the Revolutionary War, Thomas Fitzsimons commanded a militia company from Philadelphia, and he also sat on the Philadelphia Committee of Correspondence, Council of Safety, and Navy Board. George Meade and Company provided supplies to the military forces, and near the end of the war the company donated five thousand pounds to the Continental Army.[5] The company prospered during the war, but failed during an economic downturn in 1783, and the partnership was dissolved in 1784.

Catharine and Thomas Fitzsimons were devout Roman Catholics and were the largest financial contributors to the erection of St. Augustine's Catholic Church in Philadelphia. During their later lives, however, they worshipped at St. Mary's Catholic Church at Fourth and Spruce Streets in Philadelphia, where they sat in Ambassador's Pew No. 11.[6]

The Fitzsimons were considered upper middle class, and they had a few slaves for the house and garden. They entertained frequently in their pleasant home on Walnut Street in Philadelphia, and in 1782 George Washington, Alexander Hamilton, Thomas Jefferson, and John Adams, among others, came to tea and discussed affairs of state.[7] In 1805 Fitzsimons went bankrupt as a result of land speculation, and although he regained some of his wealth, his prestige was diminished.

In addition to their godchildren, the Fitzsimons lavished affection upon the children of his twin sister, Ann, who was married to Peter Maitland. Treasures were passed down from Catharine and Thomas, who gave them to Ann, including a colonial mahogany bookcase, their bed, and a lowboy. Along with the treasures of silver and wood went priceless papers. One letter was to Thomas Jefferson in which Thomas Fitzsimons unburdened his heart of its load of grief to his understanding old friend. Catharine, wrote Fitzsimons, was so very ill that he had lost all hope and feared that his wife might die any day. She had been an invalid for years, a victim of tuberculosis. Despite her illness, theirs had been a thoroughly happy marriage, and Fitzsimons could see no reason why he should go on living if the little wife he cared for so tenderly should be taken from him.[8]

The twilight of life had now come, and the shades of evening were fast approaching. The last years of the life of Thomas formed a marked contrast with his earlier period of activity when the vigor of youth spurred him on in commerce, politics, war, and religion; now the embers of that energy were smoldering into the ashes of age. As he was passing the few remaining milestones on the journey to the final goal, his burden grew heavier. His wife, Catharine, a faithful companion, a constant consolation, and ever his support, fell into decline and died on 20 June 1810.[9]

Catharine Meade Fitzsimons was laid to rest in St. Mary's graveyard. Within the short space of a year Thomas Fitzsimons followed his wife in death on 26 August 1811—close in life and close in death. He was also laid to rest with his wife in Vault 14 of St. Mary's graveyard.[10]

Notes

1. James Aloysius Farrell, "Thomas FitzSimons: Catholic Signer of the American Constitution," *Records of the American Catholic Historical Society of Philadelphia* 39 (September 1928): 182–83; Marguerite Horan Gowan, "Honoring the Memory of Thomas Fitzsimons, Last Week Serves to Recall Part Patriot, Soldier, and Financier Played in Birth of U.S. of A's Constitution," *Catholic Standard and Times* (8 October 1937).

2. Asa Earl Martin, "Thomas Fitzsimons," *Dictionary of American Biography*, Allen Johnson and Dumas Malone, eds. (New York: Charles Scribner's Sons, 1931), 6: 473–74; Farrell, "Thomas FitzSimons, Catholic Signer," 183.

3. R. W. Meade, "George Meade: A Patriot of the Revolutionary Era," *Records of the American Catholic Historical Society of Philadelphia* 3 (1888–1891): 194–96; Farrell, "Thomas FitzSimons: Catholic Signer," 183; John H. Frederick, "George Meade," *Dictionary of American Biography*, 12: 473–74.

4. Clinton Rossiter, *1787: The Grand Convention* (New York: W. W. Norton & Co., 1987), 104; Martin, "Thomas Fitzsimons," 444–45; Gowan, "Honoring the Memory."

5. Frank Donovan, *Mr. Madison's Constitution* (New York: Dodd, Mead & Co., 1965), 31; Forrest McDonald, *We the People* (Chicago: University of Chicago Press, 1958), 60, 87; Rossiter, *1787: The Grand Convention*, 104; Richard S. Bernstein and Kym S. Rice, *Are We To Be a Nation? The Making of the Constitution* (Cambridge: Harvard University Press, 1987), 184; Charles L. Mee Jr., *The Genius of the People* (New York: Harper & Row, 1987), 320; Robert K. Wright and Morris J. MacGregor Jr., "Thomas Fitzsimons," *Soldier-Statesmen of the Constitution* (Washington, D.C.: Government Printing Office, 1987), 88–90.

6. Rossiter, *1787: The Grand Convention*, 104; Farrell, "Thomas FitzSimons: Catholic Signer," 218; Thomas C. Middleton, ed. "Pew Registers of St. Mary's Church, Philadelphia, 1787–1791," *Records of the American Catholic Historical Society of Philadelphia* 5 (1894): 369.

7. Rossiter, *1787: The Grand Convention*, 143; McDonald, *We the People*, 89–90; Gowen, "Honoring the Memory."

8. Gowen, "Honoring the Memory."

9. Farrell, "Thomas FitzSimons: Catholic Signer," 219–20.

10. John J. Maitland, "St. Mary's Graveyard," *Records of the American Catholic Historical Society* 3 (1889–1891): 259; Farrell, "Thomas FitzSimons: Catholic Signer," 220.

Bibliography

Burnett, Edmund C. "The Catholic Signers of the Constitution." *The Constitution of the United States: Addresses in Commemoration of the Sesquicentennial of its Signing*

17 September 1787, ed. Herbert Wright. Washington, D.C.: Catholic University of America, 1938, 40–54.

Donovan, Frank. *Mr. Madison's Constitution.* New York: Dodd, Mead & Co., 1965.

Farrell, James Aloysius. "Thomas FitzSimons: Catholic Signer of the American Constitution." *Records of the American Catholic Historical Society of Philadelphia* 39 (September 1928): 175–224.

Ferris, Robert G., and James H. Charleton. *The Signers of the Constitution.* Flagstaff, Ariz.: Interpretive Publications, 1986.

Flanders, Henry. "Thomas Fitzsimmons." *Pennsylvania Magazine of History and Biography* 2 (1878): 306–14.

Frederick, John H. "George Meade." *Dictionary of American Biography*, ed. Allen Johnson and Dumas Malone. New York: Charles Scribner's Sons, 1933, 12: 473–74.

Gowan, Marguerite Horan. "Honoring the Memory of Thomas Fitzsimons, Last Week Serves to Recall Part Patriot, Soldier, and Financier Played in Birth of U.S. of A's Constitution." *Catholic Standard and Times* (8 October 1937).

Griffin, Martin I. J. "Thomas Fitz Simons: Pennsylvania's Catholic Signer of the Constitution." *American Catholic Historical Researches* 5 (January 1888): 2–27. Revised and expanded edition appeared in *Records of the American Catholic Historical Society of Philadelphia* 2 (1886–1888): 45–111.

Maitland, John J., comp. "Saint Mary's Graveyard." *Records of the American Catholic Historical Society of Philadelphia* 3 (1888–1891): 253–94.

Martin, Asa Earl. "Thomas Fitzsimons." *Dictionary of American Biography*, ed. Allen Johnson and Dumas Malone. New York: Charles Scribner's Sons, 1931, 6: 444–45.

McDonald, Forrest. *We the People.* Chicago: University of Chicago Press, 1958.

Meade, R. W. "George Meade: A Patriot of the Revolutionary Era." *Records of the American Catholic Historical Society of Philadelphia* 3 (1888–1891): 193–220.

Mee, Charles L., Jr. *The Genius of the People.* New York: Harper & Row, 1987.

Middleton, Thomas C., ed. "Pew Registers of St. Mary's Church, Philadelphia, 1787–1791." *Records of the American Catholic Historical Society of Philadelphia* 5 (1894): 357–84.

Pennsylvania Vital Records from Pennsylvania Genealogical Magazine and Pennsylvania Magazine of History and Biography. Baltimore: Genealogical Publishing Co., 1983, 1: 553 (marriage date).

Peters, William. *A More Perfect Union.* New York: Crown Publishers, 1987.

Rossiter, Clinton. *1787: The Grand Convention.* New York: W. W. Norton, 1987.

Scharf, J. T., and Westcott, T. *History of Philadelphia, 1609–1884.* Philadelphia: L. H. Everts & Co., 1884.

Simpson, Henry. *The Lives of Eminent Phildelphians.* Philadelphia: William Brotherhead, 1859.

Wright, Robert K., and Morris J. MacGregor Jr. "Thomas Fitzsimons." *Soldier-Statesmen of the Constitution.* Washington, D.C.: Government Printing Office, 1987, 88–90.

Deborah (Debby)
Read Rogers Franklin

Birth: c. 1704, Birmingham, England?
Parents: John Read and Sarah White
Marriages: 5 August 1725, John Rogers (d. 1745?)
             1 September 1730, Benjamin Franklin (1706–1790)
Children: Francis (Franky) Folger (1732–1736); Sarah (Sally) (1743–1808)
Death: 19 December 1774, Philadelphia, Pennsylvania

Deborah Read was born about 1704, probably in Birmingham, England, where her family originated, to John and Sarah Read. Nothing is known about her childhood. The family probably arrived in Philadelphia in about 1711. Deborah had two brothers, James and John, and a sister, Frances, who survived to maturity. Her father, a carpenter and building contractor, died in 1724.[1]

According to Benjamin Franklin, who called his wife Debby, they met on a Sunday morning in October 1723 after he had come to Philadelphia to seek his fortune. Franklin, then a seventeen-year-old, with a loaf of bread under each arm and munching a third, walked up Market Street passing the house of John Read "when she, standing at the door, saw me and thought I made, as I most certainly did, a most awkward, ridiculous appearance."[2] He took a room in the Read family home, remaining there until the following year when he left for England. In writing about these events, Franklin stated:

> I had made some courtship, during this time, with Miss Read. I had a great respect and affection for her and some reason to believe she had the same for me. But, as I was to take a long voyage and we were both very young, only a little above 18, it was thought most prudent by her mother to prevent our going too far at present as marriage. If it was to take place, it should happen after my return.[3]

Franklin went to England and returned on 11 October 1726. He wrote Deborah only one letter while he was away. Her mother and friends persuaded her to marry another man, John Rogers—a potter newly immigrated from England—on 5 August 1725 at Christ Church in Philadelphia. About four months later, Deborah was persuaded that her husband had another wife elsewhere, and she returned to her mother's house. She refused to cohabit with him or to bear his name. Rogers got into debt and in May 1728 left Philadelphia for the West Indies, where rumor said he was later killed in a brawl.[4]

Franklin pitied Debby's situation, reporting that she was "generally dejected, seldom cheerful, and avoided company."[5] Moreover, he considered that he might be the main cause of her unhappiness. Despite the difficulties, Franklin took her as his common-law wife on 1 September 1730 and later wrote that she had proved to be a good and faithful companion. Joining the household were Deborah's mother, Sarah, and William, Franklin's illegitimate son, who was born a few months later.[6]

The family thrived, with Benjamin soon being able to pay off his debts. Deborah's mother ran a shop in the front of the house, while Franklin's printing shop was in the rear. Deborah helped in both, gradually taking on more duties, keeping the books, investing in real estate, and managing the postal service after Franklin became postmaster for the colonies. After her death, Franklin maintained that his success was largely due to his wife.[7]

Although William was brought up in the Franklin household, his relationship with Deborah was strained, which grew worse after she had her own son, Francis, called Franky, on 20 October 1732. In later years, however, the antipathy between Deborah and William lessened considerably. A delight to both parents, Franky died of smallpox at age four. Seven years later, Benjamin and Debby had another child, a daughter, Sarah, whom they called Sally.[8]

In 1757 Franklin went on the first of his trips abroad and stayed five years, leaving Deborah to run the household, store, and postal service. In 1760, while he was absent, Deborah's mother died in a kitchen fire, and Debby grew more anxious about her husband's return. Franklin finally did so but hoped he could relocate the family to England. Deborah refused to cross the Atlantic, fearing the voyage. She also refused to accompany him to New York or on a tour of the colonies. Sally, who had grown into a young woman, accompanied him on the latter trip. At nineteen she resembled her mother except that she had been better educated. Deborah, although a good manager of her husband's affairs and devoted to her family, was far from his equal in intelligence or adaptability to social situations.[9]

After a short sojourn at home, Franklin left again for England in order to petition against the proprietary government. Deborah again refused to sail and also refused permission for Sally to accompany him. He told Debby that he expected to be home by the end of the summer but was absent for more than ten years. Deborah never saw her husband again.[10]

On 16 September 1765, while Franklin was in London, Deborah faced a threatened mob attack against her house by those who felt that her husband was not fighting vigorously enough against the Stamp Act. She first sent Sally off to stay with her brother, William, then governor of New Jersey. Then, with the help of relatives, Debby turned one room into a magazine and declared she would not stir. The night ended quietly without any rioting.[11]

Sally married Richard Bache in 1767, while Franklin was still in England. The Baches lived with Deborah during his absence and eventually had eight children. Franklin first met Bache in London while the latter was visiting his family and wrote Deborah that he was greatly impressed with the young merchant.[12]

Two years later Deborah had a stroke, which impaired her memory and understanding, and thereafter her health deteriorated. Her doctor, Thomas Bond, warned Franklin that although she had recovered, her constitution was weakened. In 1771 her memory failed completely, and William Franklin told his father that every day she was becoming more and more unfit to be left alone. Franklin had authorized the bank in Philadelphia to allow his wife thirty pounds a month, but when she did not send him an account of how she spent the money, he refused to increase the sum. Eventually, he justified his attitude, at least to himself, with the statement that her memory was too much impaired for the management of funds without danger of injuring the fortune of his daughter and grandchildren. As a result, she had to start borrowing from his friends. On 19 December 1774 Deborah had another stroke, from which she died. William wrote to his father after the funeral at Christ Church that "she told me that she never expected to see you unless you returned this winter, for she was sure she would not live until next summer. I heartily wish you had happened to have come over in the fall as I think her disappointment in that respect played a good deal on her spirits."[13]

Benjamin Franklin died 10 April 1790 and was laid to rest beside Deborah in Christ Church Burial Ground. A crowd of twenty thousand attended the funeral, the largest ever to assemble in Philadelphia. The tomb has his own simple wording as his will directed—Benjamin and Deborah Franklin 1790.[14]

Notes

1. Claude-Anne Lopez, "Deborah Read Franklin," *American National Biography* (New York: Oxford University Press, 1999), 8: 396.

2. Benjamin Franklin, *The Autobiography of Benjamin Franklin* (Philadelphia: Philip Altemus, 1895), 57–58.

3. Franklin, *Autobiography*, 76.

4. Franklin, *Autobiography*, 99; Lopez, "Deborah Read Franklin," 396.

5. Franklin, *Autobiography*, 136.

6. Franklin, *Autobiography*, 136.

7. Pierre-Jean Cabanis, "Notice sur Benjamin Franklin," *Oeuvres posthumes de Cabanis* 5 (1825): 233–34, as quoted in Lopez, "Deborah Read Franklin," 397.

8. Cokie Roberts, *Founding Mothers: The Women who Raised Our Nation* (New York: HarperCollins, 2004), 26–27.

9. Willard Randall, *A Little Revenge* (Boston: Little Brown, 1984), 42, 44, 186.

10. Roberts, *Founding Mothers*, 29–30.

11. Walter Isaacson, *Benjamin Franklin: An American Life* (New York: Simon & Schuster, 2004), 224.

12. Lopez, "Deborah Read Franklin," 397; Roberts, *Founding Mothers,* 34–35.

13. Ronald Clark, *A Biography of Benjamin Franklin* (New York: Random House, 1983), 235.

14. Clark, *A Biography,* 347.

Bibliography

Deborah Read Franklin's account books and letters are among the records of the American Philosophical Society in Philadelphia, and information is also available from the papers of her husband Benjamin.

Clark, Ronald. *A Biography of Benjamin Franklin.* New York: Random House, 1983.

Green, Harry Clinton, and Mary Wolcott Green. *Wives of the Signers.* Aledo, Tex.: WallBuilder Press, 1997.

James, Edward T., Janet Wilson James, and Paul S. Boyer, eds. *Notable American Women, 1607–1950: A Biographical Dictionary.* 2 vols. Cambridge, Mass.: Belknap Press of Harvard University, 1974, 1: 663–64.

Kelley, Joseph J., Jr., and Sol Feinstone. *Courage and Candlelight: The Feminine Spirit of '76.* Harrisburg: Stackpole Books, 1974, 101–38, 234.

Labaree, Leonard Woods, et al., eds. *The Papers of Benjamin Franklin.* 38 vols. New Haven, Conn.: Yale University Press, 1955–2006.

Lopez, Claude Anne. "Deborah Read Franklin." *American National Biography.* New York: Oxford University Press, 1999, 8: 396–98.

Lopez, Claude Anne, and Eugenia W. Herbert. *The Private Franklin: The Man and his Family.* New Haven, Conn.: Yale University Press, 1975.

Skemp, Sheila. "Family Partnerships; The Working Woman, Honoring Deborah Franklin." *Benjamin Franklin and Women,* ed. Larry E. Tise. University Park: University of Pennsylvania, 2000.

Van Doren, Carl. *Benjamin Franklin.* New York: The Viking Press, 1938.

Warren, Ruth. *A Pictorial History of Women in America.* New York: Crown, 1975, 47–49.

Rebecca Call Gorham

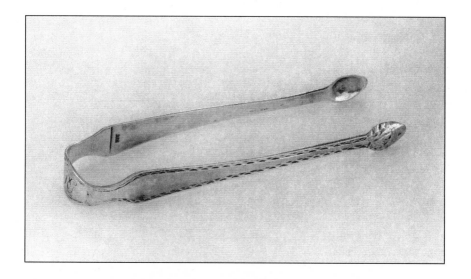

Birth:	14 May 1744, Charlestown, Massachusetts
Parents:	Caleb Call and Rebecca Stimpson
Marriage:	6 September 1763, Nathaniel Gorham (1738–1796)
Children:	Nathaniel (1763–1826); Rebecca (1765–1834); Mary (1767–1832); Elizabeth (1769–70); Ann (1771–1830); Benjamin (1775–1855); John (1772–1773); Stephen (1776–1849); Lydia (1779–1856)
Death:	18 November 1812, Charlestown, Massachusetts

Rebecca Call was born to Caleb Call (1718–1780) and Rebecca Stimpson (1719–1765) on 14 May 1744 and christened six days later. Her father, a prominent citizen of Charlestown, Massachusetts, was a baker by trade and followed that vocation there. Of Rebecca Call's thirteen siblings, seven survived to maturity: Joseph, Benjamin, Samuel, Anne, Elizabeth, John, and Martha. After their mother died, their father married Lydia Soley, widow of John Stevens and of Stephen Greenleaf.[1]

Nathaniel Gorham was also born and raised in Charlestown. He opened up a merchant house there in 1759, after having served an apprenticeship in Connecticut for several years. He married Rebecca Call on 6 September 1763 in Charlestown, where the couple made their home, and their first child, also called Nathaniel, was born the following month. The younger Nathaniel became an early supervisor of Canandaigua, New York, an Ontario County (New York) judge, and president of the Ontario Bank until his death. In all, Rebecca and Nathaniel had nine children, of whom seven lived to adulthood. Their daughter Rebecca married Warham Parks, an officer in the Revolutionary War who had been wounded at the battle of Saratoga. Mary married her cousin Dr. George Bartlett of Charlestown. Ann married Peter Chardon Brooks, a merchant who at one time was said to be the wealthiest man in New England, and their daughter married Charles Francis Adams, son of John Quincy Adams. Benjamin Gorham, an eminent Boston lawyer, served in the Massachusetts legislature and eventually became a representative in Congress from that state. Stephen remained in Charlestown as a merchant and justice of the peace and was one of the original founders of the Harvard Church. Lydia married John Phillips, founder of Andover Theological Seminary.[2]

In 1771 Nathaniel entered politics when he was elected to the Massachusetts legislature. He had early espoused the patriot cause by opposing British measures to enforce custom duties. During the Revolutionary War, British artillery fire prior to the battle of Bunker Hill largely destroyed Charlestown, and the Gorhams were forced to seek asylum in nearby Lunenburg until the British left Boston in March 1776. Although a great deal of their property was ravaged, Nathaniel managed to recoup much of the loss. He continued in politics and was elected to the Continental Congress in 1782.[3]

After the Constitutional Convention in 1787, Nathaniel Gorham retired, spending most of his time in land speculation, which eventually bankrupted him. He died suddenly of a stroke in 1796, and Rebecca died sixteen years later. Both are buried in the Phipps Street Cemetery in Charlestown.

Notes

1. George Collyer Whittier, *Genealogy of the Stimpson Family of Charlestown, Mass., and Its Allied Lines* (Boston: Press of David Clapp & Son, 1907), 26.

2. Whittier, *Genealogy of the Stimpson Family*, 30, 49–55; William Richard Cutter, *Genealogical and Family History of Western New York: A Record of the Achievements of Her People in the Making of a Commonwealth and the Building of a Nation* (New York: Lewis Publishing Co., 1912), 2: 538.

3. Robert G. Ferris and James H. Charleton, *The Signers of the Constitution* (Flagstaff, Ariz.: Interpretive Publications, 1986), 170–72.

Bibliography

Cutter, William Richard. *Genealogical and Family History of Western New York: A Record of the Achievements of Her People in the Making of a Commonwealth and the Building of a Nation.* New York: Lewis Historical Publishing Co., 1912, 2: 538.

Whittier, Charles Collyer. *Genealogy of the Stimpson Family of Charlestown, Mass., and Its Allied Lines.* Boston: Press of David Clapp & Son, 1907.

Elizabeth (Betsey) Schuyler Hamilton

Birth:	9 August 1757, Albany, New York
Parents:	Philip Schuyler and Catherine Van Rensselaer
Marriage:	14 December 1780, Alexander Hamilton (1757–1804)
Children:	Philip (1782–1801); Angelica (1784–1857); Alexander (1786–1875); James Alexander (1788–1878); John Church (1792–1882); William Stephen (1797–1850); Eliza (1799–1859); Philip (1802–1884)
Death:	9 November 1854, Washington, D.C.

Elizabeth (also known as Betsey or Eliza) Schuyler was born on 9 August 1757 in Albany, New York. Her parents were General Philip Schuyler, a well-known military and political leader in upstate New York, and Catherine Van Rensselaer. Both parents were related to some of the most affluent and socially prominent Dutch families who had settled near Albany. She was the second daughter in a close-knit family of three sons and five daughters who survived infancy. As was usual at that time, she received no formal education and learned all her domestic arts at home. Her main talents were domestic, and she is best remembered as a loving wife and devoted mother.[1]

Betsey Schuyler fell in love with the dashing Alexander Hamilton whom she met in Morristown, New Jersey, while he was serving as aide-de-camp to General George Washington. Hamilton was born on Nevis, British West Indies, and the legitimacy of his birth was somewhat in doubt, since his mother was not formally divorced from her first husband when she married Hamilton's father. Both parents died when Hamilton was quite young, and an aunt sent him to New York City in 1772, where he attended Kings College (now Columbia University). He soon became caught up with the Revolutionary spirit and left to join the staff of General Washington as aide with the rank of lieutenant colonel.[2]

Hamilton married Betsey Schuyler on 14 December 1780 at the Schuyler home, with her family's blessing. James McHenry, in attendance, even wrote a poem for the occasion.[3] There is every indication that Hamilton was deeply in love with his wife despite circulation of slanderous pamphlets concerning other women. In 1797 he wrote to a friend, "It is impossible to be happier than I am in a wife."[4] Betsey, in her turn, was ever faithful and steadfastly loyal to her husband.

The Hamiltons had eight children. Their first son, Philip, met with the same tragic fate as his father. While a student at Columbia College, he was killed in a duel on 24 November 1801 at Weehawken, New Jersey, the same place his father was fatally wounded by Aaron Burr in 1804.[5] Not long after, their eldest daughter, Angelica, sank into a fog of confusion, from which she never recovered. At first her mother cared for her, but eventually Angelica was institutionalized for insanity. None of the children ever exceeded their father in fame, but the sons all entered professional careers, and some held minor political posts in the new government. One son, John Church, took a law degree, served in the War of 1812, collected his father's papers, and wrote his biography. Betsey herself had sorted and arranged her husband's papers, letters, and manuscripts after his death prior to their acquisition by the federal government. Like their brother John Church, James and Alexander also took law degrees and served in the War of 1812. James also wrote his *Reminiscences*, which covered the administrations of Andrew Jackson and Martin Van Buren. William Stephen attended

West Point but resigned before graduating. He moved west, served in the Illinois militia, and went into mining, dying in California in 1850. In 1837, her eightieth year, Eliza made the long journey west to visit her son who was then living in Wisconsin. The last-born, called Philip after his deceased brother, also went into law practice in New York. The Hamiltons' younger daughter, Eliza, married Sidney A. Holly, a New York merchant.[6]

In 1791 Hamilton began an affair with Maria Reynolds. Her husband, well aware of the liaison, supported it to gain money from Hamilton. When Reynolds implicated Hamilton in a scheme involving financial improprieties, however, Hamilton turned Maria's letters, which proved Hamilton's innocence in any monetary corruption, over to his congressional inquirers. The inquiry was private, and the affair did not become public until 1797 when a pamphleteer gained access to Maria's letters and published them, also bringing up the previous charges of financial misconduct. Hamilton defended himself by publishing his own pamphlet, in which he acknowledged the affair but cleared himself of the other charges. In his lengthy confession and defense, he showed deep remorse for hurting his beloved wife and family.[7] Elizabeth not only forgave her husband but years later spurned the overtures of James Monroe, whom she blamed for having made the whole affair public.[8]

Eliza and her seven children reached Hamilton's bedside soon after his mortal wounding by Aaron Burr, but she was at first not told the true nature of his affliction for fear that she would become frantic. At the time of his death, Hamilton was declared insolvent. His executors proceeded to purchase his home, the Grange, built between 1800 and 1802 on Harlem Heights in New York. Elizabeth's father, General Schuyler, died four months after her husband. Her inheritance, in addition to that given to her by her siblings from their share, allowed her to live modestly in the family home for a while. In 1816 Congress also awarded her approximately $10,000 in pension funds.[9]

Elizabeth, who after her husband's death always wore the black attire befitting a widow, lived on for fifty more years. In addition to raising her children, she also found time to help establish the first private orphanage in New York and served as a director from 1821 to 1848. In 1833 Elizabeth sold the Grange and went to live for the next nine years with her son, Colonel Alexander Hamilton, and daughter, Eliza Hamilton Holly, and their spouses in a newly built townhouse in the East Village section of Manhattan.

After her husband's death, Eliza Holly and her mother moved to Washington, D.C., and it was there that Betsey Hamilton died at the age of ninety-seven on 9 November 1854. At her death a little sonnet written by her husband was found in a little bag always worn around her neck.[10] She was interred in Trinity Churchyard in New York City, beside her husband.

Notes

1. Allan McLane Hamilton, *The Intimate Life of Alexander Hamilton* (New York: Scribner's Sons, 1911), 95–96.

2. Hamilton, *The Intimate Life of Alexander Hamilton*, 1–14.

3. Hamilton, *The Intimate Life of Alexander Hamilton*, 137; Richard Brookhiser, *Alexander Hamilton: American* (New York: Touchstone, 1999), 47.

4. As quoted in Ron Chernow, *Alexander Hamilton* (New York: Penguin Press, 2004), 526.

5. Hamilton, *The Intimate Life of Alexander Hamilton*, 212–14.

6. Cuyler Reynolds, ed., *Genealogical and Family History of Southern New York and the Hudson River Valley* (New York: Lewis Historical Publishing Co., 1914), 3: 1376–91; Hamilton, *The Intimate Life of Alexander Hamilton*, 217–22.

7. The Reynolds affair is covered in several biographies of Alexander Hamilton; see Brookhiser, *Alexander Hamilton*; Chernow, *Alexander Hamilton*; Forrest McDonald, *Alexander Hamilton: A Biography* (New York: W. W. Norton, 1982), among others.

8. Hamilton, *The Intimate Life of Alexander Hamilton*, 116–17.

9. Hamilton, *The Intimate Life of Alexander Hamilton*, 405, 420–21. Jenny L. Presnell, in "Elizabeth Schuyler Hamilton," *American National Biography* 9 (www.anb.org/articles/02/02-00364.html?a=1&n=Hamilton&s=20&d=10&ss=27&q=52), states that it was not until 1837 that Congress granted Elizabeth $30,000, which included land.

10. Hamilton, *The Intimate Life of Alexander Hamilton,* 126.

Bibliography

A few of Elizabeth Schuyler Hamilton's letters are among the papers of her sister Angelica Schuyler Church in the Special Collections of the library of the University of Virginia, and some can be found in the published papers of her husband, Alexander Hamilton (see below).

Brookhiser, Richard. *Alexander Hamilton, American.* New York: Touchstone, 1999.

Chernow, Ron. *Alexander Hamilton.* New York: Penguin Press, 2004.

Cooke, Jacob Ernest. *Alexander Hamilton.* New York: Charles Scribner's Sons, 1982.

Emery, Noemie. *Alexander Hamilton: An Intimate Portrait.* New York: G. P. Putnam's Sons, 1982.

Hamilton, Allan McLane. *The Intimate Life of Alexander Hamilton.* New York: Scribner's Sons, 1911.

Hendrickson, Robert A. *The Rise and Fall of Alexander Hamilton.* New York: Dodd, Mead and Co., 1985.

McDonald, Forrest. *Alexander Hamilton: A Biography.* New York: W. W. Norton, 1982.

Mitchell, Broadus. *Alexander Hamilton.* 2 vols. New York: Macmillan, 1957–1962.

Reynolds, Cuyler. *Genealogical and Family History of Southern New York and the Hudson River Valley.* Vol. 3. New York: Lewis Historical Publishing Co., 1914

Schuyler, George Washington. *Colonial New York: Philip Schuyler and His Family.* 2 vols. New York: Charles Scribner's Sons, 1885.

Syrett, Harold C., et al., ed. *The Papers of Alexander Hamilton.* 27 vols. New York: Columbia University Press, 1962–1987.

Elizabeth (Betsy) Pettit Ingersoll

Birth: 26 December 1758, New Jersey
Parents: Charles Pettit and Sarah Reed
Marriage: 6 December 1781, Jared Ingersoll (1749-1822)
Children: Charles Jared (1782-1862); Henry (Harry) (born 1784, died young); Joseph Reed (1786-1868); Edward (1790-1841)
Death: 16 June 1846, Philadelphia, Pennsylvania

Elizabeth Pettit was born on 26 December 1758 into a family of wealth and social prominence. Of Huguenot origin, the first Pettits settled in New York in the mid-1660s. Her father, Charles Pettit (1736–1806), was a New Jersey lawyer and merchant. He was admitted to the bar in New Jersey in 1770 and the following year was appointed as aide, with the rank of lieutenant colonel, to Governor William Franklin, the son of Benjamin Franklin. When Governor Franklin was arrested as a Loyalist in 1776, Pettit cast his lot with the colonies. He served as an assistant quartermaster general in the Continental Army under General Nathanael Greene and was later a member of the Continental Congress, spending most of the war years in Philadelphia.[1]

In addition to his military duties, Pettit became an importing merchant and was the agent for the Batsto Ironworks, situated in the South Jersey Pines, about twenty-five miles southeast of Philadelphia. George Washington ordered the casting of four firebacks from Batsto, two of which remain in fireplaces at Mount Vernon.[2] A Jeffersonian Republican, Charles Pettit was a member of Congress from 1781 to 1787. He was also a founder and president of the Insurance Company of North America, a trustee of the University of Pennsylvania, and a member of the American Philosophical Society.[3]

Elizabeth's mother was Sarah Reed (1741–1785), half-sister of Joseph Reed, who was George Washington's military secretary for a time. In 1777 he was a member of the Continental Congress, while continuing to serve in the Army,

83

fighting in many engagements. In 1778 Joseph Reed was chosen as president of the Supreme Executive Council of Pennsylvania, and during his three-year administration, slavery was abolished in Pennsylvania and the University of Pennsylvania was founded.[4]

Elizabeth Pettit was the oldest of four children. Following her were Andrew (who married Elizabeth McKean, daughter of Thomas McKean, signer of the Declaration of Independence), Theodosia (who married Alexander Graydon, a memoirist of the Revolution), and Sarah (who married Andrew Bayard, a prominent Philadelphia merchant-banker).[5] Elizabeth spent her early years in New Jersey, living at various times at Burlington, Perth Amboy, and Trenton. During the war years, while Charles Pettit was on military duty in Philadelphia, his wife, Sarah, and the children lived in Trenton at the home of Joseph Reed. They may have been living there during the British occupation and certainly were under considerable tension.

Nothing is known about her schooling, but as her family was of the intellectual aristocracy, it can be assumed that she received a better than average education for a woman of her time. Her brother, Andrew, attended the Nassau Hall Grammar School in Princeton. Elizabeth and her sisters could have attended this school or been privately tutored.

On 11 April 1779, in a letter written to General Nathanael Greene during one of his brief visits with his family in Trenton, Charles Pettit added the postscript, "Mrs. Pettit and Betsy join me in best compliments to Mrs. Greene." Three days later, on 14 April, General Greene wrote from camp to Colonel Jeremiah Wadsworth, "Mrs. Greene is gone to Trenton to a Tea Frolic given by Betsy Pettit. . . . There is to be a number of Ladys from Philadelphia and some Members of Congress."[6]

Betsy Pettit married Jared Ingersoll on 6 December 1781 at the First Presbyterian Church in Philadelphia,[7] where they made their home for the rest of their lives. Jared Ingersoll, born on 27 October 1749 in New Haven, Connecticut, was the son of Jared Ingersoll and Hannah Whiting.[8] The elder Jared was a distinguished lawyer in Connecticut and friend of Benjamin Franklin. Jared the younger graduated from Yale College in 1766 at the age of sixteen. With the approach of war, his father sent him to Europe to study law. After two years at study at the Middle Temple of London, he went to Paris for two years. He returned home in 1778 as an ardent supporter of the American cause, probably having been influenced by Franklin.[9]

It may be assumed that the Ingersolls lived a life of quiet dignity. Ingersoll is said to have been the last lawyer in Philadelphia to appear in court in knee britches, silk stockings, and a powdered wig. In 1787, the year of the Constitutional Convention, the Ingersolls were living on Market Street in Philadelphia, now part of the Independence National Historical Park. On May 19 of that year,

George Washington noted in his diary that he had dined that evening at their home.[10] In Elizabeth's spare time, she probably did fine needlework and knit garments for her family. Like the other women in Philadelphia, she probably played cards, whist being a popular pastime.

Jared and Elizabeth Ingersoll had four children. Their oldest son, Charles Jared, was born on 3 October 1782. He followed his father in the field of law, but unlike Jared, he became an aggressive factor in politics, breaking away from his father's Federalist Party. Among other achievements, he served in Congress from 1813 to 1815 and was a U.S. attorney, a member of the state legislature, and a member of the Constitutional Convention of 1837–1838. In addition to his professional and public duties, Charles was the author of many published works, plays, poetry, and political pamphlets. His most noteworthy work was *A Historical Sketch of the Second War between the United States of America and Great Britain* in four volumes. Charles married, on 18 October 1804, Mary Wilcocks, daughter of Alexander and Mary (Chew) Wilcocks. To this union nine children were born. Charles Jared Ingersoll died in 1862.[11]

Of the second son, Harry, little is known beyond the fact that he is said to have gone to sea as supercargo of a vessel and that he died on one of his voyages, young and unmarried. Joseph Reed, the third son, was born on 14 June 1786. He was admitted to the Philadelphia bar in 1807. At the outbreak of the War of 1812 he was one of the organizers of the State Fencibles, a military unit. He commanded the second company of the Washington Guards and was later promoted to major in his regiment, commanded by Colonel Clement C. Biddle. In later years he was the president of the Philadelphia Common Council and served several terms in Congress. He remained a Whig, and from 1843 to 1847, he and his brother Charles were colleagues in Congress, both from Philadelphia districts, representing the two main parties of that period. Joseph was later appointed minister to Great Britain. He married Ann Wilcocks, a sister of his brother's wife, and they had three children, who predeceased him. He died in 1868.[12]

The youngest son, Edward, was born on 27 July 1790. He followed the family tradition of pursuing a career in law. He was an active participant in public affairs and was the author of several articles on politics and other subjects published in Pennsylvania periodicals. He married Catherine Ann Brinton, and they had four children. Edward died in 1841 in Florence, Italy.[13]

Jared died on 31 October 1822, and Elizabeth was named executrix of his will.[14] Like several other signers of the Constitution, Jared died a poor man because of speculation in western lands. In 1831, Stephen Girard, known at the time as the richest man in the country and for whom Jared had done a great deal of legal work, left Elizabeth an annuity of $1,000 a year in his will.[15] Elizabeth died in June 1846 in Philadelphia.[16] She and her husband, Jared, were buried in the churchyard of the First Presbyterian Church in Philadelphia. Some years later, their graves were moved to the old Pine Street (or Third) Presbyterian Church at Fourth and Pine, near the graves of Charles and Sarah Pettit. The dates on their tombstone, which was repaired or replaced at the time of the move, are incorrect. Jared's date of death is given as 1832 rather than 1822, and although it is known that Elizabeth died in 1846, her gravestone is marked 1816.

Notes

1. Roland M. Baumann, "Charles Pettit," *American National Biography* 18, www.anb.org/articles/01/01-00724.html?a=1&n=Charles%20Pettit&d=10&ss=1&q=2.

2. Arthur D. Pierce, *Family Empire in Jersey Iron* (New Brunswick: Rutgers University Press, 1964), 266–67. The state of New Jersey has restored the mansion and outbuildings at Batsto.

3. Baumann, "Charles Pettit."

4. Baumann, "Charles Pettit"; G. S. Rowe, "Joseph Reed," *American National Biography* 19, www.anb.org/articles/02/02-00272.html?a=1&n=Joseph%20Reed&d=10&ss=0&q=1.

5. DAR Application Paper #110530, Sarah Henry Clark Keys (Mrs. Alfred), DAR Seimes Technology Center, National Society, Daughters of the American Revolution, Washington, D.C.

6. *The Papers of General Nathanael Greene* (Chapel Hill: University of North Carolina Press, 1983), 3: 104.

7. "Marriage Record of the First Presbyterian Church of Philadelphia, 1760–1803," *Pennsylvania Archives*, Second Series (Harrisburg: Lane S. Hart, State Printer, 1880), 9: 91.

8. R. Sturgis Ingersoll, *Sketch of the Ingersoll Family of Philadelphia* (Philadelphia: n.p., 1966), 8.

9. Robert G. Ferris and James H. Charleton, *The Signers of the Constitution* (Flagstaff, Ariz.: Interpretive Publications, 1986), 175–76.

10. Donald Jackson and Dorothy Twohig, eds., *Diaries of George Washington* (Charlottesville: University of Virginia Press, 1979), 5: 159.

11. Ingersoll, *Sketch of the Ingersoll Family*, 9–10.

12. Ingersoll, *Sketch of the Ingersoll Family*, 10.

13. Joshua Lawrence Chamberlain, ed., *University of Pennsylvania: Its History, Influence, Equipment and Characteristics* (Boston: R. Herndon Co., 1902), 2: 25.

14. Will of Jared Ingersoll, Register of Wills, in the library of the American Philosophical Society, Philadelphia, Pennsylvania.

15. Will of Stephen Girard, published in *Arguments of the Defendants' Counsel and the Judgment of the Supreme Court, U.S. . . . .* (Philadelphia: J. Crissy, Printer, 1844), 286.

16. Philadelphia City Death Certificates, 1803–1915, Index. Original certificates housed in the Philadelphia City Archives.

Bibliography

Dexter, Franklin B., ed. *Jared Ingersoll Papers.* New Haven, Conn.: Yale University, 1918.

——. "A Selection from the Correspondence and Miscellaneous Papers of Jared Ingersoll." *Papers of the New Haven Colony Historical Society* 9 (1918): 201–472.

Ingersoll, R. Sturgis. *Sketch of the Ingersoll Family of Philadelphia.* Philadelphia, n.p., 1966.

Ann Beach Johnson

Birth:	25 April 1729, Fairfield, Stratford, Connecticut
Parents:	William Beach and Sarah Hull
Marriage:	5 November 1749, William Samuel Johnson (1727-1819)
Children:	Charity Clarissa (1750-1810); Sarah (1754-1762); Gloriana Ann (Nancy) (1757-1785); Mary (1759-1783); Samuel William (1761-1847); Elizabeth (1763-1789); Robert Charles (1766-1839)
Death:	24 April 1796, New York, New York

Ann Beach, the daughter of William Beach (1694–1751), a wealthy Anglican businessman, and Sarah Hull (1701–1763), married William Samuel Johnson on 5 November 1749 at Christ Episcopal Church in Stratford, Connecticut.[1] Johnson had begun courting Ann in the summer of 1747 but did not really fall in love until the following year. Initially he did not seem greatly impressed, writing to a friend: "She has no Beauty to recommend her being rather homely than handsome, yet her Deportment to me has been so Benevolent kind Generous . . . that I cannot but have a particular regard for her. . . . I take a vast Deal of pleasure in her acquaintance & Conversation."[2]

Ann grew up in Stratford with her older brother, Isaac, and younger brothers Abel, Abijah, and Henry. After her marriage she began to resent the long absences of her husband from Stratford on business. Gradually her father-in-law Samuel Johnson (and subsequently her stepfather) gave the family the emotional support Ann felt she lacked.[3] Ann's father died in 1751, and in 1761 her mother married William Samuel's father, Samuel. Unfortunately, she died two years later of smallpox.

William Samuel Johnson was elected to Congress in 1784, and three years later he became the president of Columbia College, a post once held by his father. While in New York Ann occasionally visited him, but it appears that she did not move there permanently until after Johnson resigned from the Senate in March 1791.[4] His absence in Philadelphia during the Constitutional Convention worried Ann. Their daughter Charity wrote her father that it "led to melancholy reflections that destroy her health and happiness."[5]

The Johnsons had seven children, five daughters and two sons (in addition to four stillborn sons), and Ann outlived four of them. During a long absence (1766–1771) of her father in London, Charity Johnson married Ebenezer Kneeland, her grandfather Samuel Johnson's successor in the Anglican church in Stratford. A Loyalist, he died almost a prisoner in his own parish in 1777.[6] In 1783 Nancy married Roger Alden, a Revolutionary War veteran and Yale classmate of Nathan Hale, who resigned his commission in 1781 to take up study of the law with Nancy's father. She died at the age of twenty-eight in 1785. Elizabeth married Daniel C. Verplanck, later a congressional representative from New York, and died in 1789 at twenty-six, leaving a son and daughter. Samuel William, who became a lawyer and state legislator, married Susan Edwards, granddaughter of Yale president Jonathan Edwards, and had several children. Robert Charles married Catherine Ann Bayard and had four children. Sarah died as a child, and Mary never married.

On 24 April 1796 Ann, whose health had been declining for some months, died in New York. Two days later her husband sailed with her remains to have them buried in the family vault at Stratford.[7]

Notes

1. Elizabeth P. McCaughey, *From Loyalist to Founding Father: The Political Odyssey of William Samuel Johnson* (New York: Columbia University Press, 1980), 33–34.
2. Quoted in McCaughey, *From Loyalist to Founding Father*, 32.
3. McCaughey, *From Loyalist to Founding Father*, 33, 135–36.
4. McCaughey, *From Loyalist to Founding Father*, 328.
5. Quoted in David O. Stewart, *The Summer of 1787: The Men who Invented the Constitution* (New York: Simon & Schuster, 2008), 44.
6. Arthur Lowndes, *Archives of the General Convention* (New York: privately printed, 1912), 4 ("The Correspondence of George Henry Hobart"): 315.
7. Eben Edwards Beardsley, *Life and Times of William Samuel Johnson, LL.D.* (New York: Hurd and Houghton, 1876), 153.

Bibliography

The Johnson family correspondence is located at the Connecticut Historical Society in Hartford.

Beach, Rachel Donaldson, and Rebecca Donaldson Gibbons. *The Reverend John Beach and His Descendants: Together with Historical and Biographical Sketches and the Ancestry and Descendants of John Sanford of Redding, Connecticut.* New Haven: The Tuttle, Morehouse, and Taylor Press, 1898.

Beardsley, Eben Edwards. *Life and Times of William Samuel Johnson, LL.D.* New York: Hurd & Houghton, 1876.

Greene, Evarts B. "William Samuel Johnson and the American Revolution," *Columbia University Quarterly* 22 (June 1930): 157–78.

Groce, G. C. *William Samuel Johnson: A Maker of the Constitution.* New York: Columbia University Press, 1937.

McCaughey, Elizabeth. *From Loyalist to Founding Father: The Political Odyssey of William Samuel Johnson.* New York: Columbia University Press, 1980.

Mary Brewster Beach Johnson

Birth:	c. 1735
Parents:	unknown
Marriages:	15 April 1753, Abijah Beach (1734–1785)
	11 December 1800, William Samuel Johnson (1727–1819)
Children:	Benjamin Beach (1753–1772); Sarah Beach (1756–1834); Elizabeth Beach (1758–1759); Isaac Beach (1760–1842); Mary (Polly) Beach (born 1765); Abijah Henry Beach (c. 1767–1854); Abel Beach (1770–1853); Ann (Nancy) Beach (1770–1856); Hannah Beach (1773–1841)
Death:	April 1827, Stratford, Connecticut

According to a history of the Beach family, the parents of Mary Brewster were Faith Ripley and James Brewster, a descendant of William Brewster, who came to America on the *Mayflower*.[1] Further research, however, has shown that this particular Mary Brewster was not born until 1751, too late to have been the subject of this essay, and in any case married to someone else. No doubt the Mary Brewster who later married William Samuel Johnson was related to the Brewsters from Massachusetts, but research thus far has failed to show the connection.

The first known reference to Mary Brewster is the record of her marriage in the Stratford Congregational Church on 15 April 1753 to Abijah Beach, brother of Ann Beach, William Samuel Johnson's first wife.[2] Abijah and his brother Abel (1731–1768) carried on the family merchant business but because of various difficulties—bad markets abroad, losses at sea, etc.—lost most of their inheritance. Abijah eventually became a virtual prisoner in his own house in order to avoid debtors and use his dwindling resources to support his family.[3]

Mary and Abijah had nine children. Benjamin, the oldest, was lost at sea in 1772. Sarah married a man named Lewis, Isaac married Lucy Chittenden, Mary married a man named Sterling, Abijah married a woman named Tamar and moved to New York, Abel married Mary Bordwell, Ann married Nathaniel

Berry, and Hannah married John Mills. Elizabeth died as an infant. Most of the children spent the remainder of their lives in Litchfield County, Connecticut.

During the Revolutionary War Mary and her family lived on a farm at Bull's Bridge in Litchfield County. In consequence of the bridge, the road across the farm became one of the main thoroughfares from Connecticut to New York. According to family lore it soon became the custom for officers to halt their commands at "Madam Beach's," the great barns giving good shelter. Having a high regard for her, General Washington is said to have been often entertained there. An ailing soldier with nearly frozen feet given shelter there in 1779 claimed to be a weaver and wove woolen cloth, coarse and fine linen, and even damask for the family. Some of the damask was reputed to be in possession of a descendant of William Samuel Johnson, author and feminist Lilly Devereaux Blake.[4]

Mary was widowed in 1785. Fifteen years later her brother-in-law William Samuel Johnson reported in his diary on 8 December that he had ridden out with his son Charles and a servant in a carriage for Kent, arriving the following day. (Johnson had returned to Stratford in 1800 from New York after retiring from his post as president of Columbia College.) His entry for the 9th read that he had executed a contract of marriage with Mrs. Beach, and that of the following day stated that he had set out with her at ten o'clock and lodged at Newtown. On the 11th they arrived in Stratford, and at six o'clock that evening they were married by the Reverend Mr. Ashbel Baldwin.[5] Johnson died in 1819, and his wife, Mary, eight years later.

Notes

1. Rebecca Donaldson Beach and Rebecca Donaldson Gibbons, *The Reverend John Beach and His Descendents: Together with Historical and Biographical Sketches . . .* (New Haven, Conn.: The Tuttle, Morehouse & Taylor Press, 1898), 136–37.

2. Beach and Gibbons, *The Reverend John Beach and His Descendants*, 137; "Marriages at Christ Episcopal Church, Stratford, CT," transcribed by Jane Devlin.

3. *The Public Records of the Colony of Connecticut [1772–1775]*, edited by Charles J. Hoadly (Hartford: Case, Lockwood, and Brainerd Co., 1887), 79–80, 180–82; Bruce H. Mann, *Republic of Debtors: Bankruptcy in the Age of American Independence* (Cambridge, Mass.: Harvard University Press, 2002), 27, 73, 75.

4. Beach and Gibbons, *The Reverend John Beach and His Descendants,* 136–38. This story appears to be unsubstantiated by any other source.

5. Eben Edwards Beardsley, *Life and Times of William Samuel Johnson, LL.D.* (New York: Hurd and Houghton, 1876), 179.

Bibliography

The Johnson family correspondence is located at the Connecticut Historical Society in Hartford.

Beach, Rachel Donaldson, and Rebecca Donaldson Gibbons. *The Reverend John Beach and His Descendants: Together with Historical and Biographical Sketches and the Ancestry and Descendants of John Sanford of Redding, Connecticut.* New Haven: The Tuttle, Morehouse, and Taylor Press, 1898.

Beardsley, Eben Edwards. *Life and Times of William Samuel Johnson, LL.D.* New York: Hurd & Houghton, 1876.

Groce, G. C. *William Samuel Johnson: A Maker of the Constitution.* New York: Columbia University Press, 1937.

McCaughey, Elizabeth. *From Loyalist to Founding Father: The Political Odyssey of William Samuel Johnson.* New York: Columbia University Press, 1980.

Mary Alsop King

Birth:	17 October 1769, New York City
Parents:	John Alsop and Mary Frogat
Marriage:	30 March 1786, Rufus King (1755–1827)
Children:	John Alsop (1788–1867); Charles (1789–1867); Caroline (1790–1793); James Gore (1791–1853); Henry (born and died 1792); Edward (1795–1836); Frederick Gore (1802–1829)
Death:	5 June 1819, Jamaica, New York

Thirty-one-year-old Rufus King, congressional delegate from Massachusetts, married, on 30 March 1786, sixteen-year-old Mary Alsop, the only child of John (1724–1794) and Mary Alsop, noted for her beauty and unspoiled nature. Bishop Samuel Provoost performed the ceremony, and Congress being in session in New York and the bridegroom belonging to it, many of its members attended, among them James Monroe and Elbridge Gerry. The ceremony was impressive, with six bridesmaids and a supper at which wine, set down at the bride's birth for the purpose, was served. According to one of her bridesmaids, "The youth, beauty, and fortune of the bride had made her a great belle and her marriage was a serious disappointment to many aspirants." The following day, accompanied by their bridesmaids and groomsmen, the couple honeymooned in nearby Jamaica, New York, returning to reside in the city three days later.[1]

John Alsop, a wealthy New York dry goods merchant whose wife had died in 1772 when Mary was only three, had served as a delegate to the Continental Congress from 1774 to1776, retiring to Connecticut during the British occupation of New York. Mary spent the war years in Connecticut with her father and uncle, returning to New York with her father after hostilities ceased. John Alsop, who also served as president of the Chamber of Commerce for New York from 1784 to 1785, opened his home to Rufus King, who soon fell in love with his host's daughter. John Jay noted to John Adams, "I am pleased with these inter-marriages. They tend to assimilate the States, and to promote one of the first wishes of my heart, viz., to see the people of America become one nation in every respect."[2]

Mary had black hair, expressive blue eyes, delicate features, a quiet nature, and radiant charm. She was widely admired in New York society; her retiring nature set her apart. The Kings moved in fashionable circles and entertained frequently. She accompanied her husband to Philadelphia, but she was not happy there where she was unknown and unable to see her friends and father. Also, she was pregnant with the couple's first child. Mary returned to New York, and four days after his election as a Massachusetts delegate, Rufus joined her, determined to stay with his wife until she delivered. Mary gave birth to a son, John Alsop King, on 3 January 1788. Bishop Provoost baptized the child with Alexander Hamilton and General and Mrs. Henry Knox as sponsors. At the end of May the Kings left their son with John Alsop and went to Massachusetts, where Rufus introduced Mary to his family and friends; they returned to New York in July.[3] A King family friend wrote to his wife, "Tell Betsy King [Rufus's half-sister] her sister is a beauty. She is vastly the best looking woman I have seen since I have been in this city. . . . She is a good hearted woman, and, I think, possesses all that Benevolence and kind, friendly disposition, that never fail to find respectable admirers."[4]

In 1788 Rufus King decided to move permanently to New York, and he was chosen as a member of the state legislature, later becoming one of the first two to represent New York in the U.S. Senate. The move was largely due to his wife and his father-in-law, who turned some of his mercantile interests over to King. When John Alsop died in 1794, Mary's inheritance brought the Kings considerable fortune. In New York, Mary attended weekly dinners, teas, and receptions with the other congressional ladies. In the meantime the family grew with several more children: Charles in 1789; Caroline in 1790 (died in 1793); James Gore in 1791; Henry in 1792 (died in infancy); and Edward in 1795. Also, King's half-brother Cyrus came to live with them while he attended Columbia College.[5]

King served as a senator until 1796, when President George Washington appointed him minister plenipotentiary to Great Britain.[6] The Kings moved with their four children and Cyrus to England. Alexander Hamilton described their home as "where everything contributed to his happiness and where a charming wife presided quietly over a household in which mutual esteem and confidence were ruling traits, attracted all who came within its hospitable and quiet influence."[7] While in England, the Kings had their last child, Frederick Gore, in 1802. There were also opportunities to travel. In 1797 they vacationed in Wales and a few years later toured the Continent, visiting Rotterdam, Delft, The Hague, Leiden, Amsterdam, Antwerp, Brussels (a favorite of Mary's), Liege, Aix-la-Chapelle, Cologne, Wiesbaden, Frankfurt, Basel, Lausanne, Geneva, and Paris. In 1803 Rufus King resigned his position, and the Kings returned home, leaving their three older sons in England and Paris to attend school.[8]

After forty days at sea, the Kings arrived in the United States, and in late 1803 rented a house in New York. In 1806 Rufus King bought ninety acres in Jamaica, Long Island, which included a house and barn. The family moved, partly because Mary's health was beginning to fail and partly because there was no immediate prospect of public office for Rufus King. Both Kings loved the country; they spent much time and money renovating the landscape to their liking. Rufus also remained politically active, spending winters in the city. In 1813 he was elected to a third term in the Senate. The Kings took rooms at Crawford's Hotel, a well-furnished mansion in Georgetown. Mary and Rebecca Gore, wife of Rufus King's fellow senator and Harvard classmate Christopher Gore, maintained a private parlor to use as a drawing room for entertaining. But Mary continued to be frail and in chronic ill health.[9]

In 1819 Rufus and Mary King left Washington because of her health and headed for New York. The journey was hard on Mary, who was weakened by digestive disorders and showing signs of scurvy. Snow delayed them in Philadelphia, but they reached New York on 19 March, although Mary was too weak to continue on to Jamaica. Instead, needing expert medical care, she stayed with her son Charles in the city. In the latter part of May she was able to go to Jamaica, but her condition soon grew grave. With her sons and their wives at her bedside, a noted physician attended her, but her strength continued to wane. On the morning of 5 June she died. She was buried in the old churchyard of Grace Church at a spot within sight of the windows of the home she had so long occupied. Rufus King was left alone; about his wife he remarked, "The example of her life is worthy of the imitation of us all."[10]

Of Mary King there are few memorials. From every respect, her married life was certainly a happy one, her gentle nature and confiding disposition being met on the part of her husband with respect, affection, and true loyalty to her. The mother of several children, of whom five sons grew up to manhood and survived her, she was ever the loving and careful parent, the prudent advisor, and the center of their affections in the home she made so pleasant for them. She and her husband had but one thought for their welfare, and they all gave their love and confidence in return. Though in every way fitted by personal beauty, attractive manners, and dignified carriage to adorn the society in which her own right and the distinguished positions occupied by her husband entitled her to move, her life was rather that of the home circle, where, with the devoted friends she made, she was always happiest. She was a faithful Christian woman, a member of Grace Episcopal Church in which she had been nurtured, by whose bishop she had been married, and by whose impressive service her mortal remains were laid at rest. Such are the estimates of her character that have been handed down, and there can be little doubt that when, after prolonged illness her presence was withdrawn, there were grief and loneliness. Rufus King continued to live alone at his house in Jamaica until a few months before his death, when he moved to New York City.[11]

The Kings had seven children, five of whom lived to adulthood. All achieved some prominence. John Alsop was educated in England and Paris while his father was minister to England. He served as a cavalry lieutenant during the War of 1812, and his political career included serving in the House of Representatives in 1849. In 1856 he was elected governor of New York. John Alsop King died at Jamaica, New York, on 7 July 1867.[12]

Charles King was born at New York City on 16 May 1789 and died at Frascati, Italy, on 27 September 1867. Like his older brother, he was educated in England and Paris. He, too, served in the War of 1812 as a captain in a volunteer regiment. He became a banker and established a newspaper, *The American*, in 1819. Charles served as the ninth president of Columbia College from 1849 until June 1864.[13]

James Gore King was born in New York City on 8 May 1791 and died at Weehawken, New Jersey, on 3 October 1853. He studied law but did not practice, preferring to enter the world of finance. He also served in Congress as a representative from New Jersey from 1849 to 1851.[14]

Edward King was born on 13 March 1795 and died at Cincinnati, Ohio, on 6 February 1836. He was a lawyer and founded the Cincinnati Law School in 1833.

Frederick Gore King was born on 6 February 1802 and died on 24 April 1829 in New York City. He took his medical degree from Columbia in 1824 and became a prominent physician. While attending his uncle's family on Long Island, he caught a fever and died.[15]

Notes

1. Edward Hale Brush, *Rufus King and His Times* (New York: Nicholas L. Brown, 1926), 23; Robert Ernst, *Rufus King, American Federalist* (Chapel Hill: University of North Carolina Press, 1968), 66–67.

2. Henry P. Johnston, ed., *Correspondence and Public Papers of John Jay*, 4 vols. (New York: G. P. Putnam's Sons, 1890–1893), 3: 194–95.

3. Ernst, *Rufus King, American Federalist*, 68, 106, 110, 119, 135–36.

4. Ernst, *Rufus King, American Federalist*, 137.

5. Ernst, *Rufus King, American Federalist*, 94, 140, 155, 168–69, 203.

6. Brush, *Rufus King and His Times*, 34, 37; Ernst, *Rufus King, American Federalist*, 220, 227, 233, 277.

7. Brush, *Rufus King and His Times*, 40.

8. Brush, *Rufus King and His Times*, 66; Ernst, *Rufus King, American Federalist*, 277.

9. Ernst, *Rufus King, American Federalist*, 278, 292, 294, 295, 322–23.

10. Ernst, *Rufus King, American Federalist*, 360.

11. Brush, *Rufus King and His Times*, 66.

12. Brush, *Rufus King and His Times*, 127–35.

13. Brush, *Rufus King and His Times*, 137–38.

14. Brush, *Rufus King and His Times*, 138–40.

15. Charles H. Weygant, *The Sacketts of America, Their Ancestors and Descendants, 1630–1907* (Newburgh, N.Y.: Higginson Book Co., 1907), 195–96.

Bibliography

Two letters of Mary Alsop King are included in the published Rufus King papers; it is unknown whether or not there are others extant.

Brush, Edward H. *Rufus King and His Times*. New York: N. L. Brown, 1926.

Ernst, Robert. *Rufus King, American Federalist*. Chapel Hill: University of North Carolina Press, 1968.

King, Rufus. *The Life and Correspondence of Rufus King: Comprising His Letters, Private and Official, His Public Documents, and His Speeches*. Edited by Charles R. King. 6 vols. New York: G. P. Putnam's Sons, 1894–1900.

————. "Letters of Rufus King," *Massachusetts Historical Society Proceedings* 49 (1915–16): 81–89.

Smith, William H. "The King Family of Maine," *The Maine Historical and Genealogical Recorder.* 1 (No. 2, 1884): 3–40.

————. "The King Family of New York," *The Maine Historical and Genealogical Recorder.* 1 (No. 4, 1884): 182–86.

Welch, Richard E. "Rufus King of Newburyport: The Formative Years (1767–1788)," *Essex Institute Historical Collections* 96 (October 1960): 241–276.

Elizabeth (Betsy) Sherburne Langdon

Birth:	1751, Portsmouth, New Hampshire
Parents:	John Sherburne and Elizabeth Moffat
Marriage:	4 February 1777, John Langdon (1741–1819)
Children:	Elizabeth (Eliza) (1777–1830); John (born and died 1779)
Death:	2 March 1813, Portsmouth, New Hampshire

Elizabeth Sherburne was born in 1751 into a prominent New Hampshire family. Her grandfather, Henry Sherburne of Portsmouth, a merchant, drew up a pedigree in 1710, tracing the family name from his grandfather to Sir Richard Sherburne of Stonyhurst, who died in 1513. His wife, Elizabeth's grandmother, was Dorothy Wentworth, the sister of the first Governor John Wentworth and an aunt of Governor Benning Wentworth. Henry and Dorothy Sherburne lived in great style in the first brick mansion built in Portsmouth.[1]

Their son, Elizabeth's father, John Sherburne, also a prominent merchant in Portsmouth, was a registrar of the Court of Vice-Admiralty and a judge of probate in Rockingham County from 1773 to 1776. He was on a committee to inform the representatives to the General Court of New Hampshire of the dangers to personal liberty that the Stamp Act posed, and he, with others chosen by Portsmouth, informed every town to oppose the sale of tea. Elizabeth's father was also a trustee of Dartmouth College from 1774 to 1777. Her mother was John Sherburne's second wife, Elizabeth Moffat, the daughter of John Moffat, of Portsmouth.[2]

Elizabeth had three siblings: John and Dorothy, who died young, and Samuel (1757–1830), who took an additional name by act of the legislature and became known as John Samuel. An officer in the Continental Army, he lost a leg during a British attack on 29 August 1778 in Rhode Island. After the war, John Samuel served in Congress and became a judge of the United States Court for the District of New Hampshire.[3]

Elizabeth Sherburne, known as both a beauty and a belle, became the bride of John Langdon on 4 February 1777 in Portsmouth, New Hampshire.[4] Elizabeth's cousin, Sarah Sherburne, married John's brother, Woodbury Langdon.

John and Woodbury Langdon came from a large family. John had spent some time at sea when he was young, eventually went into the mercantile business, and prospered. A vigorous supporter of the American Revolution, he attended various assemblies, sat on the New Hampshire Committee of Correspondence, and participated in the seizure of Fort William and Mary in the Portsmouth harbor in 1774. The following year he served as speaker of the New Hampshire assembly and sat in the Continental Congress. In 1776 he accepted a colonelcy in the New Hampshire militia and became the state's agent for British prizes on behalf of the Continental Congress, a lucrative position he held throughout the war. He also organized and paid for General John Stark's expedition in 1777 from New Hampshire against the British forces of General John Burgoyne and was in command of a militia unit at Saratoga when Burgoyne surrendered.[5]

The Langdons' daughter Elizabeth was born on 4 December 1777, less than two months after a fine dinner party they gave to honor Baron von

Steuben. Elizabeth was baptized on 21 December 1777, and a few days later the proud parents presented the clergyman with a gift of two yards of Genoa velvet for a jacket.[6] The Langdons also had a son born in March 1779, but the child did not survive.

From 1777 to 1781 John Langdon was the speaker of the New Hampshire legislature. In 1783 he was elected to the Continental Congress, in 1784 to the New Hampshire senate, and in 1785 he became the chief executive of the state.[7] Langdon built a large home in 1784, now known as the Governor John Langdon Mansion. General Washington said that it was the most beautiful house in Portsmouth. An early reminiscence of Elizabeth Buckminster, a childhood friend of Elizabeth, was that of seeing the Langdon family carriage waiting, with two liveried black servants in attendance, at the gate of their fine mansion. She described Elizabeth Langdon as stately and powdered in the style of the time. The Marquis de Chastellux in 1782 wrote of his meeting and conversations with John and Elizabeth Langdon, describing her as being "young, fair, and tolerably handsome."[8] Noah Webster, on the other hand described her as "a most beautiful woman 20 years younger than her husband."[9]

Between 1786 and 1787 John Langdon was again speaker of the New Hampshire legislature and in the latter year was elected to the Continental Congress for the third time. The following year, once again New Hampshire's chief executive, Langdon took part in the ratifying convention. From 1789 to 1801 John Langdon served in the U.S. Senate and was president pro tem for several sessions. Elizabeth and John were able to participate in several social occasions while living in New York.[10]

In 1801 John Langdon declined Thomas Jefferson's offer to be Secretary of the Navy but continued to be active in New Hampshire politics. He served in the state legislature from 1801 to 1805 and as governor of the state from 1805 to 1808 and from 1809 to 1811. In the meantime Dartmouth College awarded him an honorary doctor of laws degree in 1805.[11]

John Langdon's only brother, Woodbury, died on 13 January 1805, and afterward John became more interested in religious affairs. The Langdons had for a long time regularly attended church services at the North Meetinghouse, where they had the best pew. In 1806 John became the founder and first president of the New Hampshire Bible Society, the chief aim of which was to place a Bible in every New Hampshire home.[12]

Refusing the Democratic-Republican nomination as vice president in 1812 on grounds of age and health, Langdon retired and spent his remaining years in Portsmouth until his death in 1819.[13] Elizabeth Langdon had died in the early spring of 1813 and was buried in the North Cemetery. Their daughter, Elizabeth, married Thomas Elwyn, originally from England, who had served as an aide to John Langdon in 1808. The couple eventually had nine children, one of whom—Alfred—married Mary Middleton Mease, granddaughter of Pierce Butler, also a signer of the Constitution.

Notes

1. Edward Raymond Sherburne, *Some Descendants of Henry and John Sherburne of Portsmouth, N.H.* (Boston: New England Genealogical Society, 1984). Some sources state that Elizabeth Sherburne was born in 1761, making her sixteen at the time of her marriage, but her gravestone gives the date as 1751.

2. *The New England Genealogical and Historical Register and Antiquarian* 9 (1855): 180.

3. George T. Chapman, *Sketches of the Alumni of Dartmouth College* (Cambridge: Riverside Press, 1867), 20; Charles Henry Bell, *The Bench and Bar of New Hampshire* (Cambridge: Riverside Press, 1894), 635–36.

4. Fred Myron Colby, "The Langdon Mansion," *The Granite Monthly* 3 (1880): 80–81.

5. Charles Robert Corning, *John Langdon* (Concord: Rumford Printing Co., 1903), 9–16.

6. Lawrence Shaw Mayo, *John Langdon of New Hampshire* (Concord: Rumford Press, 1937), 170–71.

7. Corning, *John Langdon*, 23.

8. Mayo, *John Langdon of New Hampshire*, xi, 190; Colby, "The Langdon Mansion," 80–81.

9. Mayo, *John Langdon of New Hampshire*, 140–41. Elizabeth Langdon was actually about ten years younger than her husband.

10. William Spohn Baker, *Washington after the Revolution* (Philadelphia: J. B. Lippincott, 1898), 135, 144, 157.

11. Corning, *John Langdon*, 25.

12. Robert Sobel and John Raimo, *Biographical Directory of the Governors of the United States, 1789–1978* (New York: Meckler Books, 1988), 3: 943.

13. Robert G. Ferris and James H. Charleton, *The Signers of the Constitution* (Flagstaff, Ariz.: Interpretive Publications, 1986), 184.

Bibliography

Cleary, Barbara Ann. "The Governor John Langdon Mansion Memorial: New Perspectives in Interpretation." *Old-Time New England* 69 (Summer–Fall 1978): 23.

Corning, Charles R. *John Langdon.* Concord: Rumford Printing Co., 1903.

Elwyn, Alfred Langdon. "Some Account of John Langdon." *Early State Papers of New Hampshire* 20 (1891): 850–80.

————. *Letters by Washington, Adams, Jefferson, and Others, Written during and after the Revolution, to John Langdon, New Hampshire.* Philadelphia: H. B. Ashmead, 1880.

Lacy, Harriet S. "The Langdon Papers, 1716–1841." *Historical New Hampshire* 22 (Autumn 1967): 55–65.

Mayo, Lawrence Shaw. *John Langdon of New Hampshire.* Concord: Rumford Press, 1937.

Sherburne, Edward Raymond. *Some Descendants of Henry and John Sherburne of Portsmouth, N.H.* Boston: New-England Historic and Genealogical Society, 1904.

"The Sherburne Family." *New England Historical and Genealogical Register* 9 (July 1855): 208.

Susannah French Livingston

Birth:	June 1723 (christened 19 June), New York, New York
Parents:	Philip French and Susannah Brockholst
Marriage:	2 March 1747, William Livingston (1723–1790)
Children:	Son (born and died 1746); Son (born and died 1747); Susanna (Sukey) (1748–1840); Catherine (Kitty) Wilhelmina (1751–1813); Mary (Molly) (1753–1839); William (1754–1817); Philip van Brugh (born and died 1755); Sarah (Sally) van Brugh (1756–1802); Henry (Harry) Brockholst (1757–1823); Judith (Judy) Philipa (1758–1843); Philip French (1760–1768); John Lawrence (1762–1781); Elizabeth Clarkson (1764–1765)
Death:	17 July 1789, Elizabethtown, New Jersey

Susannah French, one of four surviving daughters of Philip French and Susannah Brockholst, came from a family with impeccable social credentials, but whose fortunes had waned. When she was a child the family moved to New Brunswick, New Jersey, where Philip French had a large estate. In 1730, when Susannah was seven, her mother died, and her father remarried. Eleven years later a disastrous fire destroyed Kells Hall, the family home. Susannah then went to live in New York with her maternal aunt Mary Brockholst.[1]

Susannah's courtship by her cousin William Livingston met with his father's disapproval. Susannah and William finally married on 2 March 1747 at the Dutch church in Acquackanonck, New Jersey, which stood on land formerly belonging to the Brockholst family.[2]

While William was occupied in furthering a distinguished public career, Susannah was equally engaged at home. The young Livingstons moved in the best circles of New York society, and both were interested in maintaining their position. An early biographer described Susannah's character as "plain and unpretending" and that although she had "received only an imperfect education," she was "endowed with a strong intellect, ardent in her affections, devoted to her husband, and adapt[ed] herself with success to the peculiarities of his temper . . . possess[ing] his love and respect undiminished to the end of her life."[3]

Until 1773, when they moved to Elizabethtown, New Jersey, the couple occupied a prominent place in the social, artistic, and cultural life of New York City. Not all was bright, however. In 1746 and again in 1747, Susannah gave birth to sons, both of whom died in infancy. She was experiencing a tragedy all too common to families in the eighteenth century—the loss of children in infancy and childhood. Thirteen children were born to Susannah and William, and William boasted that they had as many children as states in the Union. But they lost four of them in infancy, and there were other tragedies as well. One son, Philip French, drowned in a boating accident on the Hackensack River as a child, and another, John Lawrence, was lost at sea on 18 March 1781 while serving on the ill-fated sloop *Saratoga*.[4]

The remaining children fared better. Their daughter Sarah married John Jay, subsequently the first Chief Justice of the Supreme Court, in 1774 at the family estate in Elizabethtown, New Jersey. Another son, Henry Brockholst, was an officer in the Revolutionary War, serving as aide-de-camp to General Philip Schuyler, and in 1807 was appointed associate justice of the Supreme Court. Susanna, "pretty Susan" of Major John Andre's poem "Cow Chase," married John Cleve Symmes, who had served in the New Jersey militia during the Revolutionary War and was later a jurist in New Jersey and the Northwest Territory. The marriage also made her the stepmother of William Henry Harrison's future wife. Son William also served in the New Jersey militia. The Livingstons' daughter Kitty married Matthew Ridley, a Baltimore merchant, and secondly her first cousin, John Livingston; Molly married James Linn, a representative to Congress from New Jersey; and Judy married John W. Watkins, a New York merchant and veteran of the Revolutionary War.[5]

In 1773 the Livingstons moved to Elizabethtown, New Jersey, where William built a large house, Liberty Hall, surrounded by lovely gardens for his family. After the move William served as delegate to the Continental Congress, and Susannah saw him installed in 1776 as the first governor of New Jersey.[6] During the Revolutionary War, because of threats of assassination, he was frequently away for long periods of time in hiding from the British.[7] When they invaded in 1776, Susannah and two of her daughters fled to take refuge with her brother-in-law, returning to the family home in 1779. Enemy troops broke into Liberty Hall in February, when only the daughters were at home. Susanna protected her father's papers by telling the enemy they were her private letters; although the library was ransacked, Livingston's official papers were thus saved.[8] Livingston's wife, Susannah, was left to cope with her family and large estate at Elizabethtown as best she could. The farm was neglected, income was negligible, and the once beautiful gardens were overrun. When the war was over, William Livingston returned to an impoverished estate. He and Susannah set about rebuilding the family fortune. The gardens were restored, and the family farm once again became productive.

Susannah spent her last years as an invalid. In 1786 she traveled to Lebanon Springs, New York, hoping to derive some benefit from its waters. In a letter that year her husband wrote that he loved her most affectionately and that when he returned (from Trenton), he would, by his attentions and assiduities, give her the greatest demonstrations possible of his sincerity.[9] Susannah died three years later on 17 July 1789 at Liberty Hall. William's later letters expressed his great depression over the loss of a beloved wife and companion of more than forty years.[10] The following year William died on 25 July of heart failure at his estate in Elizabethtown. Originally buried in the local Presbyterian church cemetery, they were moved to their son's vault in Trinity Church, Manhattan. In 1844 they were reinterred with their son Brockholst in Green-Wood Cemetery, Brooklyn.

Notes

1. *Papers of William Livingston*, ed. by Charles E. Prince et al. (Trenton: New Jersey Historical Commission, 1979): 5: 554–55.

2. *Papers of William Livingston*; Claire Brandt, *An American Aristocracy: The Livingstons* (Garden City, N.Y.: Doubleday and Co., 1986), 95; Paul A. Stellhorn and J. Birkner, eds., *The Governors of New Jersey, 1644–1974. Biographical Essays* (Trenton:

New Jersey Historical Commission, 1982), 77; Theodore Sedgwick, *A Memoir of the Life of William Livingston* (New York: J. & J. Harper, 1833), 60. The Acquackanonck Dutch Reformed Church records show a Livingston and a Susan marrying on 2 March 1747 (Arthur C. M. Kelly, *Vital Records of the Protestant Dutch Reformed Church at Acquackanonck Dutch . . .* [New York: Holland Society of New York, 1977], 218).

   3. Sedgwick, *A Memoir of the Life of William Livingston*, 60.

   4. Sedgwick, *A Memoir of the Life of William Livingston*, 127; Cuyler Reynolds, comp., *Genealogical and Family History of Southern New York and the Hudson River Valley* (New York: Lewis Publishing Co., 1914), 3: 1335.

   5. Sedgwick, *A Memoir of the Life of William Livingston*, 345–48; Reynolds, *Genealogical and Family History of Southern New York*, 3: 1335; Thomas Streatfield Clarkson, *A Biographical History of Clermont, or Livingston Manor* (Clermont, N.Y.: s.n., 1869), 291–92.

   6. Sedgwick, *A Memoir of the Life of William Livingston*, 77–81.

   7. Sedgwick, *A Memoir of the Life of William Livingston*, 77–81.

   8. Clarkson, *A Biographical History of Clermont, or Livingston Manor*, 300; Elizabeth Fries Ellet, in *Revolutionary Women in the War for American Independence* (New York: Charles Scribner, 1856), 118–20, tells another story, which took place the following year, in which a drunken enemy soldier took one of the daughters as the ghost of a woman (Hannah Caldwell) they had killed earlier in the day.

   9. Clarkson, *A Biographical History of Clermont, or Livingston Manor*, 306; Sedgwick, *A Memoir of the Life of William Livingston*, 390–91.

   10. Sedgwick, *A Memoir of the Life of William Livingston*, 434.

Bibliography

Susannah French Livingston left very few letters, some of which are included with her husband's papers at the New York Public Library. Some are published in *The Papers of William Livingston* cited below.

American Association of University Women, New Jersey Division. *Ladies at the Crossroads, Eighteenth Century Women of New Jersey.* Morristown, N.J.: Compton Press, 1978.

Brandt, Claire. *An American Aristocracy: The Livingstons.* Garden City, N.Y.: Doubleday and Co., 1986.

Clarkson, Thomas Streatfield. *A Biographical History of Clermont, or Livingston Manor.* Clermont, N.Y.: s.n., 1869.

Elizabeth, N.J., Sesqui-centennial Committee. *Revolutionary History of Elizabeth, New Jersey.* Elizabeth, N.J.: n.p., 1926.

Hatfield, Edwin Francis. *History of Elizabeth, New Jersey; including the early history of Union County.* New York: Carlton & Lanahan, 1868.

Livingston, Edwin. *The Livingstons of Livingston Manor.* New York: Knickerbocker Press, 1910.

Livingston, William. *The Papers of William Livingston*. Ed. Carl E. Prince et al. Trenton: New Jersey Historical Commission, 1979–.

Piwonka, Ruth. *A Portrait of Livingston Manor, 1686-1986*. Clermont, N.Y.: Friends of Clermont, c. 1986.

Prince, Carl E. *William Livingston, New Jersey's First Governor*. Trenton: New Jersey Historical Commission, 1975.

Sedgwick, Theodore Jr. *A Memoir of the Life of William Livingston, Member of Congress in 1774, 1775, and 1776; Delegate to the Federal Convention in 1787, and Governor of the State of New-Jersey from 1776 to 1790*. New York: J. & J. Harper, 1833.

Thayer, Theodore. *As We Were: The Story of Old Elizabethtown*. Newark: New Jersey Historical Society, 1964.

Van Rensselaer, Florence. *The Livingston Family in America and Its Scottish Origins*. New York, 1949.

Dolley Payne Todd Madison

Birth:	20 May 1768, New Garden, North Carolina
Parents:	John Payne and Mary (Molly) Coles
Marriages:	7 January 1790, John Todd (1763–1793)
	15 September 1794, James Madison (1751–1836)
Children:	John Payne Todd (1792–1852); William Temple Todd (July–October 1793)
Death:	8 July 1849, Washington, D.C.

Dolley Payne was born on 20 May 1768 in New Garden, near Guilford, North Carolina, one of eight surviving children of John (1739–1792) and Mary Coles (1743–1807) Payne.[1] Her parents were Quakers, who had come from Hanover County, Virginia, with their son Walter in 1765 to a new settlement in North Carolina. A second son, William Temple, was born in 1766, and Dolley arrived two years later. After only a few years in North Carolina, the Payne family decided to move back to Virginia. John Payne sold his land and returned with his family to Hanover County in 1769.[2]

Dolley's mother came from an old Quaker family that had immigrated to Virginia from Yorkshire, England. Among Dolley's maternal relatives was her second cousin, Patrick Henry. Her father was the son of a prosperous landowner who had served in the House of Burgesses in Virginia. He had converted to the Quaker faith, and he and his wife had joined the Cedar Creek Meeting of Friends in 1764. The Paynes and other members of their faith were wrestling with the question of slavery, which their faith held as immoral. John and Mary Payne were among the first to free their slaves, and others followed.[3]

After returning to Virginia five more children were born to the Paynes: Isaac, Lucy, Anna, Mary, and John. The three oldest children—Walter, William Temple, and Dolley—went to a nearby log schoolhouse where they were taught reading, writing, and grammar, with some mathematics taught for an additional fee. The children later went to a school held in the Cedar Creek Meeting.[4] Walter, the oldest, eventually went to work in Philadelphia, leaving the second son, Temple, to help his father with the farm. In 1781 Mary Payne visited Walter and her old Quaker friends there. After her return to Virginia, the Payne family decided to move to Philadelphia, arriving in 1783, when Dolley was fifteen years old.[5]

Soon after their arrival in Philadelphia, the Paynes were accepted into the Quaker community. They moved into a small rented house, where the front room was used as an office by John Payne, who established himself as a laundry starch manufacturer. There, their last child, Philadelphia, who died in infancy, was born.

Among the young men interested in Dolley Payne was John Todd Jr., who attended the Pine Street Meeting and who was also a friend of her father. He came from an old Quaker family, who, for three generations, had lived in Chester County and Philadelphia. John Todd Sr. had been principal of the Friends Academy and had gained the reputation of being a strict disciplinarian. His son was kind, patient, and serious. He had studied law and was a practicing attorney. He had long devoted himself to winning Dolley, but she was enjoying her youth and was not ready to settle down as a Quaker wife.

John Payne's starch-making business proved a failure, and the Pine Street Meeting disowned him in 1789 for failure to pay his debts. It was a terrible blow to this devoted Quaker and to his family. During this time, John Todd Jr. was a faithful friend and tried to help in any way he could. Dolley was twenty-one when this misfortune to her father occurred, and soon after the crisis the young couple became engaged. The wedding took place on 7 January 1790 at the Pine Street Meeting.[6] Within two years they moved into their own house, an imposing three-story brick home on the northeast corner of Fourth and Walnut Streets in Philadelphia. There Dolley's two sons were born, John Payne Todd on 29 February 1792, named for his father and Dolley's father, and William Temple Todd in July 1793, named for Dolley's brother.[7]

To support her family, Molly Payne had opened a boardinghouse in 1791. After continuing to decline in health, Dolley's father died on 24 October 1792.[8] In August of the following year Dolley's sister Lucy eloped with George Steptoe Washington, ward and nephew of President George Washington; she was fifteen, and he was seventeen.

Also in the summer of 1793 a terrible scourge of yellow fever broke out in Philadelphia. To keep his family safe John Todd sent Dolley, her mother, and the two children to stay outside the city. His brother James had also sent his family away, but their parents hesitated to leave because of certain commitments, and John Todd, too, felt his commitments should keep him in the city. John Todd's parents died, and in late October he, too, contracted yellow fever and died. The baby, William Temple, also died, and Dolley became seriously ill. Nursed by her mother, Dolley recovered. It was estimated that five thousand people had died during the epidemic and that seventeen thousand had fled the city. Mrs. Payne decided to give up the boardinghouse and went to live with Lucy and George Steptoe Washington in Virginia, along with her two younger children, Mary and John. Anna remained with Dolley until Anna's marriage in 1804. Their brother Walter had been lost at sea in 1786, and Temple and Isaac were out on their own (both brothers died in 1794).[9]

Dolley was twenty-five years old when she returned to Philadelphia in December 1793 and gradually resumed her life in the Quaker community. James Madison was in Philadelphia at the time, serving as a representative in Congress from Virginia. He was forty-three and came from a successful planter family in Virginia. His career had already been a very distinguished one. Along with so many others, he had noticed the beautiful young widow. He asked their mutual friend, Senator Aaron Burr, if he would arrange a meeting, which took place in Dolley Todd's Philadelphia home on a May evening in 1794. Soon afterward Dolley, her sister Anna, and her son Payne went to Virginia to visit family. While she was gone, she wrote Madison a letter accepting his proposal. He met her at her sister Lucy's home at Harewood, Virginia, where they were married on 15 September 1794. As expected, the Pine Street Meeting disowned her for marrying outside the Quaker faith, but Dolley was apparently not greatly disturbed.

The Madisons lived in Philadelphia for the next three years while James Madison served in Congress after which they retired to Montpelier, Madison's home in Virginia. Dolley soon established a reputation as a great hostess, and her invitations became very popular. In 1800 the government moved from Philadelphia to the new city of Washington. When Thomas Jefferson became president in 1801, he appointed Madison as his secretary of state, an office he retained until 1809. Jefferson often asked Dolley, as the wife of the highest-ranking cabinet officer, to be his official hostess. She and her husband often entertained at their own house as well, and Dolley soon became Washington's most important hostess. She was charming and had a talent for bright conversation. "As in costume and manners she was elegant, so in conversation she was easy."[10]

On 4 March 1809 James Madison became the fourth president of the United States, and Dolley became its first lady. During the next two years Dolley decorated the White House with the help of the architect Benjamin Latrobe. She chose American-made furniture of high quality and with funding from Congress made the president's house an important building in America. Her style of entertaining took a middle road between European elegance and republican simplicity.[11] Dolley loved fashion, and she was noted for her beautiful clothes, especially those from Paris.

On 17 August 1814, during the War of 1812, the British began marching toward the city. On the afternoon of 24 August, Dolley packed a wagon to be stored at the Bank of Maryland and then decided to save the portrait of George Washington, thus becoming one of the heroines of the war. But the president's house was burned, and James and Dolley Madison spent the remainder of his term in rented houses, initially in the Octagon House and later in a house on 19th Street, where Dolley resumed entertaining in style.

The Madisons retired to Montpelier in 1817, remaining there until James Madison's death in 1836. The following year Dolley moved back to Washington, taking a house on Lafayette Square across from the White House. Her later life was marred by the mounting debt created by her son Payne. Delaying poverty, she sold Madison's papers to Congress but eventually had to sell the entire Montpelier estate. Dolley continued to entertain and be entertained in her Washington house. She had many influential friends and relatives that made it possible for her to be the consummate hostess and guest. When she died in 1849, at the age of eighty-one, her funeral was a state occasion. Dolley was eventually laid to rest near her husband James at Montpelier.

Notes

1. Ethel Stephens Arnett, *Mrs. James Madison, The Incomparable Dolley* (Greensboro, N.C.: Piedmont Press, 1972), 9.

2. Arnett, *Mrs. James Madison*, 17.

3. Katherine Anthony, *Dolly Madison, Her Life and Times* (Garden City, N.Y.: The Country Life Press, 1949), 9–11, 14.

4. Ella Kent Barnard, *Dorothy Payne, Quakeress: A Sidelight upon the Career of "Dolly" Madison* (Philadelphia: Ferris and Leach, 1909), 53.

5. Arnett, *Mrs. James Madison*, 31.

6. Barnard, *Dorothy Payne, Quakeress*, 67–70.

7. Barnard, *Dorothy Payne, Quakeress*, 44–45.

8. Allen Culling Clark, *Life and Letters of Dolly Madison* (Washington, D.C.: W. F. Roberts, 1914), 16.

9. Clark, *Life and Letters of Dolly Madison*, 29.

10. Anthony, *Dolly Madison, Her Life and Times*, 124.

11. Holly Cowan Shulman, "Dolley Madison," *American National Biography* (New York: Oxford University Press, 1999), 15: 302.

Bibliography

Most of Dolley Madison's letters are included in the Papers of James Madison, Alderman Library, University of Virginia. Some of her papers are also in the Library of Congress and the Greensboro (North Carolina) Historical Museum. In addition to Allen Clark's *Life and Letters of Dolly Madison* and Lucia Cutts's *Memoirs and Letters of Dolly Madison* (see below), Holly C. Shulman has digitized a collection of her letters; see rotunda.upress .virginia.edu/dmde/. (There are many biographies of Dolley Madison; below are listed some of the more important ones.)

Allgor, Catherine. *A Perfect Union: Dolley Madison and the Creation of the American Nation.* New York: Macmillan, 2006.

Anthony, Katherine. *Dolly Madison, Her Life and Times.* Garden City, N.Y.: The Country Life Press, 1949.

Arnett, Ethel Stephens. *Mrs. James Madison: The Incomparable Dolley.* Greensboro, N.C.: Piedmont Press, 1972.

Barnard, Ella Kent. *Dorothy Payne, Quakeress: A Sidelight on the Career of "Dolly" Madison.* Philadelphia: Ferris and Leach, 1909.

Clark, Allen Cullen. *Life and Letters of Dolly Madison.* Washington, D.C.: W. F. Roberts, 1914.

Cote, Richard N. *Strength and Honor: The Life of Dolley Madison.* Mount Pleasant, S.C.: Corinthian Books, 2005.

Cutts, Lucia B. *Memoirs and Letters of Dolly Madison.* Cambridge, Mass.: The Riverside Press, 1886.

Dean, Elizabeth Lippincott. *Dolly Madison, The Nation's Hostess.* Boston: Lothrop, Lee & Shepherd Co., 1928.

Gerson, Noel B. *The Velvet Glove: A Life of Dolly Madison.* Nashville: T. Nelson, 1975.

Goodwin, Maud Wilder. *Dolly Madison.* New York: Charles Scribner's Sons, 1896.

Hunt-Jones, Conover. *Dolley and the "Great Little Madison."* Washington, D.C.: American Institute of Architects Foundation, 1977.

Mattern, David B., and Holly C. Shulman. *The Selected Letters of Dolley Madison.* Charlottesville: University of Virginia Press, 2001.

Moore, Virginia. *The Madisons: A Biography.* New York: McGraw-Hill, 1979.

Pflueger, Lynda. *Dolley Madison: Courageous First Lady.* Springfield, N.J.: Enslow, 1999.

Shulman, Holly Cowan. "Dolley Madison." *American National Biography.* New York: Oxford University Press, 1999, 15: 302.

Shulman, Holly Cowan, and David B. Mattern. *Dolley Madison: Her Life, Letters, and Legacy.* New York: The Rosen Publishing Group, 2003.

Zall, Paul M. *Dolley Madison.* Presidential Wives Series. Hauppauge, N.Y.: Nova History Publications, 2001.

Margaret (Peggy) Caldwell McHenry

Birth:	8 October 1762, Philadelphia, Pennsylvania
Parents:	David Caldwell and Grace Allison
Marriage:	8 January 1784, James McHenry (1753–1816)
Children:	Grace (1784–1789); Daniel William (1786–1814); Anna (1788–1837); Margaretta (1794–1809); John (1797–1822)
Death:	20 November 1833, Baltimore, Maryland

In 1771 eighteen-year-old James McHenry emigrated from Ireland to Philadelphia, where his host was Captain William Allison, a successful merchant and fellow Presbyterian. His stepdaughter Peggy, whom James was later to marry, was then nine years old. In 1763 Captain Allison had married his cousin, Grace Allison Caldwell, a widow with three children. Grace had been married to David Caldwell, also a successful merchant, but he died in 1762 leaving two children, John (Jack) and Elizabeth, as well as a pregnant wife. Margaret Caldwell, always called Peggy, was born after her father's death. Grace and William Allison had four more children of their own: Mary (Polly), William, Grace, and Jane. Elizabeth Caldwell and Polly and William Allison all died young.[1]

While James McHenry's family settled in Baltimore, James studied medicine in Philadelphia, thus remaining close to the Allison family. He served in the Revolutionary War as a surgeon, on George Washington's staff, and ultimately as the Marquis de Lafayette's aide-de-camp. After the war he was elected to the Maryland legislature.

Until his father died in 1782, James was not in a position to marry as he was financially dependent upon him. At his father's death, however, the estate was divided between James and his brother, both of whose financial woes appear to have abated.[2] James, a minor poet, turned his eyes once again to Peggy Caldwell, penning her romantic verses. He continued writing her poems on almost every wedding anniversary. Peggy, too, wrote some poetry. When Congress moved in November 1783 from Princeton to Annapolis, James paid a visit to Peggy in Philadelphia and gained her consent to marry. McHenry was anxious to marry as soon as possible, January 1784 being his desired date. Peggy wanted to wait until spring to give her time to find a house as well as spend the winter in Philadelphia with her family. Peggy's mother resolved the dilemma by suggesting that they marry in January but that Peggy stay in Philadelphia until spring.[3] Eventually the McHenrys built an elegant new house they called "Fayetteville" on the outskirts of Baltimore.

In 1796 McHenry was appointed Secretary of War, and the family prepared to move to Philadelphia. Among the many complications that faced Peggy in moving her family was that of their five household slaves. Because Pennsylvania was in the process of gradually abolishing slavery, the McHenrys could have their slaves with them only with great difficulty. At first she thought to sell the slaves but was upset at the financial loss in the long run and at the thought of having strange servants in her new home. They could have been converted to indentured servants, thereby gaining their freedom in seven years. The slaves themselves had mixed feelings. Going to Philadelphia might mean possible freedom, but it would also mean leaving their families behind in Baltimore. In the end three slaves accompanied the McHenrys to Philadelphia and eventual freedom, one gained her freedom because of age, and the fate of the other is unknown.[4]

Peggy was deeply religious and concentrated her efforts on being a good housewife and mother, not much interested in public affairs.[5] The McHenrys had five children, and Peggy outlived all but one. Grace, born in 1784, died at age five. Years later her father wrote to Alexander Hamilton, "I lost my eldest child, a daughter, after she had discovered whatever can promise to flatter parental expectations."[6] Daniel William, named for his grandfather and Peggy's stepfather, married and had one son, who died without issue. Daniel William himself died young, killed in 1814 after being thrown from his horse. Anna married James P. Boyd in 1808 and had four children who died without issue. Margaretta died in 1809 of tuberculosis at the age of fifteen, and John, who was educated for the bar, died at twenty-five from a fever, leaving one son.

The McHenrys also assumed responsibility for John McHenry, the son of James's brother, John, as well as Peggy's two younger sisters, Grace and Jane, after both their parents died.[7] Grace married Hugh McCurdy, a successful Baltimore merchant who had succeeded McHenry's brother, John, in the family business,[8] while Jane married Larkin Dorsey, a member of an old Maryland family.

Peggy lived on after her husband's death in 1816 until 1833 and is buried in Baltimore with her husband and children.

Notes

1. Karen Evelyn Robbins, "James McHenry: His American Experience," Ph.D. dissertation, Columbia University, 1994, 7–9.

2. Robbins, "James McHenry," 132–33; Bernard C. Steiner, *The Life and Correspondence of James McHenry, Secretary of War under Washington and Adams* (Cleveland: Burrows, 1907), 50.

3. Robbins, "James McHenry," 155, 159; Steiner, *The Life and Correspondence of James McHenry*, 59–60.

4. Robbins, "James McHenry," 278–83; Karen Robbins, "Power among the Powerless: Domestic Resistance by Free and Slave Women in the McHenry Family of the New Republic," *Journal of the Early Republic* 23 (Spring 2003): 47–68.

5. Steiner, *The Life and Correspondence of James McHenry*, 77.

6. McHenry to Hamilton, in Harold C. Syrett, ed., *The Papers of Alexander Hamilton*, 27 vols. (New York and London: Columbia University, 1961–1987), 25: 439.

7. Robbins, "James McHenry," 240.

8. Robbins, "James McHenry," 254.

Bibliography

The McHenry family papers, including those of Margaret McHenry, are in the collections of the Maryland Historical Society in Baltimore. Some of Margaret's letters are included in the John McHenry Papers in the same institution. Other letters are among the James McHenry Papers in the Clements Library, University of Michigan, and one often-quoted letter of James to Margaret, relating to the resignation of George Washington as commander-in-chief, is among the records of the Maryland Archives in Annapolis.

Brown, Frederick J. *A Sketch of the Life of Dr. James McHenry.* Baltimore: Maryland Historical Society, 1877.

Caldwell, Charles Tufts. *William Coaldwall, Caldwell, or Coldwell of England, Massachusetts, Connecticut, and Nova Scotia.* Washington, D.C.: Higginson Book Co., 1910.

Coad, Oral S., ed. "James McHenry, a Minor Poet." *Rutgers University Library Journal* 8 (June 1945): 3364.

Robbins, Karen. "James McHenry: His American Experience." Ph.D. dissertation, Columbia University, 1994.

———. "Power among the Powerless: Domestic Resistance by Free and Slave Women in the McHenry Family of the New Republic." *Journal of the Early Republic* 23 (Spring 2003): 47–68.

Steiner, Bernard C. *The Life and Correspondence of James McHenry.* Cleveland: The Burrows Brothers Co., 1907.

Sarah (Sally) Morris Mifflin

Birth:	5 April 1747, Philadelphia, Pennsylvania
Parents:	Morris Morris and Elizabeth Mifflin
Marriage:	4 March 1767, Thomas Mifflin (1744–1800)
Children:	Emily (1770–1850)
Death:	1 August 1790, Philadelphia, Pennsylvania

The daughter of prominent Quakers, Morris Morris and his wife, Elizabeth Mifflin, Sarah Morris was born in Philadelphia on 5 April 1747. The family also included two sisters: Susannah and Rebecca. Nothing of her early life is known until she married a cousin, Thomas Mifflin, the son of John and Elizabeth Bagnell Mifflin, at the Fair Hill Meeting on 4 March 1767.[1] The young couple were notable socialites during the early years of their marriage, a lifestyle doubtless supported by Mifflin's budding mercantile career. Pre-revolutionary Philadelphia was not only the largest city in the colonies but one particularly well blessed with educational, cultural, and recreational amenities. Evidence suggests that the Mifflins enjoyed every advantage.

On 12 November 1770 the Mifflins became parents of Emily, who married Joseph Hopkinson, son of Francis Hopkinson, signer of the Declaration of Independence, on 27 February 1794.[2] Joseph Hopkinson also was the author in 1798 of a popular poem, "Hail Columbia." After her mother's death, Emily served as hostess for her father.[3]

In 1773 Thomas and Sarah Mifflin sat for a painting by John Singleton Copley, thought by the artist himself to have been his masterpiece. Now owned by the Philadelphia Museum of Art, the unusual double portrait shows a plainly dressed and delicate Sarah weaving a fringe, looking clearly at the viewer. It has been described by art historians as a "modern" representation of an egalitarian and affectionate marriage. Reportedly, Sarah sat twenty different times for the painting of her hands alone.[4]

The political career of Thomas Mifflin began rather inauspiciously with his appointment as warden of Philadelphia in 1771, but it led, the following year, to a seat in the colonial legislature, and in 1774, he was elected as a member of the Continental Congress. The British march on Lexington in April 1775 raised the alarm in Philadelphia. It was now clear that war was imminent, and volunteer companies began to organize and drill. Mifflin joined the ranks and was commissioned a major. His increasing military activities earned him, in July 1774, the dubious distinction of being expelled from the Society of Friends of Philadelphia.[5]

Sarah proclaimed her commitment to the Revolution at its outset by writing to a friend in Boston:

> I have retrenched every superfluous expense in my table and family. Tea I have not drank since last Christmas, nor bought a new cup or gown since the affair at Lexington, and what I never did before, have learned to knit, and am now making stockings of wool for my servants; and this way do I throw in my mite to the public good. I know this, that as free I can die but once; but as a slave I shall not be worthy of life. I have the pleasure to assure you that these are the sentiments of my sister Americans. They have sacrificed assemblies,

parties of pleasure, tea-drinkings and finery to that great spirit of patriotism which actuates all degrees of people throughout this extensive country.[6]

Appointed aide-de-camp to General George Washington, Thomas Mifflin set out for the army's camp at Boston on 23 June 1775. It was here that Mifflin first made the acquaintance of John and Abigail Adams. Shortly thereafter, the sharp-eyed and sharp-witted Abigail wrote from Weymouth to her husband in Philadelphia, asking that she be remembered to Mrs. Mifflin, adding: "I do not know whether her husband is safe here. Bellona and Cupid have a contest about him. You hear nothing from the ladies but about Major Mifflin's easy address, politeness, complaisance, etc. 'Tis well he has so agreeable a lady at Philadelphia."[7]

We may only guess at what then led Sarah, in September of that year, to set out for camp to join Thomas. As she made her progress toward Boston, Silas Deane, representative from Wethersfield, Connecticut, wrote his wife: "If she pass thro' Wethersfield, wish you to be acquainted with her. She is a most agreeable lady, and worthy your notice on every account."[8] In January 1776 John Adams wrote his wife, Abigail, reporting upon a dinner he had attended at the Mifflins:

> I went to Cambridge where I dined at Coll. Mifflins with the General, and Lady and a vast Collection of other Company, among whom were six of seven Sachems and Warriours, of the French Cagnawaga Indians, with several of their Wives and Children. A savage Feat they made of it, yet were very polite in the Indian style. One of these sachems is an Englishman, a Native of this Colony, whose Name was Williams, captivated in his Infancy with his Mother, and adopted by some kind Squaw—another I think is half French blood.
>
> I was introduced to them by the General as one of the grand Council Fire at Philadelphia which made them prick up their Ears, they came and shook Hands with me, and made me low Bows, and scrapes &c. In short I was much pleased with this Days entertainment.[9]

Quite likely during the summer of 1776 Sarah became the temporary guardian of young Margaret Moncreiffe, the teenaged daughter of a British officer on General William Howe's staff. Margaret, suspected of spying for the enemy British, was being held under virtual house arrest on the direct orders of General Washington. She reported having been treated "tenderly" by Mrs. Sarah Mifflin for a time until she was finally released into British custody.[10]

When, in September 1777, the British took Philadelphia, Sarah moved to the relative safety of the Mifflin's Reading, Pennsylvania, property. It was reported that there she lived quietly but, with her neighbors there, prepared delicacies for the sick and wounded quartered nearby.[11] Following the British evacuation of Philadelphia in June 1778, the city became a center of financial speculation, with wealth easily acquired and as frivolously spent. Timothy Pickering, then a member of the Board of War of the Continental Congress, wrote to his wife in Salem, Massachusetts:

> I have mentioned to you the enormous head-dresses of the ladies here. The more I see, the more I am displeased with them. 'Tis surprising how they fix such loads of trumpery on their polls; and not less so that they are by anyone deemed ornamental. The Whig ladies seem as fond of them as others. I am told by a French gentleman they are in the true French taste, only that they want a few very long feathers. The married ladies, however, are not at all infected. One of the handsomest (General Mifflin's lady) I have seen in the State does not dress her head higher than was common in Salem a year ago. But you know, my dear, I have old, old-fashioned notions.[12]

And, upon at least two occasions, General Washington himself expressed in writing his regard for and wish to be remembered to Mrs. Mifflin, once on 19 March 1777 and again on 14 January 1784.[13]

When hostilities ended, the Mifflins lived alternately on Market Street in Philadelphia and their country home near Reading, but Thomas's political career had far to run. He was successively a member of the Continental Congress (1782–1784; president, 1783), a member of the Pennsylvania State House of Representatives (1785–1788), a delegate to the Federal Constitutional Convention (1787) and signer of the Constitution (1788), president of the Supreme Executive Council of Pennsylvania (1788–1790), president of the Pennsylvania Constitutional Convention (1790–1800), and again a member of the Pennsylvania State House of Representatives (1799–1800). Sarah Morris Mifflin died on 1 August 1790 "after a six months' illness,"[14] just before her husband became the first governor of the Commonwealth of Pennsylvania. She was buried in the Friends Burial Ground at Arch Street in Philadelphia. Thomas Mifflin died on 20 January 1800 in Lancaster, Pennsylvania, and is buried there in the Trinity Lutheran Churchyard.

Notes

1. William Henry Egle, *Some Pennsylvania Women during the War of the Revolution* (Harrisburg, Pa.: Harrisburg Publishing Co., 1898. Reprint, Cottonport: Polyanthos, 1972), 127–29; Wilfred Jordan, ed., *Colonial and Revolutionary Families of Philadelphia* (New York: Lewis Historical Publishing Co., Inc., 1933), 1: 37; Kenneth R. Rossman, "Thomas Mifflin: Revolutionary Patriot," *Pennsylvania History* 15 (January 1948): 10.

2. Jordan, *Colonial and Revolutionary Families of Philadelphia*, 12: 284.

3. According to one family account (Benjamin C. Mifflin, *Charles Mifflin, M.D. with an Account of his Ancestors and Ancestral Connections* [Cambridge: Riverside Press, 1876], 24), however, there were four daughters, "all beautiful women." The given names of the other three are unknown, but the family source believed that one married a Mr. Siebenstein of Mifflin County, Pennsylvania; one married a "Southern gentleman," possibly from New Orleans; and that the fourth "died insane." This source appears to be the only reference to any children other than Emily of Thomas and Sarah Mifflin. Furthermore, some other sources imply that the marriage was childless.

4. Kenneth Rossman, *Thomas Mifflin and the Politics of the American Revolution* (Chapel Hill: University of North Carolina Press, 1952), 9; Philadelphia Museum of Art, press release, 15 January 1999, available at philamuseum.org/information/pr/990127.shtml.

5. Rossman, *Thomas Mifflin*, 41.

6. Egle, *Some Pennsylvania Women*, 127.

7. Charles Francis Adams, ed., *Familiar Letters of John Adams and his Wife Abigail Adams during the Revolution* (New York: Hurd and Houghton, 1876), 93, quoted in Rossman, *Thomas Mifflin*, 44.

8. Rossman, *Thomas Mifflin*, 44.

9. John and Abigail Adams, *The Book of Abigail and John: Selected Letters of the Adams Family, 1762–1784*, ed. L. H. Butterfield, Marc Friedlaender, and Mary-Jo Kline (Cambridge, Mass.: Harvard University Press, 1975), 114.

10. Philip Young, *Revolutionary Ladies* (New York: Alfred A. Knopf, 1977), 146–47.

11. Egle, *Some Pennsylvania Women*, 129.

12. Octavius Pickering, *Life of Timothy Pickering*, 4 vols. (Boston: Little, Brown and Co., 1867), 1: 215, quoted in Frederick D. Stone, "Philadelphia Society One Hundred Years Ago, or, The Reign of Continental Money," *The Pennsylvania Magazine of History and Biography* 3 (1879): 363–64.

13. George Washington Papers, 1741–1799, Library of Congress. Available at memory.loc.gov/cgi-bin/query/r?ammem/mgw@field.

14. Jacob Hiltzheimer, "Extracts from the Diary of Jacob Hiltzheimer, 1668–1798," *The Pennsylvania Magazine of History and Biography* 16 (1892): 414; Rossman, *Thomas Mifflin*, 198.

Bibliography

The letter quoted is included in William Henry Egle's essay in *Some Pennsylvania Women during the War of the Revolution* (see below). The location of this and other papers of Sarah Morris Mifflin are unknown.

Egle, William Henry. *Some Pennsylvania Women during the War of the Revolution.* Harrisburg, Pa.: Harrisburg Publishing Co., 1898. Reprint, Cottonport: Polyanthos, 1972.
Jordan, Wilfred, ed. *Colonial and Revolutionary Families of Philadelphia.* New York: Lewis Historical Publishing Co., 1933.

Merrill, John Houston. *Memoranda Relating to the Mifflin Family.* Philadelphia: privately printed, 1890.

Mifflin, Benjamin C. *Charles Mifflin, M.D. with an Account of his Ancestors and Ancestral Connections.* Cambridge: Riverside Press, 1876.

Rawle, William. "Sketch of the Life of Thomas Mifflin." *Pennsylvania Historical Society Memoirs* 2 (1830): 105–26.

Rossman, Kenneth R. "Thomas Mifflin: Revolutionary Patriot." *Pennsylvania History* 15 (January 1948): 9–23.

———. *Thomas Mifflin and the Politics of the American Revolution.* Chapel Hill: University of North Carolina Press, 1952.

Ann (Nancy) Cary
Randolph Morris

Birth: 16 September 1774, Tuckahoe Plantation, Virginia
Parents: Thomas Mann Randolph and Ann Cary
Marriage: 25 December 1809, Gouverneur Morris (1752–1816)
Children: Gouverneur (1813–1888)
Death: 28 May 1837, Morrisania, Bronx, New York

The life of Ann Cary Randolph Morris is a story of tragedy and triumph, of a life filled with high drama, much of it played out in the public eye of the Virginia courts and in high political circles of the post-revolutionary era. Ann Cary not only survived, she rose like a phoenix above the ashes of poverty and disgrace to soar into an age of respectability.

Ann, called Nancy, was the eighth of thirteen children born to Thomas Mann Randolph (1741–1793) and his wife, Ann Cary (1745–1789), both members of Virginia's aristocracy.[1] Her parents were second cousins, and although intermarriage with cousins was not unusual in colonial times, the custom seemed especially pronounced with the Randolphs, creating a confusing tangle of relationships.

Nancy's troubles began when her mother died, and her father married a young woman not much older than she. Friction was inevitable, and Nancy began visiting her married brothers and sisters, spending as much time as possible away from Tuckahoe, her family home. In 1790, at the age of sixteen, Nancy went to stay with her older sister Judith, who had married their cousin Richard Randolph and lived in rural Cumberland County at Richard's plantation "Bizarre." Richard's parents had died, and his two younger brothers, Theodorick and John, lived with them. Richard's widowed cousin and her children completed the family circle.[2]

On 1 October 1792, during a visit to a cousin's plantation, screams were heard in the night from Nancy's room, which opened off that of Richard and Judith. Rumors soon spread that Nancy had delivered a baby (or had a miscarriage), that Richard was the father, and that he had hidden the body on the grounds of the plantation. For months the family tried to rise above the rumors. St. George Tucker, Richard's stepfather, with whom Richard, Judith, and Nancy spent the winter, distributed a broadside defending his family, but to no avail. Apparently upon Richard's initiative, the affair ended up in a courtroom in April 1793, with Patrick Henry and John Marshall as two of his attorneys. John Randolph testified that Theodorick had told him prior to his death in early 1792 that he and Nancy were "engaged." Judith testified that there was no dissension, and indeed others testified likewise. Both Richard and Ann were exonerated for lack of evidence, but the scandal did not die.[3]

For over ten years Nancy continued to live at Bizarre under increasing strain for both sisters, Nancy complaining that she was treated little better than a servant. Their father had died a few months after the trial, and Nancy, with little chance of marrying well, was dependent upon her remaining family. Then Richard died in 1796, and his brother John took over the family estates. The sisters got along reasonably well when John was absent, but friction increased when he was there.[4] Nancy finally left Bizarre with her maid Phoebe in 1805, first going to Richmond. She soon decided to quit Virginia and went to Newport, Rhode Island, where a distant cousin lived.

After a stay in Fairfield, Connecticut, Nancy moved to a rented room in New York City, where Gouverneur Morris found her in October 1808. Twenty years earlier, he had met Nancy as a young girl at her home at Tuckahoe while visiting her father.[5] He began to correspond with her and then asked if she would consider coming to Morrisania, his family home in New York, to manage his household. Nancy at first refused his offer, for Morris had a reputation as a womanizer. Eventually she agreed to come, and Morris's diary for 23 April 1809 says that he drove to Armstrong's tavern and brought Miss Randolph of Virginia home. Eight months later, at a family Christmas dinner, he announced to his surprised guests that they were to witness his wedding. The two were married that evening by the Reverend Isaac Watkins, Morris's brother-in-law.[6] The following June the couple journeyed west to inspect the land where the Erie Canal was to be built, returning home in September.[7]

In 1813 the marriage was blessed with a son, also called Gouverneur.[8] Carrying on the Randolph family tradition, the second Gouverneur married his cousin, Martha (Patsey) Jefferson Cary, the daughter of his mother's youngest sister, Virginia Randolph. Although not as famous as his father, Gouverneur Jr. was a railway executive and in 1854 became one of the founders of the Republican Party.[9]

Judith's younger son, Tudor, who suffered from tuberculosis, was studying at Harvard in 1814 when he became ill. Morris wrote John Randolph, inviting John, Judith, and Tudor to stay at Morrisania. Tudor arrived desperately ill. After Nancy had nursed her nephew for almost three months, Tudor's mother and uncle appeared. Believing that his nephew was on the mend, John began his trip back to Virginia, stopping in New York City. While in New York, he wrote Nancy a vitriolic letter filled with accusations of her alleged transgressions. Nancy retaliated by writing a long letter of defense, sending it to twenty of John Randolph's political opponents. Tudor went to England for his health, dying there in August 1815. His mother Judith died a year later.[10]

Gouverneur Morris Sr. died on 6 November 1816 at his home Morrisania. Ann successfully survived challenges to his will, continued to live at Morrisania, and raised her son.

Although Morris had provided generously in his will for both Nancy and their son, his wealth had been diminished by the mismanagement of one of his nephews. Through various economies and good management, Ann was able to pass the estate unencumbered to her son.[11]

Partly to dissuade others from believing rumors damaging to her reputation as a chaste and honorable wife and mother, Nancy submitted some of her husband's correspondence, including a poem written to her during a prolonged absence, to the Columbia College alumni magazine for publication. Afterward she felt that her good character was somewhat restored.[12]

Nancy died in 1837 and was buried at Saint Ann's Church, commissioned by her son in her honor, in the Bronx, New York.[13]

Notes

1. "The Last of the Randolphs," *The Living Age* (1858) 56: 294 (from the *Petersburgh Virginia Express*).

2. Hugh A. Garland, *The Life of John Randolph of Roanoke*, 9th ed. (New York: D. Appleton and Co., 1854), 63.

3. William Cabell Bruce, *John Randolph of Roanoke* (New York: G. P. Putnam's Sons, 1922), 1: 106–23.

4. Bruce, *John Randolph of Roanoke*, 132, 134–35.

5. Alan Pell Crawford, *Unwise Passions: A True Story of a Remarkable Woman* (New York: Simon & Schuster, 2000), 53, 173–75, 177, 184, 191.

6. William Howard Adams, *Gouverneur Morris: An Independent Life* (New Haven, Conn.: Yale University Press, 2003), 283–84.

7. Gouverneur Morris, *The Diary and Letters of Gouverneur Morris*, ed. Ann Cary Morris (New York: Charles Scribner's Sons, 1888), 2: 522.

8. Adams, *Gouverneur Morris*, 291.

9. Obituary, Gouverneur Morris Jr., *New York Times* (21 August 1888).

10. Crawford, *Unwise Passions*, 226–27, 228, 245, 257, 260.

11. Crawford, *Unwise Passions*, 274; Cynthia A. Kierner, *Scandal at Bizarre: Rumor and Reputation in Jefferson's America* (Charlottesville: University of Virginia Press, 2004), 148–49.

12. Kierner, *Scandal at Bizarre*, 155–56; James J. Kirschke, *Gouverneur Morris: Author, Statesman, and Man of the World* (New York: St. Martin's Press, 2005), 265.

13. Adams, *Gouverneur Morris*, 296.

Bibliography

The Nancy Randolph Papers, 1805–1962, are located in the Earl Gregg Swem Library, College of William and Mary, Williamsburg, Virginia. Other papers, mainly financial, are included in the Gouverneur Morris Papers in the Library of Congress. Copies of letters concerning the trial are among the Randolph Family of Virginia Papers, Princeton University.

Adams, William Howard. *Gouverneur Morris: An Independent Life*. New Haven, Conn.: Yale University Press, 2003.

Bruce, William Cabell. *John Randolph of Roanoke*. 2 vols. New York: G. P. Putnam's Sons, 1922.

Crawford, Alan Pell. *Unwise Passions: A True Story of a Remarkable Woman*. New York: Simon & Schuster, 2000.

Doyle, Christopher L. "The Randolph Scandal in Early National Virginia, 1792–1815: New Voices in the 'Court of Honor.'" *Journal of Southern History* 69 (May 2003): 283–318.

Kierner, Cynthia A. *Scandal at Bizarre: Rumor and Reputation in Jefferson's America*. Charlottesville: University of Virginia Press, 2004.

Kirschke, James J. *Gouverneur Morris: Author, Statesman, and Man of the World*. New York: St. Martin's Press, 2005.

Morris, Gouverneur. *The Diary and Letters of Gouverneur Morris*. Ed. Anne Cary Morris. 2 vols. New York: Charles Scribner's Sons, 1888.

Sparks, Jared. *The Life of Gouverneur Morris, with Selections From his Correspondence, and Miscellaneous Papers; Detailing Events in the American Revolution, the French Revolution, and in the Political History of the United States*. 3 vols. Boston: Gray & Brown, 1832.

Swiggett, Howard. *The Extraordinary Mr. Morris*. Garden City, N.Y.: Doubleday, 1952.

Mary (Molly) White Morris

Birth:	13 April 1749, Philadelphia, Pennsylvania
Parents:	Thomas White and Esther Heulings
Marriage:	2 March 1769, Robert Morris (1734–1806)
Children:	Robert (1769–1804); Thomas (1771–1849); William White (1772–1798); Hester (Hetty) (1774–1817); Charles (1777–1801); Maria (1779–1852); Henry (1784–1842)
Death:	16 January 1827, Philadelphia, Pennsylvania

Mary White, known informally as Molly, was born on 13 April 1749 at the home of her parents in Philadelphia and baptized in Christ Church on 21 May 1749. She was the second and last child of the socially prominent Colonel Thomas White (1704–1779) and Esther Heulings (1719–1790). Her mother, the daughter of Abraham and Mary Heulings of Burlington, New Jersey, and widow of John Newman, was a lady of much force and character, coming from a family that lived among Quakers but had adhered to the Church of England.[1] Thomas White had moved from Maryland to Philadelphia in about 1745, and he participated actively in the life of the city. He was a trustee of Philadelphia College from 1749 until his death in 1779.[2]

Mary probably enjoyed all the pleasantries a beloved child of well-to-do parents could expect. The beautiful home of her childhood was considered to be a fine example of a proper and socially prominent colonial family. Mary was blessed with lovely features, and she must have been carefully trained and educated in all the womanly accomplishments to have been able to fill with so much ease, dignity, and grace the prominent social position in which she was placed after her marriage. A poem of the day mentioned her:

> In lovely White's most pleasing form,
> What various graces meet!
> How blest with every striking charm!
> How languishingly sweet![3]

Mary's brother, William (1748–1836), known as Billy, was educated in Philadelphia schools and graduated from the College of Philadelphia, now the University of Pennsylvania, in 1765, having just completed his seventeenth year. He had resolved to enter the ministry, and therefore, in October 1770, he sailed for England to become an Episcopalian priest. Returning to Christ Church, Philadelphia, in 1777, he was chosen as the chaplain of the Continental Congress and later of the United States Congress, serving whenever those government bodies met in Philadelphia.[4] Mary also had three half-sisters from her father's first marriage, one of whom died in early childhood.

Robert Morris was born in Liverpool, England, on 31 January 1734. He came to this country with his father and settled at Oxford, Maryland. His father, also Robert Morris, died in 1750, when his son was in his seventeenth year. In March 1749 young Robert came to Philadelphia and entered the counting house of Charles Willing, considered to be the first-rate merchant of his day. In 1754, at the age of twenty, young Robert formed a partnership with Thomas, the son of Charles Willing, which lasted for a period of thirty-nine years. The firm of Willing and Morris became the best known and largest import house in the colonies, which led Morris to become involved in the vital and explosive political situation of the pre-revolutionary era.[5]

The marriage of Robert Morris to Mary White took place on 2 March 1769 at the same Christ Church where, almost twenty years earlier, Mary had been baptized. The Reverend Richard Peters performed the ceremony.[6] To this union seven children were born: Robert, Thomas, William, Hester, Charles, Maria, and Henry.

The following year Robert Morris purchased "The Hills," a summer residence outside Philadelphia, where he erected a large house on the knoll of the hill overlooking the boathouses of the Schuylkill River, together with extensive hothouses where he raised all kinds of tropical fruit, a fishpond, and an icehouse. The hothouses and the icehouse were possibly the first introduced into the colonies.[7]

Near the end of 1776, five years after the Morrises' marriage, the British approached Philadelphia, and Congress went to Baltimore. Robert remained behind in Philadelphia, while Mary fled to stay with her half-sister, Sophia (Mrs. Aquila) Hall, in Harford County, Maryland, not far from Baltimore, remaining there until March the following year. On 20 December 1776 Mary wrote to her husband: "I long to give you an account of the many difficulties and uneasiness we have experienced in this journey. Indeed, my spirits were very unable to the task after the greatest conflict flying from home . . . but after all the dangers, I've the pleasure to inform you we are safely housed in a hospitable mansion."[8]

And on 15 January 1777, following the battle of Princeton, she wrote, "I suppressed mine [fear] all in my power, as I wish to make myself as agreeable as possible to this family, and as they had invited a party of young folks to a Twelfth Cake, I tryed to be cheerful."[9]

The Morris family had not been home a month before fears of the approach of the British necessitated preparations for once again seeking safer refuge. Mary wrote her mother, "We are preparing for another flight in packing up our furniture and removing them to a new purchase Mr. Morris has made ten miles from Lancaster."[10] Two weeks later she wrote, "We intend sending off our best furniture, with all the linen we can spare, and stores of all kinds, that our flight may be attended with as few incumbrances as possible."[11] The house in Lancaster, which Robert Morris bought, had been built by Baron Henry William Steigel, who had come to America about 1757, from Mannheim, Germany. The magnificent mansion, known as "The Castle," was very large and contained a chapel. The wainscotings, mantle pieces, and cornices are described as having been very massive and rich, while the arras tapestry that covered the parlor walls and the porcelain tiles encircling the fireplace were of the finest order. To this "famous house" the Morris family repaired when, in September 1777, the near approach of the British Army obliged Congress to move from Philadelphia.[12]

In the summer of 1778 the British evacuated Philadelphia, and Congress returned. Mary Morris wrote again to her mother: "We have a great many balls and entertainments, and soon the Assemblys will begin."[13] Robert and Mary often entertained, and their hospitality enjoyed an international reputation. In the fall of 1781, they sent their two older sons, Robert and Thomas, to Europe for their education, accompanied by Matthew Ridley, who later married William Livingston's daughter Kitty. In Geneva, the two boys went to school with Benjamin Franklin's grandson, Benjamin Bache. In 1786 they attended the University of Leipzig, returning home two years later, much to the joy of their parents.[14]

Robert and Thomas both set out to superintend their father's land interests, Robert in Pennsylvania and Thomas in western New York. Thomas practiced law in New York and served as a representative in Congress. The other sons were not so fortunate as to be educated abroad. Both William and Charles attended the University of Pennsylvania but were a bit wild and caused their father much worry. William studied law but died in the yellow fever epidemic of 1798. Charles, after several false starts, presumably died at sea. Hetty and Maria, the Morrises' daughters, both married—Hetty to James Marshall, a judge and brother of Chief Justice John Marshall, and Maria to Henry Nixon. The youngest child, Henry, came of age during his father's financial misfortunes and went into manufacturing.

While the Constitutional Convention was being held in Philadelphia, the Washingtons resided with the Morris family. When Martha Washington and her grandchildren traveled to join her husband after his inauguration as president in 1789, they stayed at the Morrises' house, after which Mary and her daughter Maria accompanied them to New York.[15] When the capital was moved to Philadelphia, the Morris house was offered as the presidential mansion.[16]

In 1798 Morris became bankrupt through land speculation and was arrested for debt. He remained in debtors' prison in Philadelphia until a bankruptcy law passed in 1801 liberated him. During this disastrous time, Mary stood by her husband, dining with him each evening and making arrangements for his return. She obtained an annuity of $2,000 per year from certain interests in the Holland Land Company bequeathed to her by Gouverneur Morris in return for her indispensable signature on certain papers. When her husband was released, there was a home waiting for him.[17]

Robert Morris died on 8 May 1806, at seventy-two years of age and was buried in the family vault adjoining Christ Church. After his death, Mary moved into another Philadelphia house, and it was there that General Lafayette, on his grand tour of America, visited her. At his request she attended a ball in his honor. Even at seventy-five she was still tall, graceful, and commanding, with a stately dignity of manner. Mary White Morris died in her seventy-eighth year on 16 January 1827 and was buried beside her husband.[18]

Notes

1. Charles Henry Hart, *Mary White—Mrs. Robert Morris* (Philadelphia: Collins, 1878), 1.
2. Emma Siggins White and Martha Humphreys Maltby, *Genesis of the White Family* (Kansas City, Mo.: Tiernan Dart Printing Co., 1920), 135–36.
3. Thomas Balch, *Letters and Papers Relating Chiefly to the Provincial History of Pennsylvania . . .* (Philadelphia: Crissy and Markley, Printers, 1855), 3: lxxii. The poem was written by Col. Joseph Shippen and included the names of many Philadelphia "belles."
4. White and Maltby, *Genesis of the White Family*, 136–37; Gillis J. Harp, "William White," *American National Biography* 23, www.anb.org/articles/08/08-01644.html ?a=1&n=William%20White&d=10&ss=0&q=4.
5. Hart, *Mary White—Mrs. Robert Morris*, 2; Robert G. Ferris and James H. Charleton, *The Signers of the Constitution* (Flagstaff, Ariz.: Interpretive Publications, 1986), 197–99.
6. Hart, *Mary White—Mrs. Robert Morris*, 2.
7. Hart, *Mary White—Mrs. Robert Morris*, 5–6; William Graham Sumner, *Robert Morris: The Financier and the Finances of the American Revolution* (New York: Dodd Mead & Co., 1891; reprint, Washington, D.C.: Beard Books, 2000), 2: 227.
8. Hart, *Mary White—Mrs. Robert Morris*, 2–3.
9. Hart, *Mary White—Mrs. Robert Morris*, 3–4.
10. Hart, *Mary White—Mrs. Robert Morris*, 5.
11. Hart, *Mary White—Mrs. Robert Morris*, 5.
12. Hart, *Mary White—Mrs. Robert Morris*, 5–6.
13. Hart, *Mary White—Mrs. Robert Morris*, 7.
14. Hart, *Mary White—Mrs. Robert Morris*, 12–14.
15. Hart, *Mary White—Mrs. Robert Morris*, 16.
16. Hart, *Mary White—Mrs. Robert Morris*, 17; Harry Clinton Green and Mary Wolcott Green, *Wives of the Signers* (Aledo, Tex.: WallBuilder Press, 1997), 166.
17. Hart, *Mary White—Mrs. Robert Morris*, 19–24.
18. Hart, *Mary White—Mrs. Robert Morris*, 26–27.

Bibliography

In addition to the letters quoted in Hart's *Mary White,* cited below, a few letters written to Catherine (Kitty) Livingston Ridley are included among the Matthew Ridley Papers in the Massachusetts Historical Society, and some other letters are among the papers of Robert Morris in the Henry E. Huntington Library, San Marino, California. The Morris papers are scattered among many institutions, and it is possible that additional letters of Mary could be among them.

Chernow, Barbara Ann. *Robert Morris, Land Speculator, 1790–1801*. Manchester, N.H.: Ayer Publishing Co., 1974.

Ferguson, James, John Catanzariti, Elizabeth M. Nuxoli, and Mary A. Gallagher. *Papers of Robert Morris, 1781–1784*. 8 vols. Pittsburgh: University of Pittsburgh Press, 1973–1995.

Green, Harry Clinton, and Mary Wolcott Green. *Wives of the Signers*. Aledo, Tex.: WallBuilder Press, 1997.

Griswold, Rufus W. *The Republican Court, or, American Society in the Days of Washington*. New York: D. Appleton and Co., 1867.

Hart, Charles Henry. "Mary White—Mrs. Robert Morris." *Pennsylvania Magazine of History and Biography* 2 (1878): 177. Reprint, Philadelphia: Collins, 1878.

Oberholtzer, Ellis Paxton. *Robert Morris: Patriot and Financier*. New York: Macmillan Co., 1903.

Ver Steeg, Clarence L. *Robert Morris, Revolutionary Financier; with an Analysis of his Earlier Career*. Philadelphia: University of Pennsylvania Press, 1954.

White, Emma Siggins, and Martha Humphreys Maltby. *Genesis of the White Family*. Kansas City, Mo.: Tierman Dart Printing Co., 1920.

Young, Eleanor May. *Forgotten Patriot: Robert Morris*. New York: Macmillan, 1950.

Cornelia Bell Paterson

Birth:	1755, Philadelphia, Pennsylvania
Parents:	John Bell and Hannah Smith
Marriage:	9 February 1779, William Paterson (1745–1806)
Children:	Cornelia Bell (1780–1844); Frances (1782–1783); William Bell (Billy) (1783–1832)
Death:	13 November 1783, New Brunswick, New Jersey

Cornelia, the first child and only daughter of John Bell, who had come to Philadelphia from England in the 1740s, was born in 1755. Her younger brother Andrew was born two years later. On 27 April 1763 John Bell married a widow, Anna Meyer Tilden, with one son, John Bell Tilden.[1] The will that John Bell drew up in September 1769 made clear that the mother of his children was Hannah Smith, daughter of Frederick Smith of Philadelphia.[2]

In 1769, when Cornelia was fourteen, her father bought an estate of fifty acres in Somerset County, New Jersey, which he called Bellfield, where the Bells resided until the outbreak of the Revolutionary War. The war divided the family. Both her father, John, who died in October 1778, and her brother Andrew were Loyalists, and Andrew joined the British Army. In the summer of 1777 Cornelia, who espoused the patriot cause, went to live with the family of neighbor Anthony White at Union Farm in Hunterdon County. She intended remaining only a couple of months but ended up staying two years, feeling it more of a home than the one she left.[3] In the meantime, John Bell Tilden was a student at Princeton until 1779 when he joined the 2nd Pennsylvania Regiment. After the war, he settled with his family, including his mother, in Frederick County, Virginia.[4]

It was at the Whites' home that Cornelia met William Paterson, New Jersey's attorney general and prominent patriot. After more than a year of letter writing, they were married on 9 February 1779 by Presbyterian minister Samuel Blair at the home of Anthony White. The newlyweds remained with the Whites until April, when Paterson bought Raritan Plantation, a property that had been forfeited by a Loyalist.[5]

Despite their differences, Cornelia and her brother kept up a correspondence throughout the war. In her letters she expressed how much happiness her marriage had brought her: "We are united by indissoluble ties, those of affection, tenderness, sentiment, delicacy—an union of hearts" and "we experience what you so kindly wish us, domestic felicity, untainted, uninterrupted!"[6] On his part William Paterson expressed his affection for his wife in his letters to her during their many separations. During one such separation, Cornelia wrote that she was lonely, indisposed, and looking forward to a visit from her mother.

The Patersons had three children: Cornelia Bell, Frances, and William Bell. Frances, born in January 1782, died in June 1783, and Cornelia took her death very hard. At the time she was pregnant with her third child. Her spirits briefly rose when Andrew paid her a visit in July after a seven-year separation, but in October Cornelia became ill. Four days after her son was born, she died on 13 November 1783 at the age of twenty-eight and was buried in the First Presbyterian Church graveyard in New Brunswick.[7]

Her daughter Cornelia Bell married General Stephen van Rensselaer (1765–1839), whose mother was Catherine Livingston (daughter of Philip Livingston, signer of the Declaration of Independence) and who had been married first to Margaret Schuyler, Elizabeth Schuyler Hamilton's sister. Stephen and Cornelia had nine children. William Bell went to Princeton, as did his father. He became an attorney, married Jane Eliza Neilson, and had four children.

Notes

1. Ann Copeland, "Cornelia Bell Paterson, 1775–1783," *Past and Promise: Lives of New Jersey Women*, ed. by Joan N. Burstyn (Syracuse, N.Y.: Syracuse University Press, 1997), 33–34; John Blair Linn and William Henry Egle, *Pennsylvania Marriages Prior to 1790* (Baltimore: Genealogical Publishing Co., Inc., 2001), 27, 247.

2. Copeland, "Cornelia Bell Paterson," 34; also see Theodore Frelinghysen Chambers, *The Early Germans of New Jersey: Their History, Churches, and Genealogy* (German Valley, N.J.: T. F. Chambers, 1895), 261.

3. Copeland, "Cornelia Bell Paterson," 34.

4. "Extracts from the Journal of Lieutenant John Bell Tilden, Second Pennsylvania Line, 1781–1782," *The Pennsylvania Magazine of History and Biography* 19 (1895): 51. John Bell Tilden was born in Philadelphia on 9 December 1761 and died in Virginia on 31 July 1838. Anna Meyer Tilden Bell was born 31 August 1731 in New York and died 10 June 1819 in Virginia.

5. Copeland, "Cornelia Bell Paterson," 34.

6. Quoted in Copeland, "Cornelia Bell Paterson," 34.

7. Copeland, "Cornelia Bell Paterson," 34.

Bibliography

Cornelia Bell Paterson papers are included in the Andrew Bell Papers (Manuscript Group 45) and William Paterson Papers (Manuscript Group 42), New Jersey Historical Society. Information about Cornelia is also available from Box 10, Folder 26, Inventory to the Records of the Women's Project of New Jersey, 1984–2004, by Carla B. Zimmerman, Special Collections and University Archives, Rutgers University Archives.

American Association of University Women, New Jersey Division. *Ladies at the Cross-roads, Eighteenth-Century Women of New Jersey.* Morristown, N.J.: Compton Press, 1978.

Boggs, J. Lawrence, ed. "The Cornelia (Bell) Paterson Letters." *Proceedings of the New Jersey Historical Society* 15 (1930): 508–17; 16 (1931): 56–67, 186–201.

Copeland, Ann. "Cornelia Bell Paterson, 1755–1783." *Past and Promise: Lives of New Jersey Women.* Metuchen, N.J.: Scarecrow Press, 1990. Reprint, Syracuse, N.Y.: Syracuse University, 1997, 32–35.

O'Connor, John E. *William Paterson: Lawyer and Statesman, 1745–1806.* New Brunswick, N.J.: Rutgers University Press, 1979.

Wood, Gertrude Sceery. *William Paterson of New Jersey, 1745–1806.* Fair Lawn, N.J.: Fair Lawn Press, 1933.

Euphemia (Affa)
Morris White Paterson

Birth:	10 December 1746, White House Farm, New Jersey
Parents:	Anthony White and Elizabeth Morris
Marriage:	November 1785, William Paterson (1745–1806)
Children:	None
Death:	29 January 1832, New Brunswick, New Jersey

Euphemia Morris White was the third child and daughter of Anthony White (1717–1787) and Elizabeth Morris (1712–1784) and granddaughter of Governor Lewis Morris of New Jersey. Her father, Anthony, was a New Jersey landholder and judge in Somerset County. She had two older sisters, Isabella and Johanna Kelsall, and a younger brother, Anthony Walton. Isabella died unmarried in 1789, leaving her sister Euphemia a "wench," her niece Cornelia Paterson a silver coffeepot, and her brother-in-law William Paterson $100 plus a lot in New York to be shared with her sister Johanna.[1] Johanna married Colonel John Bayard and died in 1831. Anthony served as a cavalry officer in the Revolutionary War and died in 1803.

Anthony White sold White House Farm in 1774, and the family moved to Union Farm in Hunterdon County. William Paterson had Euphemia's father as a legal client and often visited the house where he met his first wife, Cornelia Bell. In February 1779 Euphemia, her father, and her sisters were present at their wedding, which took place at their home in Hunterdon County. The newlyweds remained with the Whites until William bought an estate in Raritan two months later.

Cornelia died in 1783, and two years later, Paterson married Euphemia, moving his family from Raritan to New Brunswick, where they lived comfortably on his legal business. Euphemia had some means of her own, inheriting one-fifth of her father's estate when he died in 1787.[2]

Their marriage, like many of their contemporaries, included many separations. In 1793 William wrote to Euphemia from New York, addressing her as Affa, admonishing her not to let her spirits sink as he was in the course of his duty. He expressed his affection and love and commended her for always treating his children "most tenderly."[3] William Paterson's children remained close to her, and Cornelia Paterson even named her youngest daughter after her.

In the winter of 1803–1804 William Paterson was seriously injured in a carriage accident, from which he never fully recovered.[4] On his way to Saratoga Springs, New York, for his health in 1806, he died at the home of his daughter Cornelia in Albany and was buried in the van Rensselaer family vault. Euphemia lived another twenty-six years. In her later life, she resided near her sister Johanna in Franklin, the town next to New Brunswick.[5] Johanna died in 1831 and Euphemia in 1832. Both are buried in the graveyard of the First Presbyterian Church in New Brunswick.

Notes

1. *Calendar of New Jersey Wills, Book 7* (1786–1790): 251.
2. William Nelson, "Anthony White I, II, and III," *The Magazine of History with Notes and Queries* 4 (July–December 1906): 77.

3. Quoted in Maeva Marcus, ed. *The Documentary History of the Supreme Court of the United States, 1789–1800* (New York: Columbia University Press, 1998), 2: 358.

4. Gertrude Sceery Wood, *William Paterson of New Jersey, 1744–1806* (Fair Lawn, N.J.: Fair Lawn Press, 1933), 185–86.

5. The census for 1830 shows Johanna Bayard and Euphemia Paterson living near each other in Franklin.

Bibliography

Some Euphemia White Paterson papers are included in the Andrew Bell Papers (Manuscript Group 45) and William Paterson Papers (Manuscript Group 42), New Jersey Historical Society.

American Association of University Women, New Jersey Division. *Ladies at the Crossroads, Eighteenth-Century Women of New Jersey.* Morristown, N.J.: Compton Press, 1978.

Nelson, William. "Anthony White I, II, and III." *The Magazine of History with Notes and Queries* 4 (July–December 1906): 73–78.

O'Connor, John E. *William Paterson: Lawyer and Statesman, 1745–1806.* New Brunswick, N.J.: Rutgers University Press, 1979.

Wood, Gertrude Sceery. *William Paterson of New Jersey, 1745–1806.* Fair Lawn, N.J.: Fair Lawn Press, 1933.

Mary (Polly) Eleanor Laurens Pinckney

Birth:	27 April 1770, South Carolina
Parents:	Henry Laurens and Eleanor Delamere Ball
Marriage:	27 April 1788, Charles Pinckney (1757–1824)
Children:	Frances (Fan) Henrietta (1790–1818); Mary Eleanor (1792–1846); Henry Laurens (1794–1863)
Death:	6 October 1794, South Carolina

Mary Eleanor Laurens, born in 1770, was the youngest of the fourteen children of Henry and Eleanor Laurens, and her mother died shortly after her birth. Only four of the children lived to adulthood, and only two survived their parents. Polly, as she was known in the family, was reared with her sister Martha, known as Patsy, by their uncle James Laurens and his wife, Mary, who were childless. In 1775 they moved to England and then to France because of James's deteriorating health and because of British hostility.[1] Henry Laurens had earlier taken his sons, Henry Jr. (Harry), John (Jack), and James (Jemmy, who died in England in 1775 from an accidental fall), to Europe so that the brothers could be educated.

Polly's brother Harry described her as a child as being rather spoiled by their aunt but still admired by everyone. She also appears to have been somewhat of a tomboy, for, being envious of Harry's freedom, she asked quite innocently if she couldn't be allowed to wear breeches and be rechristened a boy.[2]

In 1780 Henry Laurens was captured while on a diplomatic mission to Holland and imprisoned in England. He was released on bail in 1781 and exchanged the following year for Lord Cornwallis. Also during the Revolution, Polly's brother John, who had served as an aide to General George Washington, was killed in a skirmish in 1782, a great blow to his father. John's orphaned daughter Frances (Fanny) then joined the household. The family remained in Europe until 1785, after the death of the elder Henry's brother James, and then returned to Charleston and the Laurens' Mepkin Plantation.

Polly, still in skirts and more French than American, was fifteen when the family returned to Charleston. The following year she asked her father for permission to marry Charles Pinckney, who called her his "little French girl." Henry Laurens at first objected, ostensibly because of her youth and because Pinckney was more than thirteen years older than she. Political differences may have also contributed to his opposition. Laurens managed to delay the wedding two years, which took place at Mepkin on Polly's eighteenth birthday.[3] The following year, Pinckney became the governor of South Carolina.

In the meantime, Polly's sister Patsy had married Dr. David Ramsay, a well-known physician, historian, and politician, in 1787. Her brother Harry married Elizabeth Rutledge, daughter of John Rutledge and Elizabeth Grimke, in 1792.

Polly and Charles Pinckney had three children before her death in 1794 after the birth of their son, Henry. She was buried in the Laurens Family Cemetery at Moncks Corner, South Carolina. The Pinckneys' daughter Frances Henrietta married Robert Young Hayne, who later became a U.S. senator. Daughter Mary Eleanor married her first cousin David Laurens Ramsay, who died in 1831. The Pinckneys' only son, Henry, became a lawyer and mayor of Charleston, served in the House of Representatives, and founded the Charleston *Mercury*.

Notes

1. Gregory D. Massey, *John Laurens and the American Revolution* (Columbia: University of South Carolina Press, 2000), 21, 24, 92.

2. Marty D. Matthews, *Forgotten Founder: The Life and Times of Charles Pinckney* (Columbia: University of South Carolina Press, 2004), 60.

3. Matthews, *Forgotten Founder*, 59–60, quotation from 61; Daniel J. McDonough, *Christopher Gadsden and Henry Laurens: The Parallel Lives of Two American Patriots* (Sellinsgrove, Pa.: Susquehanna University Press, 2000), 276; David Duncan Wallace, *The Life of Henry Laurens* (New York: G. P. Putnam's Sons, 1915), 430; *The Papers of Henry Laurens* (Columbia: University of South Carolina Press, 1968), 16: 688.

Bibliography

Bowen, William E. *Charles Pinckney, A Forgotten Statesman.* Greenville, S.C.: n.p., 1928.

Edgar, Walter B., et al., comps. *Biographical Dictionary of the South Carolina House of Representatives.* Columbia: University of South Carolina Press, 1974–.

Hennig, Helen K. *Great South Carolinians from Colonial Days to the Confederate War.* Chapel Hill: University of North Carolina Press, 1940.

Johnson, Joseph. *Traditions and Reminiscences, Chiefly of the American Revolution in the South.* Charleston: Walker & James, 1851.

Matthews, Marty D. *Forgotten Founder: The Life and Times of Charles Pinckney.* Columbia: University of South Carolina Press, 2004.

McCrady, Edward. *History of South Carolina in the Revolution, 1775–1780.* New York: Macmillan, 1901.

Webber, Mabel L. "The Thomas Pinckney Family of South Carolina." *South Carolina Historical and Genealogical Magazine* 39 (January 1938): 15–35.

Sarah (Sally)
Middleton Pinckney

Birth:	5 July 1756, Charleston, South Carolina
Parents:	Henry Middleton and Mary (Molly) Baker Williams
Marriage:	28 September 1773, Charles Cotesworth Pinckney (1746–1825)
Children:	Maria Henrietta (1774–1836); Harriott (1776–1866); Charles Cotesworth (born and died 1779); Charles Cotesworth (born and died 1780); Eliza Lucas (1781–1851)
Death:	8 May 1784, South Carolina

Sarah Middleton, known as Sally, was one of the seven children who lived to maturity of Henry Middleton (1717–1784), a wealthy South Carolina planter, and Mary (Molly) Baker Williams (1721–1761), an heiress of considerable property. Through the marriage, Henry acquired Middleton Place and eventually owned about fifty thousand acres and more than eight hundred slaves. After his wife died, when Sally was four, Henry Middleton married Mary Henrietta Bull (1722–1772) and in 1776 Lady Mary MacKenzie (c. 1720–1788) but had no more children.

The family was quite prominent in the Revolutionary War. Sarah's father was briefly president of the Continental Congress in 1774, and in 1776 her brother Arthur (1742–1787), who also served as president, signed the Declaration of Independence. Her sister Henrietta (1750–1792) married Edward Rutledge, also a signer of the Declaration of Independence. Her brother Thomas (1753–1797) was a member of the South Carolina legislature from 1774 to 1776. Hester (1754–1789) married Charles Drayton, a physician, artist, and botanist, who served as a captain of volunteers during the war and later as a representative in the state legislature. Mary (1757–1825) married Peter Smith, who, along with Drayton, voted to ratify the Constitution in 1788. Susannah (1760–1834) married John Parker, an attorney who was a delegate to the Continental Congress. Sally's first cousin Mary Middleton married Pierce Butler, a signer of the Constitution.[1]

Sally married Charles Cotesworth Pinckney on 28 September 1773 in Charleston.[2] The couple had five children. Two sons, also named Charles Cotesworth, died in infancy. Their daughter, Maria Henrietta, described as "a woman of masculine intellect," never married and sometimes served as her father's hostess. She also wrote a treatise on nullification for a younger relative.[3] Harriott, known for her "benevolence and cheerful piety," also never married and managed her own plantation on Pinckney Island off the South Carolina coast, as well as others.[4] The youngest daughter, Eliza Lucas, married Ralph De Lancey Izard (1785–1824), a naval hero of the Barbary Wars, as his second wife but had no children. Thus, there are no descendants of Charles Cotesworth Pinckney.

During the Revolutionary War Sally's husband served in the army, rising to the rank of brigadier general. He participated in an expedition to East Florida in 1778; in the defense of Savannah, also in 1778; and in the defense of Charleston in 1780. When the British marched on Charleston, Sally and the children took refuge with several relations and friends, including her sisters, at Hampton Plantation on the Santee River, the home of Harriot Pinckney Horry, her sister-in-law.[5] During the fall of Charleston, Charles Cotesworth Pinckney was taken prisoner. Upon his parole he took his family to Philadelphia where they shared a house with the families of Thomas Pinckney and Edward Rutledge. The house, lent by Dr. George Logan and called "Stenton," was in nearby Germantown. When they returned to Charleston after Pinckney's exchange, they found that the British had sequestered their estates and slaves, as well as damaged their property.[6]

Sally, who suffered from tuberculosis, stayed at her brother's plantation outside Charleston and died in 1784 of a fever at age twenty-seven, while her husband was away on circuit court business.[7]

Notes

1. Langdon Cheves, "Middleton of South Carolina," *South Carolina Historical and Genealogical Magazine* 1 (1900): 239–42.

2. Cheves, "Middleton of South Carolina," 241; Frances Leigh Williams, *A Founding Family: The Pinckneys of South Carolina* (New York: Harcourt, Brace, Jovanovich, 1978), 55.

3. Harriet Horry Ravenel, *Eliza Pinckney* (New York: Charles Scribner's Sons, 1896), 320; John L. Wakelyn, ed. *Southern Pamphlets on Secession, November 1860–April 1861* (Chapel Hill: University of North Carolina Press, 1996), 3. Some plays and essays have also been attributed to her.

4. Ravenel, *Eliza Pinckney*, 320; Marli Frances Weiner, *Mistresses and Slaves: Plantation Women in South Carolina, 1830–1850* (Champaign: University of Illinois Press, 1978), 36–37.

5. Lori Glover, *All Our Relations: Blood Ties and Emotional Bonds among the Early South Carolina Gentry* (Baltimore: Johns Hopkins University Press, 2000), 133.

6. Williams, *A Founding Family*, 174, 180–81.

7. Caroline Winterer, *The Mirror of Antiquity: American Women and the Classical Tradition, 1750–1900* (New York: Cornell University Press, 2007), 59; Henry Benbridge, Maurie Dee McInnis, and Angela D. Mack, *Henry Benbridge: Charleston Portrait Painter (1743–1812)* (Charleston: Gibbes Museum of Art, 2000), 82.

Bibliography

One letter of Sarah Middleton Pinckney is included in Volume 15, *Colonial and State Records of North Carolina* (Ancestry.com).

Cheves, Langdon. "Middleton of South Carolina." *South Carolina Historical and Genealogical Magazine* 1 (1900): 228–62.

Johnson, Joseph. *Traditions and Reminiscences, Chiefly of the American Revolution in the South*. Charleston: Walker & James, 1851.

McCrady, Edward. *History of South Carolina in the Revolution, 1775–1780*. New York: Macmillan, 1901.

Webber, Mabel L. "The Thomas Pinckney Family of South Carolina." *South Carolina Historical and Genealogical Magazine* 39 (January 1938): 15–35.

Williams, Frances Leigh. *A Founding Family: The Pinckneys of South Carolina*. New York: Harcourt, Brace, Jovanovich, 1978.

Zahniser, Marvin R. *Charles Cotesworth Pinckney, Founding Father*. Chapel Hill: University of North Carolina Press, 1967.

Mary Stead Pinckney

Birth: 1751, Charleston, South Carolina
Parents: Benjamin Stead and Mary Johnson
Marriage: 23 July 1786, Charles Cotesworth Pinckney (1745-1825)
Children: None
Death: 4 January 1812, Charleston, South Carolina

Mary Stead was one of three children of Benjamin Stead (1706–1776), a wealthy Charleston merchant, and Mary Johnson (1724–1759), the daughter of South Carolina governor Robert Johnson. Their father served as the London factor for Peter Manigault, a South Carolina planter, and kept a residence in London. While in London his younger daughter Elizabeth married, in 1773, Ralph Izard (c. 1750–1812), who served several terms in the South Carolina Assembly. The sisters also had a brother, called Benjamin after his father.

The family was still living in London in 1776, when Benjamin Sr. died, leaving most of his property to Mary, Benjamin, and Elizabeth. Under the Banishment Act of 4 May 1782, his property in Georgia was confiscated and sold. In June of that year Mary wrote Henry Laurens requesting his assistance in regaining it. Laurens responded that he would do so but recommended that a personal appeal might be even more effective. That summer the family returned to Charleston, but a quick settlement was not forthcoming.[1]

In July 1786 Mary married Charles Cotesworth Pinckney, who had been widowed two years before and whose daughters were still young. She brought to the marriage a fortune of fourteen thousand pounds (some of which was in the wrongfully confiscated Georgia land), which did much to replenish the fortune Pinckney had lost during the Revolution. After the marriage, Pinckney became involved to attempts to recover the Stead estate.[2]

In the spring of 1787 the Pinckneys sailed to Philadelphia for the Constitutional Convention, considering the trip "their honeymoon." Unfortunately, they became terribly seasick but were given a surprise welcome by George Washington upon their arrival. Not wishing to repeat the difficulties of sea travel, the Pinckneys returned to Charleston by coach, stopping at Mount Vernon to visit the Washingtons.[3]

In the late 1790s the couple moved to Paris, along with his daughter Eliza, when Pinckney became the first minister to France and later as the member of a negotiating team. They traveled the Continent, sometimes with the Middletons and Rutledges, visiting the Louvre, Versailles, and porcelain and furniture factories and seeing plays and the opera.[4] Mary saw waltzing for the first time in Amsterdam. While she was pleased to see the young people having such a good time, she became anxious upon hearing that the waltz, although danced with a great deal of decency, was not performed with as much spirit as in Paris.[5]

Mary was well traveled and very interested in French porcelain and furniture.[6] After their return from Europe, the Pinckneys settled down in Charleston and his retreat on Pinckney Island. Their house in Charleston typified Charlestonian taste for gilded painted furniture—the highest end of English Regency design. In 1803 the couple, again with Eliza, toured New England, hoping to restore Mary's health. Mary died nine years later and was buried in Charleston.[7]

Notes

1. David R. Chesnutt and Philip May Hamer, *The Papers of Henry Laurens: September 1, 1782–December 1792* (Columbia: University of South Carolina Press, 1968), 16: 203–6.

2. Chesnutt and Hamer, *The Papers of Henry Laurens*; Frances Leigh Williams, *A Founding Family: The Pinckneys of South Carolina* (New York: Harcourt, Brace, Jovanovich, 1978), 210–11.

3. Joseph C. Morton, *Shapers of the Great Debate of the Constitutional Convention of 1787* (Westport, Conn.: Greenwood Publishing Group, 2006), 250, 252; Williams, *A Founding Family*, 270.

4. Maurie D. McInnis, *In Pursuit of Refinement: Charlestonians Abroad, 1740–1860* (Columbia: University of South Carolina Press, 1999), 16.

5. Marvin R. Zahniser, *Charles Cotesworth Pinckney, Founding Father* (Chapel Hill: University of North Carolina Press, 1967), 18.

6. Mary Stead Pinckney, *Mary Stead Pinckney Letterbook* (New York: Grolier Club, 1946), passim.

7. Harold C. Syrett, ed., *The Papers of Alexander Hamilton* (New York: Columbia University Press, 1978), 26: 154; Williams, *A Founding Family*, 468.

Bibliography

Letters written by Mary Stead Pinckney while in Europe have been published (see below).

Cheves, Langdon. "Middleton of South Carolina." *South Carolina Historical and Genealogical Magazine* 1 (1900): 228–62.

Johnson, Joseph. *Traditions and Reminiscences, Chiefly of the American Revolution in the South*. Charleston: Walker & James, 1851.

McCrady, Edward. *History of South Carolina in the Revolution, 1775–1780*. New York: Macmillan, 1901.

Pinckney, Mary Stead. *Mary Stead Pinckney Letterbook*. New York: Grolier Club, 1946.

Webber, Mabel L. "The Thomas Pinckney Family of South Carolina." *South Carolina Historical and Genealogical Magazine* 39 (January 1938): 15–35.

Williams, Frances Leigh. *A Founding Family: The Pinckneys of South Carolina*. New York: Harcourt, Brace, Jovanovich, 1978.

Zahniser, Marvin R. *Charles Cotesworth Pinckney, Founding Father*. Chapel Hill: University of North Carolina Press, 1967.

Gertrude (Gitty) Ross Till Read

Birth:	c. 1732, New Castle, Delaware
Parents:	George Ross and Anna Catherine van Gezel
Marriages:	18 June 1752, Thomas Till (c. 1721–1760)
	11 January 1763, George Read (1733–1798)
Children:	William Till (c. 1757–1762); John Read (born and died 1763); George Read (1765–1836); William Read (1767–1846); John Read (1769–1854); Mary Howell Read (1770–1814)
Death:	2 September 1802

Gertrude Ross was born in New Castle, Delaware, about 1732, the daughter of George Ross (1679–1754), the rector of Immanuel Episcopal Church for almost fifty years, and his wife Anna Catherine van Gezel. She was one of five children of the marriage (her father had six other children—David, Margaret, John, Aeneas, Ann Catherine, and Jacob—by a previous marriage); the others were her brother, George, who became a signer of the Declaration of Independence, and three sisters, Catherine, Elizabeth, and Mary. She was highly educated by her father, and it was said that "her person was beautiful, her manners elegant, and her piety exemplary."[1]

On 18 June 1752, at the age of twenty, she married Thomas Till in Trinity Church, Oxford, in Philadelphia.[2] Till's family was in the shipping business, and Thomas's father, William Till, who died in 1766, was a justice and a mayor of Philadelphia. Thomas Till, who was also a justice, and Gertrude resided at Prime Hook in Sussex County, Delaware. Thomas Till died in October 1760, and their son, William, died on 11 December 1762 when he was five years old.[3]

On 11 January 1763 Gertrude, known informally as Gitty, married George Read, the son of an Irish immigrant, who eventually settled in New Castle, Delaware. Read, an attorney in New Castle, was described by a contemporary as "tall, slight, agreeable, austere, and sternly moral."[4] In the same year as their marriage, Read began his public career, becoming the attorney general for the Three Lower Counties (the colonial name for Delaware). In time the Reads had four sons and one daughter: John, who died in infancy;[5] George, born in 1765; William, born in 1767; a second John born in 1769; and Mary, born in 1770. Gertrude Read was known for her fondness of flowers and taste for horticulture, and she was proud of her profusion of flowers, tulips in particular, in her New Castle garden. She spent most of her life there, except when she was forced for safety during the Revolutionary War to go to Philadelphia, Maryland, or Wilmington.[6] Although the house burned in 1824, the site is now the gardens of their son George's home, a historic site.

During the Revolutionary War, Gertrude Read and her husband were often separated, and her life was a troubled one. The enemy was almost constantly on the Delaware coastline, keeping the province in continual alarm. While George Read was serving in the Continental Congress (1774–1776) and performing other duties, he often wrote to his wife about public affairs.[7] In October 1777 the family narrowly escaped capture by British troops en route from Philadelphia to Dover.[8]

After the Constitutional Convention, George Read was elected as one of Delaware's first senators (1789–1793). He resigned in 1793 to accept a position as chief justice of Delaware, a post he retained until his death in 1798. After her husband's death, his old friend John Dickinson gave a valuable Delaware farm to Gertrude Read and their children.[9] Gertrude died four years after her husband, in September 1802. Both are buried in the Immanuel Church Cemetery in New Castle, Delaware. Of their children, George, U.S. district attorney for

Delaware for thirty years, married his first cousin Mary Thompson. William became consul-general for Naples at Philadelphia and married Ann McCall. John, a prominent member of the Philadelphia bar and judge of the Superior Court of Pennsylvania, married Martha Meredith, eldest daughter of Samuel Meredith, George Clymer's brother-in-law. The Reads' only daughter, Mary Howell, married Matthew Pearce of Maryland.[10]

Notes

1. William Thompson Read, *Life and Correspondence of George Read* (Philadelphia: J. B. Lippincott, 1870), 20.

2. Historical Society of Pennsylvania, *Historic Pennsylvania Church and Town Records*, Reel 336. Marriage license issued by Gov. James Hamilton of Pennsylvania.

3. *Colonial and Revolutionary Families of Pennsylvania*, 3 vols. (New York, 1911; reprint, Baltimore Genealogical Publishing Co., 1978), 1: 525–26; *Colonial Families of the Eastern Shore of Maryland* (Westminster, Md.: Family Line Publications, 1996), 2: 70.

4. Quoted in Robert K. Wright Jr. and Morris J. MacGregor Jr., *Soldier-Statesmen of the Constitution* (Washington, D.C.: Government Printing Office, 1987), 167.

5. Letter, Dec. 1763, S. L. Wharton to George Read, congratulating him on the birth of his son, Box 37, Folder 2, George Read (I), Delaware Historical Society.

6. Read, *Life and Correspondence of George Read*, 575; Harry Clinton Green and Mary Wolcott Green, *Wives of the Signers* (Aledo, Tex.: WallBuilder Press, 1997), 214.

7. Green and Green, *Wives of the Signers*, 211–14. There are several additional examples of letters George Read wrote to his wife in the collections of the Delaware Historical Society.

8. Read, *Life and Correspondence of George Read*, 276.

9. Read, *Life and Correspondence of George Read*, 575.

10. Green and Green, *Wives of the Signers*, 214–15.

Bibliography

Boughner, Daniel T. "George Read and the Founding of the Delaware State, 1781–1798." Ph.D. dissertation, Catholic University of America, 1970.

Colonial and Revolutionary Families of Pennsylvania. 3 vols. New York, 1911. Reprint, Baltimore: Genealogical Publishing Co., 1978, 1: 525–26.

Green, Harry Clinton, and Mary Wolcott Green. *Wives of the Signers*. Aledo, Tex.: WallBuilder Press, 1997.

Read, William T. *Life and Correspondence of George Read, Signer of the Declaration of Independence*. Philadelphia: J. B. Lippincott and Co., 1870.

Wright, Robert K., Jr., and Morris J. MacGregor Jr. *Soldier-Statesmen of the Constitution*. Washington, D.C.: Government Printing Office, 1987.

Elizabeth Grimke Rutledge

Birth:	29 November 1741, Charleston, South Carolina
Parents:	Frederick Grimke and Martha Emms Williamson
Marriage:	1 May 1763, John Rutledge (1739–1800)
Children:	Martha Henrietta (1764–1806); Sarah (born and died 1765); John (1766–1819); Edward James (1767–1811); Frederick Wilkes (1769–1821); William Spencer (1771–1822); Charles Wilson (1773–1821); Thomas Littlebury (1774, died young); Elizabeth (1776–1842); States Whitcomb (1783–1829)
Death:	6 June 1792, Charleston, South Carolina

Elizabeth Grimke, the younger daughter of Frederick and Martha Grimke, was born on 29 November 1741 and christened the following month. Her elder sister, Mary, who married Alexander Fraser in 1755, was described at the time as a young lady of merit, beauty, and fortune. Their father had come from Germany to Charleston in 1733 at the age of twenty-eight to make his fortune as a merchant.[1] Elizabeth and her sister grew up in a house that still stands on Tradd Street in Charleston.

On 1 May 1763 at St. Phillips Church in Charleston, Elizabeth Grimke married John Rutledge, an attorney-at-law who had studied at the Middle Temple in London.[2] There was no announcement or marriage settlement, and no guests were invited. One biographer noted that the bride was attractive with dark hair and blue eyes, of small stature and refined.[3]

The couple lived in a house that today operates as a bed and breakfast, on 116 Broad Street in Charleston.[4] They eventually had ten children, of whom eight lived to maturity, Sarah dying in infancy and Thomas in childhood. Their daughter Martha married Francis Kinloch, a wealthy South Carolina planter, who had served as an officer in the Continental Army and as a member of the Continental Congress. Son John served in the House of Representatives and in the War of 1812 as an officer in the South Carolina militia. Edward also served in the state legislature, as did Frederick, who married Harriot Pinckney Horry and became a prosperous planter. William married a cousin, Ann Grimke Coslett, and became a merchant in Charleston. Charles went into medicine and also married a cousin, Caroline Smith. Elizabeth married Henry Laurens, the brother of Charles Pinckney's wife, Mary Eleanor Laurens. The last-born, States Rutledge, after receiving a naval appointment, became a South Carolina planter.

In August 1774 John Rutledge, his wife, son, and sister Sarah, left Charleston on the *Betsey* bound for Philadelphia, where the First Continental Congress was meeting, returning to Charleston in 1775.[5] As the war drew closer to Charleston, Elizabeth left with the children before the city fell and spent the remaining war years in Philadelphia. In 1783, while critically ill, she gave birth to her last child, States. The family returned to South Carolina in the spring of 1784 to find devastation. Rutledge's library was destroyed and his home damaged.[6]

After a few years in the state legislature and on the circuit court, John Rutledge once again traveled to Philadelphia for the Constitutional Convention and was joined by his wife, Elizabeth, returning home the following year. In 1791 George Washington came to Charleston and breakfasted with Elizabeth, an occasion noted in his diary.[7]

The following year Elizabeth Rutledge died after a short illness, within six weeks of the death of John Rutledge's mother, and was buried in Charleston. According to an early biographer, John Rutledge was passionately attached to his wife, and her death was at least partially responsible for his later mental illness.[8] John Rutledge died eight years later, in 1800.

Notes

1. Charles Fraser, "Fraser Family Memoranda," *South Carolina History and Genealogical Magazine* 5 (January 1904): 57. Richard Barry, in *Mr. Rutledge of South Carolina* (reprint, Salem, N.H.: Ayer Company, Publishers, 1971), 72, mentions a brother James Grimke who was at the Middle Temple with John Rutledge and who became his lifelong friend, but there appears to be no other evidence of this brother. Elizabeth had a first cousin, South Carolina jurist John Faucheraud Grimke, who was a Templar, but fifteen years later than Rutledge.

2. A. S. Salley Jr., comp., *Marriage Notices in the South-Carolina Gazette and its Successors (1732–1801)* (Albany, N.Y.: Joel Munson's Sons, Publishers, 1902), 24.

3. Barry, *Mr. Rutledge of South Carolina*, 74.

4. Barry, *Mr. Rutledge of South Carolina*, 73. The Rutledges sold the house in 1790.

5. James Haw, *John and Edward Rutledge of South Carolina* (Athens: University of Georgia Press, 1997), 61–62.

6. Haw, *John and Edward Rutledge of South Carolina*, 61–62, 75, 136, 156, 169.

7. Fraser, "Fraser Family Memoranda," 57, quoting from Washington's *Diary*.

8. Henry Flanders, *The Lives and Times of the Chief Justices of the Supreme Court of the United States* (Philadelphia: J. B. Lippincott & Co., 1874), 451.

Bibliography

Barry, Richard. *Mr. Rutledge of South Carolina*. Reprint, Salem, N.H.: Ayer Company, Publishers, 1971.

Flanders, Henry. *The Lives and Times of the Chief Justices of the Supreme Court of the United States*. Philadelphia: J. B. Lippincott & Co., 1874.

Haw, James. *John and Edward Rutledge of South Carolina*. Athens: University of Georgia Press, 1997.

Webber, Mabel L. "Dr. John Rutledge and His Descendants." *The South Carolina Historical and Genealogical Magazine* 31 (January and April 1930): 7–25, 93–106.

Elizabeth Hartwell Sherman

Birth: 11 September 1726, Stoughton (now Canton), Massachusetts
Parents: Joseph Hartwell and Mary Tolman
Marriage: 17 November 1749, Roger Sherman (1721-1793)
Children: John (1750-1802); William (1751-1789); Isaac (1753-1819);
            Chloe (1754-1757); Oliver (1756-1757); Chloe (1758-1840);
            Elizabeth (1760-1762)
Death: 19 October 1760, New Milford, Connecticut

Elizabeth Hartwell was born on 11 September 1726 in Stoughton, Massachu-setts, where Roger Sherman lived in his early years. Her parents were Deacon Joseph Hartwell (1698–1786) and Mary Tolman (1697–1782) of Stoughton. Elizabeth had five younger siblings: Joseph (who married Roger Sherman's sister Rebecca), John, Abigail, Moses, and Ruth. Elizabeth had a solid family background but not an educated one; by at least one account, she was illiterate.[1]

After the death of Roger Sherman's father in 1741, Roger had moved with his mother and younger siblings to New Milford, Connecticut, where his elder brother William had already settled. In his youth Roger Sherman had learned the trade of cordwainer, or shoemaker, and reportedly carried his tools on his back when he walked to his new home in Connecticut.[2] In 1748 Roger and Wil-liam began operating a general store, and Roger bought one of the finest houses in the village. He then returned to Stoughton to marry Elizabeth Hartwell. Tradition in Stoughton relates that Elizabeth had another suitor for her hand, a young lawyer, and that her father favored Roger Sherman, while her mother favored the lawyer.[3] Nevertheless, Roger Sherman and Elizabeth were married on 17 November 1749 by the Reverend Samuel Dunbar, Sherman's mentor, of Stoughton.[4] Elizabeth was twenty-three, and Roger was twenty-eight. At the time of his marriage, Roger Sherman had been appointed surveyor of New Haven County, serving in that capacity until 1758. He also became the surveyor of Litchfield County in 1752 and accumulated considerable land during this period, eventually becoming the largest landowner in the county. In 1754 Roger was admitted to the Litchfield bar and in 1755 elected to the General Assembly, where he served continuously, with the exception of 1756–1757, until 1761.

Elizabeth Hartwell Sherman died on 19 October 1760 at the age of thirty-four, soon after the birth of her seventh child. She was buried in the old burying place at New Milford, and her husband made the appropriate entry in the family Bible. Four of her seven children lived to adulthood. Her daughter Chloe married a physician, John Skinner; one of their grandchildren was Roger Sherman Skinner, an eminent mayor of New Haven, Connecticut, while another, Jane Wakeman Skinner, married Timothy Dwight, president of Yale University. Although two of Elizabeth Sherman's sons graduated from Yale and all three served in the Revolutionary War—Isaac with distinction—none of them achieved as much success as their father in civilian life. John, the oldest son, became the father of the Reverend John Sherman, the owner of Trenton Falls and a very accomplished person in his day. He also had two other sons who became ministers.[5]

Notes

1. Roger Sherman Boardman, *Roger Sherman—Signer and Statesman* (Philadelphia: University of Pennsylvania Press, 1938), 55; Christopher Collier, *Roger Sherman's Connecticut: Yankee Politics and the American Revolution* (Middletown, Conn.: Wesleyan University Press, 1971), 332. Her brother Moses was a Yale graduate, and so her illiteracy seems unlikely.

2. Collier, *Roger Sherman's Connecticut*, 6–10.

3. Lewis Henry Boutell, *The Life of Roger Sherman* (Chicago: A. C. McClurg and Co., 1896), 23.

4. Collier, *Roger Sherman's Connecticut*, 10; Boardman, *Roger Sherman—Signer and Statesman*, 40.

5. Boardman, *Roger Sherman—Signer and Statesman*, 181–82, 332–33; Frank Dempster Sherman, *Ancestry of James Morgan Sherman and His Descendants* (New York: privately printed, 1915), 43–46.

Bibliography

Boardman, Roger Sherman. *Roger Sherman—Signer and Statesman*. Philadelphia: University of Pennsylvania Press, 1938. Reprint, 1971.

Boutell, Lewis Henry. *The Life of Roger Sherman.* Chicago: A. C. McClurg and Co., 1896.

Boyd, Julian P. "Roger Sherman: Portrait of a Cord-Wainer Statesman." *The New England Quarterly* 5 (1932): 221–36.

Collier, Christopher. *Roger Sherman's Connecticut: Yankee Politics and the American Revolution.* Middletown, Conn.: Wesleyan University Press, 1971.

Green, Harry Clinton, and Mary Wolcott Green. *Wives of the Signers.* Aledo, Tex.: Interpretive Publishers, 1997.

Rommel, John G. *Connecticut's Yankee Patriot: Roger Sherman.* Hartford: American Revolution Bicentennial Commission of Connecticut, 1979.

Sherman, Frank Dempster. *Ancestry of John Taylor Sherman and His Descendants.* New York: privately printed, 1915.

Sherman, Thomas Townsend. *Sherman Genealogy . . .* New York: Tobias A. Wright, Printer and Publisher, 1920.

Rebecca Prescott Sherman

Birth:	31 May 1742, Salem (now Peabody), Massachusetts
Parents:	Benjamin Prescott and Rebecca Minot
Marriage:	12 May 1763, Roger Sherman (1721–1793)
Children:	Rebecca (1764–1795); Elizabeth (1765–1850); Roger (1768–1856); Mehetabel (born and died 1772); Mehetabel (1774–1851); Oliver (1777–1820); Martha (1779–1806); Sarah (1783–1866)
Death:	19 April 1813, New Haven, Connecticut

Roger Sherman journeyed on horseback from New Haven, where he had moved after his wife Elizabeth's death, to visit his brother Josiah, who was then settled over his church in Woburn, Massachusetts. Upon his departure, his brother accompanied him some little distance, when they stopped to say a few parting words. As they were bidding each other good-bye, there appeared on horseback a beautiful young girl. She was Rebecca Prescott, riding from Salem to visit her aunt, Josiah Sherman's wife. Rather than conclude his visit, Roger Sherman rode back with her. Rebecca Prescott was the eldest child of Benjamin Prescott (1717–1778) and Rebecca Minot (1720–1761), and her younger siblings were Martha, James, Elizabeth, Mercy, Mary, and Benjamin. Her mother was the daughter of a magistrate in Danvers, Massachusetts, and her father was a merchant and justice of the peace. Rebecca's paternal grandfather was the Reverend Benjamin Prescott, who for many years was the pastor in Salem.[1]

Roger Sherman and Rebecca Prescott were married on 12 May 1763 by Rebecca's grandfather at his home.[2] According to the family, Rebecca had been engaged to a Mr. Curran, who had died before the marriage could take place. At her wedding to Roger Sherman she received a large silver pepper caster from Curran's sister Sarah, and Rebecca later named her youngest child after Sarah.[3] Roger Sherman brought his bride back to New Haven, where they became the parents of eight children—five daughters and three sons, all but one of whom grew to maturity. Upon the young Rebecca fell the duty of caring for both her own children and Roger's four surviving children by Elizabeth Hartwell.

Their son Roger graduated from Yale and became a merchant in New Haven, highly esteemed for integrity and benevolence. Martha Sherman married Dr. Jeremiah Day, who was president of Yale College for thirty years. Rebecca married Judge Simeon Baldwin, a member of Congress and judge of the Supreme Court of Connecticut and also a member of the Peace Congress of 1861. After Rebecca's death, Simeon married her widowed sister, Elizabeth, by whom he had one son, Simeon, who became a merchant in New York. Mehetabel became the wife of Jeremiah Evarts and mother of William M. Evarts of New York, senator, secretary of state, and attorney general of the United States. Oliver, a Boston merchant, died unmarried in Havana, Cuba. Sarah, the youngest daughter, was the wife of Samuel Hoar of Concord, Massachusetts, an eminent advocate esteemed for his integrity and ability.[4]

By all accounts Rebecca was a lovely, intelligent young woman, blessed with a cheerful ready wit, a good horsewoman, and literate. Her husband once remarked that he disliked settling any perplexing matter without the benefit of the opinion of an intelligent woman. Another family story was that at a state dinner party, George Washington selected Rebecca to escort into dinner, incurring the jealousy of Mrs. John Hancock. Washington said he chose Rebecca because she was the handsomest woman in the room.[5] Another family story was that she made the first U.S. flag in Connecticut after visiting Betsy Ross and sewing some of the stars on her flag.[6]

Three years after their marriage, Sherman became the treasurer of Yale University. In 1768 this self-educated man received an honorary degree from Yale, and in 1772 he retired from business to devote the remainder of his life to public service. Sherman served in the Connecticut Assembly for many years, he was a member of the first Continental Congress, and he was active in the Council of Safety. He was the only person to have signed all four key documents: Declaration of Independence, Articles of Association of 1774, Articles of Confederation, and the Constitution. In 1789 he was elected to Congress, and in 1791 he was elected to fill the place of William Samuel Johnson in the Senate, an office he held until his death of typhoid fever on 23 July 1793 at the age of seventy-two.[7] Rebecca Prescott Sherman survived her husband by nineteen years, passing away on 19 April 1813 at the age of seventy-one. They are buried in the Grove Street Cemetery in New Haven.[8]

George Sherman, a son of Roger Sherman Jr., wrote on 6 April 1894, "Grandmother, who was a Prescott, took interest in everybody and in everything, was very clear and quick in calculating, much more so than grandfather. I wish more of her character and work had been appreciated and handed down to us. Her influence and good counsel were felt wherever she was known."[9]

Notes

1. Thomas Townsend Sherman, *Sherman Genealogy . . .* (New York: Tobias A. Wright, Printer and Publisher, 1920), 152; Lewis Henry Boutell, *The Life of Roger Sherman* (Chicago: A. C. McClurg and Co., 1896), 46; Katherine Prescott Bennett, "American Mothers of Strong Men," *Journal of American History* 3 (1909): 54.

2. Roger Sherman Boardman, *Roger Sherman—Signer and Statesman* (Philadelphia: University of Pennsylvania Press, 1938), 76.

3. Sherman, *Sherman Genealogy*, 152.

4. Boardman, *Roger Sherman—Signer and Statesman*, 332–33.

5. Sherman, *Sherman Genealogy*, 75–77; Christopher Collier, *Roger Sherman's Connecticut: Yankee Politics and the American Revolution* (Middletown, Conn.: Wesleyan University Press, 1971), 43–44; Boutell, *The Life of Roger Sherman*, 45, 48; Bennett, "American Mothers of Strong Men," 58.

6. Bennett, "American Mothers of Strong Men," 58.

7. Boardman, *Roger Sherman—Signer and Statesman*, 335.

8. Boardman, *Roger Sherman—Signer and Statesman*, 335.

9. Boutell, *The Life of Roger Sherman*, 47.

Bibliography

Bennett, Katherine Prescott. "American Mothers of Strong Men." *Journal of American History* 3 (1909): 49–52.

Boardman, Roger Sherman. *Roger Sherman—Signer and Statesman*. Philadelphia: University of Pennsylvania Press, 1938. Reprint, 1971.

Boutell, Lewis Henry. *The Life of Roger Sherman*. Chicago: A. C. McClurg and Co., 1896.

Boyd, Julian P. "Roger Sherman: Portrait of a Cord-Wainer Statesman." *The New England Quarterly* 5 (1932): 221–36.

Collier, Christopher. *Roger Sherman's Connecticut: Yankee Politics and the American Revolution*. Middletown, Conn.: Wesleyan University Press, 1971.

Green, Harry Clinton, and Mary Wolcott Green. *Wives of the Signers*. Aledo, Tex.: Interpretive Publishers, 1997.

Ireland, Norma Olin. *Index to Women of the World from Ancient to Modern Times, Biographies and Portraits*. Westwood, Mass.: F. W. Faxon, 1970.

Prescott, William. *The Prescott Memorial or a Genealogical Memoir of the Prescott Families in America*. Asheville, N.C.: Ward Publishing Co., 1870. Reprint, 1983.

Rommel, John G. *Connecticut's Yankee Patriot: Roger Sherman*. Hartford: American Revolution Bicentennial Commission of Connecticut, 1979.

Sherman, Frank Dempster. *Ancestry of John Taylor Sherman and His Descendants*. New York: privately printed, 1915.

Sherman, Thomas Townsend. *Sherman Genealogy . . .* New York: Tobias A. Wright, Printer and Publisher, 1920.

Mary (Polly) Jones
Leech Spaight

Birth:	1765, New Bern, North Carolina
Parents:	Joseph Leech and Mary Jones
Marriage:	24 September 1788, Richard Dobbs Spaight (1758–1802)
Children:	William Wilson (1794–1809); Richard Dobbs Jr. (1796–1850); Charles George (1798–1831); Margaret Elizabeth (1800–1831)
Death:	1810, Philadelphia, Pennsylvania

Mary Spaight, during her entire married life, lived in New Bern, bore her children, attended Christ Church, and supported her husband in his political career. It was generally agreed that Polly was lovely, well educated, and articulate. Her days were spent raising her children and supervising life at her country estate, Clermont, and the family home in New Bern. Her final years as a widow were lived out in Raleigh and Philadelphia, Pennsylvania.

Polly Spaight was descended from two prominent families—the Leeches and the Vails. Her father was Colonel Joseph Leech (1720–1803), and her mother was Mary Jones. The couple had three surviving children: son George and daughters Frances and Mary (Polly). Their grandmother, Mary Vail Jones Wilson Moore, was also the grandmother of Richard Dobbs Spaight Sr., making Mary Spaight his cousin. Colonel Leech was a prominent soldier and statesman, justice of the peace, one of the first councilors of state, judiciary of the Admiralty Court for the port of Beaufort, one of the custodians of the palace square, and mayor of New Bern. He was a wealthy landowner and farmer and built several homes. One of his homes was opposite Tryon Palace, and he was a confidant and supporter of the royal governor. Leech also served the Craven County militia and was an acquaintance of Richard Spaight's father.[1]

Mary Leech married her cousin Richard Dobbs Spaight, on 24 September 1788 in New Bern, North Carolina. The following notice appeared in *Columbian Magazine* for October of that year: "At New Bern, The Honorable Richard Dobbs Spaight, Esq., late member of the Federal Convention, to Miss Mary Leech, daughter of Col. Joseph Leech, a young lady whose amiable character and beautiful person, added to an extensive fortune, promise much felicity to this worthy pair."[2]

The following year Spaight sought retirement from public life for reasons of health, and his name was withdrawn from nomination to the U.S. Senate. He spent his time traveling, both in the United States and West Indies. Upon his return, he was elected governor of South Carolina.[3]

The Spaights were among the few who enjoyed wealth, great landholdings, and political power. Both Mary's father and husband served in the military, and Spaight was given the honorable title of general. Mary's background and social standing augured well for her to become the wife of Governor Spaight and to assume the position of first lady of North Carolina. One of the most impressive of social events, and probably one of the more happy occasions for Mary Spaight, was the welcome given to President George Washington when he made a grand tour of the South, visiting New Bern on 20–21 April 1791: "A delegation headed by John Sitgreaves and Mayor Joseph Leech, and a committee of the Masonic Lodge welcomed the President to New Bern. . . . At four o'clock in the afternoon a banquet was held at Tryon Palace, and that evening . . . a ball was given. . . . Mrs. Richard Dobbs Spaight, whose husband was soon to be the first native-born

Governor, led the minuet with the distinguished guest as partner." After attending the ball, Washington is said to have gone to a smaller party at the Leech home.[4]

After Richard Dobbs Spaight became governor in 1792, much entertaining was required of his wife, Mary. It was during his tenure as governor that the University of North Carolina was founded at Chapel Hill, and it is said that Mary Spaight was the first woman to attend a university commencement in July 1795.[5]

Upon completion of his term as governor, Spaight served in the House of Representatives in Philadelphia and Washington from 1798 to 1801. In 1802 he decided to run for Senate, but on 5 September, he was struck down by a political rival in a duel, leaving Mary a grieving widow with four children. She and the children moved to Raleigh and in the summer of 1809, after her oldest son, William, died,[6] moved to Philadelphia. There she became a recluse with her children, nearly undermining their health. Mary Spaight died the following year and was buried with other members of her family in the Clermont graveyard near New Bern. After her death, Charles Biddle, a friend of the family, cared for the children until their health improved, after which they returned to live in New Bern.[7]

The Spaights' second son, Richard Dobbs Jr., was educated at the University of North Carolina, graduating in 1815. After becoming a lawyer, he served as a member of Congress from 1823 to 1825 and was then elected to the state legislature. He became the governor of North Carolina in 1834, the only instance in North Carolina where father and son each held the gubernatorial chair. He died unmarried in 1850. The youngest son, Charles George, also became a lawyer. He represented the borough town of New Bern in the 1830 state House of Commons and was reelected in that year only to die prior to taking his seat. The Spaights' only daughter, Margaret, married John Robert Donnell, a native of Ireland and distinguished North Carolina jurist.[8]

Notes

1. Alan D. Watson, *Richard Dobbs Spaight* (New Bern, N.C.: Griffin & Tilghman, 1987), 14, 46.

2. Quoted in Alexander B. Andrews, "Richard Dobbs Spaight," *North Carolina Historical Review* 1 (April 1924): 112, and Rufus Wilmot Griswold, *The Republican Court: Or, American Society in the Days of Washington* (New York: D. Appleton and Co., 1855), 105.

3. Watson, *Richard Dobbs Spaight*, 15; William S. Powell, *Dictionary of North Carolina Biography* (Chapel Hill: University of North Carolina Press, 1994), 5: 403.

4. Daniel W. Barefoot, *Touring North Carolina's Revolutionary War Sites* (Winston-Salem, N.C.: J. F. Blair, 1998), 79.

5. Albert Coates, *By Her Own Bootstraps: A Saga of Women in North Carolina* (Chapel Hill: University of North Carolina, 1975), 39; Kemp Plummer Battle, *History of the University of North Carolina* (Raleigh: Edwards & Broughton Printing Co., 1907), 1: 69–70.

6. Newbern *Herald* (15 April 1809). The grave marker, however, says 1812.

7. Watson, *Richard Dobbs Spaight*, 27; Charles Biddle, *Autobiography of Charles Biddle* (Philadelphia: E. Claxton and Co., 1883) 3: 328–29.

8. Watson, *Richard Dobbs Spaight*, 27.

Bibliography

Andrews, Alexander B. "Richard Dobbs Spaight." *North Carolina Historical Review* 1 (April 1924): 95–120.

Ashe, Samuel A., ed. *Biographical History of North Carolina from Colonial Times to the Present.* 8 vols. Greensboro: C. L. Van Noppen, 1905–1917.

Watson, Alan D. *Richard Dobbs Spaight.* New Bern, N.C.: Griffin & Tilghman, 1987.

Wheeler, John H. *Sketch of the Life of Richard Dobbs Spaight of North Carolina.* Baltimore: W. K. Boyle, 1880.

Martha (Patsy) Dandridge Custis Washington

Birth:	2 June 1731, New Kent County, Virginia
Parents:	John Dandridge and Frances Jones
Marriages:	15 May 1749, Daniel Parke Custis (1711–1757)
	6 January 1759, George Washington (1732–1799)
Children:	Daniel Parke Custis (1751–1754); Frances Parke Custis (1753–1757); John (Jacky) Parke Custis (1754–1781); Martha (Patsy) Parke Custis (1756–1773)
Death:	22 May 1802, Mount Vernon, Virginia

Martha Dandridge was born on 2 June 1731 to John Dandridge (1701–1756) and his wife, Frances Jones (1710–1785). Her father had come from London to New Kent County where he became the Clerk of courts and a vestryman and church warden in St. Peter's parish. She grew up at Chestnut Grove, a tobacco plantation, with her younger siblings, John, William, Bartholomew, Anna Frances (Nancy), Frances, Elizabeth, and Mary.

Daniel Parke Custis, a wealthy plantation owner, was also a vestryman at St. Peter's. Although much older than Martha, he began courting her. Initially his father opposed the match but eventually pronounced Martha to be "beautifull & sweet temper'd" and consented to the marriage.[1] Martha and Daniel were married on 15 May 1749 at Chestnut Grove by the Reverend Chichley Thacker. The newlyweds went to live in one of the Custis residences known as White House Plantation. They eventually had four children, two of whom died in early childhood. Soon after the death of their daughter Frances, Daniel became ill and died at the age of forty-six, leaving Martha as one of the wealthiest widows in the colony. Daniel had died intestate with the result that Martha had to act as executor. The Custis estate of approximately 17,500 acres was divided among Martha and her surviving children.

Eight months after her husband's death, Martha was visiting at Poplar Grove Plantation, where she met George Washington. Martha was about five feet tall with large eyes, and she was known for her easy but dignified manner. George and Martha were married on 6 January 1759 at her White House home by candlelight, with the Reverend Peter Mossom, rector of St. Peter's, performing the ceremony. The following April the new family moved to George Washington's home at Mount Vernon.

During the next fifteen years, Martha remained active in raising her children, looking after the Custis estate, accompanying her husband to Williamsburg when the House of Burgesses met, as well as to other places, and enjoying visits with friends and relatives. There was sadness, however, because in 1773 Martha's daughter Patsy, who had been in delicate health for some years, died at Mount Vernon at seventeen, leaving Martha devastated. Jacky, who had been attending King's College (now Columbia University) in New York, returned home. He and Eleanor (Nelly) Calvert of Maryland had known each other for some time, and their parents finally consented to their marriage despite their youth. George Washington attended the wedding, but Martha, still in mourning, did not. The young couple made their home near Mount Vernon and had four children reach maturity.

After the war began in 1775 and Washington took command of the Continental Army, he managed to return to Mount Vernon only twice in the next eight years. Martha joined her husband in Cambridge, Massachusetts, in 1776, by way of Philadelphia, where she was feted and titled "Lady Washington" for the first time. When she reached Cambridge, the house became a center for young officers to gather, and her first social event was the celebration of Twelfth Night, her wedding anniversary; a few days later the Washingtons hosted a dinner that included members of a French Indian tribe, as well as John Adams and General and Mrs. Horatio Gates. From Cambridge, Martha went to New York, where Washington had moved his headquarters, and thence to Philadelphia, before returning to Mount Vernon.

Throughout the war years, Martha joined her husband each winter in camp—in Massachusetts, New Jersey, and Pennsylvania, the most notable camp being that of Valley Forge. While in camp, she, the officers' wives, and others spent their days knitting socks, mending and sewing clothes, and tending to the needs of the soldiers. Many writers have noted how much she raised the spirits of her husband and how she impressed all those who met her.

In 1781 the army moved south to Yorktown, and her son Jack, as an aide-de-camp to his stepfather, moved with it, only to fall ill with "camp fever," possibly typhus. His wife and mother reached his bedside just in time to soothe his last hours. Martha was left childless.

After spending a few days at Mount Vernon, the Washingtons traveled to Philadelphia, remaining there for some months, then moving on to Newburgh, New York, where they stayed until August 1783, and thence to New Jersey. Martha took leave of the general in November and arrived back home at last to Mount Vernon. The following month, however, she rejoined her husband at Annapolis when he took his leave of the army before returning to Mount Vernon. The following years were anything but quiet, for visitors and relatives were constantly coming to see the Washingtons, and in 1784 the general remarked that it was more than a year since he and Martha had been able to dine alone.[2] The house also underwent considerable expansion and improvement to make it a comfortable home for its inhabitants and their guests.

In the fall of 1783 Martha's daughter-in-law, Eleanor, remarried, and George and Martha offered a home to her two younger children, Eleanor (Nelly) (1779–1852) and George Washington Parke (Wash) (1781–1857). The two older girls, Elizabeth and Martha, remained with their mother, although they spent much of their time at Mount Vernon.

Martha did not accompany her husband to the Constitutional Convention in Philadelphia in 1787, but remained at Mount Vernon with her grandchildren entertaining friends and relatives. When Washington became president in 1789, however, she, Nelly, and Wash joined him in New York and later in Philadelphia, temporary capitals of the new United States. Martha did not altogether enjoy her new status as the wife of the first president, for, as she said, "grandchildren and domestic connections make up a great portion of the felicity" she looked for, and she did not expect to find such felicity in public life.[3] In another letter to a niece, she wrote that life was dull, that she never went to any public place, and that she felt like a state prisoner.[4] Philadelphia appeared to be more to her liking, and Washington's diary and correspondence mention plays, balls, dinners, traveling in the countryside, and all manner of entertainments. After two terms, however, both George and Martha Washington were relieved to become private citizens again and resume the relatively tranquil domesticity of their previous life.

On General Washington's last birthday in 1799, Nelly Custis married Lawrence Lewis, his nephew, at Mount Vernon. In December the first president of the United States died and was buried at Mount Vernon. Martha moved out of their bedroom to an attic room where she spent most of her remaining days. After contracting a severe fever in 1802, Martha Dandridge Custis Washington died and was laid to rest beside her husband on the estate.

Notes

1. *The Letterbook of John Custis IV of Williamsburg, 1717–1742*, ed. Josephine Little Zuppan (Lanham, Md.: Rowman & Littlefield, 2005): 15.
2. Quoted in Anne Hollingsworth Wharton, *Martha Washington* (New York: Charles Scribner's Sons, 1897), 156.
3. Wharton, *Martha Washington*, 203.
4. Wharton, *Martha Washington*, 205–6.

Bibliography

The Mount Vernon Ladies' Association has custody of the Martha Washington Collection of Manuscripts and Books, most of which have been published in Joseph E. Fields' *Worthy Partner* cited below. A large collection of papers is also in Richmond, Virginia, among the records of the Virginia Historical Association. Many biographies have been published about Martha Washington; a select bibliography follows.

Brady, Patricia. *Martha Washington: An American Life*. New York: Viking, 2006.
Bryan, Helen. *Martha Washington: First Lady of Liberty*. New York: John Wiley and Sons, 2002.
Fields, Joseph E., ed. *"Worthy Partner": The Papers of Martha Washington*. Westport, Conn.: Greenwood Press, 1994.
Lindsey, Rae. "Martha Dandridge Custis Washington." *The Presidents' First Ladies*. New York: R&R Writers, Inc., 2001, 11–16.
Thane, Elswyth. *Washington's Lady*. New York: Dodd, Mead, 1960.
Wharton, Anne Hollingsworth. *Martha Washington*. New York: Charles Scribner's Sons, 1897.

Maria Apthorp Williamson

Birth: c. 1767, "Elmwood," Bloomingdale, New York
Parents: Charles Ward Apthorp and Mary McEvers
Marriage: 3 January 1789, Hugh Williamson (1735–1819)
Children: Charles Apthorp (1789–1811); John (1790–1815)
Death: 14 October 1790, New York, New York

Charles Ward Apthorp (1726–1797), Maria's father, was the eldest son of Charles Ward and Grizzel Apthorp of Boston. Both father and son were wealthy merchants with imperial trading connections.[1] Charles Ward settled early in New York City and there married Mary, daughter of John McEvers, who died of a fever in 1779.[2] Six children reached adulthood, three sons and three daughters. Their home was referred to as a mansion and was one of the most classic and monumental examples of English renaissance architecture in the colonies.[3] "Elmwood" was located on the north side of Ninety-first Street, west of Ninth Street (now Ninety-sixth Street at Riverside Drive), Bloomingdale. During the Revolutionary War the house was used as a hospital, and in its last years was used as a beer garden before being demolished in 1891.[4]

New York in the decade preceding the Revolution was that of a Dutch town slowly changing into a provincial English city. It was here that Charles Ward Apthorp established himself as a merchant.[5] The year 1776 was marked by a succession of revolutionary changes and trade restrictions that made life difficult for merchants. Furthermore, because Apthorp was a Tory, the times were even more difficult for him. Apthorp remained in the city at least until June 1776. His oldest son, Charles, was a captain in the 23rd Regiment, Royal Welch Fusiliers.[6] In August 1776, when additional space was needed, the Provincial Council of New York authorized General Washington to use the Apthorp house in Bloomingdale as a hospital.[7]

Hugh Williamson was born in Pennsylvania and studied medicine. He had a diverse range of scientific interests and was elected to the American Philosophical Society in 1768. After a three-year sojourn in England, Williamson returned in 1776 and went into the mercantile business with his brother John in Charleston, South Carolina. He subsequently moved to Edenton, North Carolina, and during the Revolutionary War served as surgeon general of that state. He entered politics in 1782, first in the North Carolina House of Commons and then in the Continental Congress, which took him to New York where he met his future bride.[8]

Maria Apthorp married Hugh Williamson on 3 January 1789 at her family home. The officiant, Bishop Samuel Provoost, was the same man who had married Mary Alsop and Rufus King three years earlier and who was one of the chaplains of Congress. The announcement mentioned the lovely and accomplished bride.[9] To underline this description, John Dawson wrote James Madison on 29 January 1789 describing her as "a beautiful girl about twenty-two. She appears pleased with her bargain—may she never repent."[10] He may have been prompted to write this as Hugh Williamson, at fifty-three, was many years her senior.

Maria gave birth to two sons, Charles Apthorp and John, within two years, but she died in October 1790, soon after the birth of her second son.[11] She was buried in the Apthorp family vault in Trinity Church in New York City. The

Williamsons' son Charles died in 1811, shortly after graduating from Columbia College in New York. There is a very poignant paragraph in the preface to Hugh Williamson's *History of North Carolina*, which alludes to the death of Charles: "The publication, as I thought, might have been trusted with great safety to my oldest son; a young man, whose moral and Christian virtue could not be praised above his merits. But it pleased the heavenly Father lately to remove him to 'a house not made with hands.'"[12]

A biographical memoir of Hugh Williamson noted that his elder son was "a good classical scholar, well versed in astronomical and philosophical knowledge and still more remarked for his correct deportment, his benevolence of character, and his sincere piety."[13] The Williamsons' younger son, John, died on 19 November 1815 after an eight-day illness. Williamson never remarried and died suddenly in 1819 while riding in a carriage with his niece and heir, Maria Hamilton.[14]

Notes

1. Wendell D. Garrett, *Apthorp House, 1760–1960* (Cambridge, Mass.: Harvard University Press, 1960), 14.

2. E. Alfred Jones, *The Loyalists of Massachusetts: Their Memorials, Petitions, and Claims* (London: Saint Catherine Press, 1930), 7; *Rivington's New York Newspaper Excerpts from the Loyalist Press*, comp. Kenneth Scott (New York: The New-York Historical Society, 1973), 196.

3. Talbot Hamlin, *The American Spirit in Architecture* (New Haven, Conn.: Yale University Press, 1926), 64.

4. Bruce Bliven Jr., *Under the Guns: New York 1775–1776* (New York: Harper & Row, 1972), 195.

5. James Kirby Martin, *Men in Rebellion: Higher Governmental Leaders and the Coming of the American Revolution* (New Brunswick, N.J.: Rutgers University Press, 1973), 89.

6. Jones, *The Loyalists of Massachusetts*, 7.

7. Thomas Jefferson Wertenbaker, *Father Knickerbocker Rebels: New York City during the Revolution* (New York: Charles Scribner's Sons, 1948), 80.

8. Robert G. Ferris and James H. Charleton, *The Signers of the Constitution* (Flagstaff, Ariz.: Interpretive Publications, 1986), 218–20.

9. *New York Daily Gazette*, 1789 (5 January 1789), 1: 16.

10. Robert A. Rutland and Charles F. Hobson, eds., *The Papers of James Madison* (Charlottesville: University of Virginia), 11: 410–11.

11. Record of the Chancery Court, New York, Guardianships 1681–1915, Petition, 30 May 1804, 151.

12. Hugh Williamson, *History of North Carolina* (Philadelphia: Thomas Dobson, 1812), preface.

13. David Hosack, *Biographical Memoir of Hugh Williamson* (New York: C. S. Van Winkle, 1820), 163.

14. Maria Hamilton was actually his wife's niece, daughter of her sister Charlotte Augusta Apthorp van den Huevel, who married John C. Hamilton, son of Alexander Hamilton.

Bibliography

Ashe, Samuel A., ed. *Biographical History of North Carolina from Colonial Times to the Present.* 8 vols. Greensboro: C. L. Van Noppen, 1905–1917.

Garrett, Wendell D. *Apthorp House, 1760–1960.* Cambridge, Mass.: Harvard University Press, 1960.

Hosack, David. *A Biographical Memoir of Hugh Williamson.* New York: C. S. Van Winkle, 1820.

Jones, E. Alfred. *The Loyalists of Massachusetts: Their Memorials, Petitions, and Claims.* London: Saint Catherine Press, 1930.

Kagarise, Mary Jane, and George F. Sheldon. "Hugh Williamson, M.D., LL.D. (1735–1819): Soldier, Surgeon, and Founding Father." *World Journal of Surgery* 29 (2005): 580–84.

Mitchell, Memory F. *North Carolina's Signers.* Raleigh: North Carolina Division of Archives and History, 1964, 22–27.

Neal, John W. "Life and Public Services of Hugh Williamson." *Trinity College Historical Society Papers* 13 (1919): 62–115.

Sheldon, George F. *Hugh Williamson: Physician, Patriot, and Founding Father.* Amherst, N.Y.: Prometheus Books, 2009.

Williamson, Hugh. *History of North Carolina.* Philadelphia: Thomas Dobson, 1812.

Rachel Bird Wilson

Birth:	c. 1749, Birdsboro, Pennsylvania
Parents:	William Bird and Bridgetta Huling
Marriage:	5 November 1771, James Wilson (1742–1798)
Children:	Mary (Polly) (1772–1832); William (Billy) (1774–c. 1820); Bird (1777–1859); James (Jem) (1779–1808); Emily (1782–1809); Charles (1785–1810)
Death:	14 April 1786, Philadelphia, Pennsylvania

The news of young Mrs. Wilson's death appeared in the *Pennsylvania Gazette* on 19 April 1786: "Died on Friday morning last, Mrs. Rachel Wilson, the wife of the Honorable James Wilson, Esq. Her remains were deposited in Christ Church yard, attended by a numerous train of respectable citizens and sorrowing friends. The religious and social virtues of her heart were manifested by a uniform and exemplary exercise of the important duties of mother, wife, and friend. . . . Well may the tears of sorrow flow for the loss of one so valued and so beloved."[1]

Born Rachel Bird in about 1749, she was the daughter of William Bird (1706–1761) and Bridgetta Huling (1710–1792), one of five children who survived to adulthood. William Bird came to Pennsylvania at an early age and made his fortune in ironworks in Berks County. In 1750 he laid out a town, calling it Birdsboro, and the following year erected a two-story cut-stone mansion. (This house stands today and is being used as the community center of Birdsboro.) Rachel's father died of apoplexy in 1761, and Rachel's mother remarried the following year John Patton, also a landowner and pioneer iron manufacturer.[2]

Mark Bird, the oldest son and brother of Rachel, took over much of the family ironworks after their father's death. He was also a colonel in the Pennsylvania militia and active in the political affairs of the Revolutionary War. Mark married Mary Ross, daughter of the Reverend George Ross, and their son William married his cousin Mary Ross, daughter of George Ross, signer of the Declaration of Independence. Mark and Rachel's sister Mary Bird married George Ross, the son of the signer of the Declaration of Independence and grandson of the Reverend George Ross. Their sister Rebecca married first Peter Turner, a Philadelphia merchant, and after his death in 1776 married Dr. Joseph Redman, also of Philadelphia. Rachel's brother William went to Alexandria, Virginia, where, with George Washington, he was a vestryman of the Pohick Church. After marrying Catherine Dalton in 1781, William moved to Georgia where he established Georgia's first ironworks in Warren County at the shoals of the Ogeechee River.

James Wilson was admitted to the bar in November 1767, and the following summer he began to practice law in Reading, Pennsylvania, near Birdsboro, the home of Rachel Bird, whom he had met in Philadelphia at the home of Mary Harrison. From their first meeting in 1768, James was "taken" with the charming Rachel. After many pleasant visits to her home in Birdsboro on the Schuylkill River, the immigrant from Scotland blurted out his feelings of love. Rachel demurely replied, "I am much obliged to you for the good opinion you hold of me. Indeed I do not know a gentleman of whose friendship I would be more glad than I would of yours. Your frequent visits give me pleasure, but you must visit me in the character of a friend and not that of a lover, for I do not propose to marry."[3] James chided Rachel gently about her determination to be an old maid, but her response caught him off guard. "I know not how it may be with other girls in pretense, but it is a serious matter with me."[4] And she proceeded to lecture him, as he later wrote a close friend, "with some of the finest observations I have ever heard on the dangers of the married state and the source from which those dangers arose."[5]

Rachel's reasons for not considering James Wilson as a serious love did not dissuade him. He would, he declared, continue to visit her as a lover and would never visit her "in any other character." Rachel then declared that she would not see him at all. But she relented, and their "friendship" continued, sometimes by way of long, ardent letters from James when he was away in nearby towns or Philadelphia. James then begged for "some distant hint that he need not despair," pointing out that she herself had admitted that "the married state may be a happy one." "What are you afraid of? How delightfully would I run the risk with you. Do you think favorably of me, I will do all in my power to deserve it," he assured her. Love cast a warm glow over everything when he was with her, and he was full of wonder at the way in which "a thousand little trifles which are wholly unentertaining and indifferent to others become so many sources of delight to those who love."[6]

James finally turned to his close friend and confidant William White, later bishop of Philadelphia, to help bring a successful conclusion to his courtship of Rachel. By coincidence, Rachel's close friend Mary Harrison was White's fiancée. James entreated White to prevail upon Mary to make discreet inquiries of Rachel to discover Rachel's true feelings toward her suitor. White encouraged Wilson to continue courting his reluctant Rachel.[7] In the fall of 1770 Wilson had moved to Carlisle, Pennsylvania, on the prospect of much greater business for his law practice, but he continued to besiege Rachel with ardent letters and visits to Birdsboro. At last she consented to marry him, and the wedding took place on 5 November 1771 at St. Gabriel's Episcopal Church, across the river from Birdsboro. The young couple established their first home in Carlisle, where James had purchased a handsome house and furnished it to Rachel's liking.[8]

Their first child, Mary, affectionately called Polly, was born in 1772, followed by William (Billy) in 1774. Rachel played gracefully the role of the wife of a rising young frontier lawyer, almost single-handedly taking care of the home, the children, and the farm during the many absences of her husband, who became more and more involved in riding the circuit and in the evolving government of the thirteen colonies and in acquiring land and businesses. Their third child, a son, Bird, was born on 8 January 1777. This child was said to be his father's favorite. Initially practicing law like his father, Bird later fulfilled the role of clergyman so desired for James by his parents. He was ordained by his father's old friend Bishop White. After James Wilson's death, Bird edited his father's writings and wrote a biography of Bishop White. He never married and died in 1859.[9]

In 1778 James and Rachel moved to Philadelphia, where James purchased a house on Chestnut Street, a block from the state house. The following year 1779 James Jr. was added to the family, followed by Emily in 1782, and Charles in 1785, bringing the number of children to six. Although the Wilsons often rode out to the Schuylkill to visit, to listen to concerts, or to stroll through Gray's Gardens, James Wilson had established his own country seat at Somerset on the Delaware near the ironworks that he and Mark Bird, Rachel's brother, owned.

In 1779 Rachel and the children had to leave the house on Chestnut Street during what became known as the "Fort Wilson Riot." After the British had left Philadelphia, Wilson had successfully defended twenty-three people from the radical government of Pennsylvania. Spurred to action by the president of Pennsylvania's Supreme Executive Council, Joseph Reed, a mob descended on Wilson's house, where he and thirty-five others had barricaded themselves. In the fight, six people died and seventeen to nineteen were injured.[10] Despite the riot, the Wilsons remained patriots, and in the winter of 1780 Rachel and other ladies of Philadelphia raised money for the Continental Army.[11]

The Wilsons had no reputation for elegant parties but were gracious hosts. The Marquis de Chastellux, who had served in the Revolutionary War with the Americans, was invited to dinner. He found the fare "excellent" and was pleased by the "plain and easy politeness" of his host. "Mrs. Wilson," Chastellux noted, "did the honours of the table with all possible attention." Their circle of friends was a close and congenial one. Silas Deane, in Paris, recalled nostalgically the evenings he had spent in the Wilson household, and Bushrod Washington, taken into the family during his law apprenticeship, wrote of his affection and gratitude for the Wilsons' kindness to him.[12]

In the spring of 1786, after Charles's christening, James left Philadelphia to take his seat once more in Congress, then meeting in New York. Reluctant to leave Rachel, still weak and unwell, and distracted by the illness of young James, he left his formal commission in his desk. He wrote his wife upon his arrival in New York, asking her to forward it and inquiring anxiously about the invalid. A few days later word reached him that Rachel was very ill. Apparently in nursing James, she had caught the baby's malady. Wilson hurried home to be with his wife. Benjamin Rush, called in for consultation, could do nothing but bleed her. It was a futile remedy if not a disastrous one. Rachel sank rapidly, and with her husband and children beside her, she died on 14 April 1786. Although a reluctant bride, Rachel had been a devoted wife and mother. Annis Boudinot Stockton, wife of Declaration of Independence signer Richard Stockton, wrote "An Elegy on the Death of Mrs. Wilson" in her honor.[13]

Of their children, only Polly married. She wed Paschal Hollingsworth, a Philadelphia merchant, and had one child, Emily Hollingsworth, the last of Wilson's descendants. James entered the army but resigned to become a merchant and died in Santo Domingo in 1808; Emily died in Philadelphia in 1809; Charles entered the navy but also resigned for a mercantile career, dying in Havana, Cuba, in 1810; and Bird died in 1859 after a long, distinguished career in the ministry.[14]

Notes

1. *Pennsylvania Gazette*, 19 April 1786, as quoted in Charles Page Smith, *James Wilson: Founding Father: 1742–1798* (Chapel Hill: University of North Carolina Press, 1956), 212–14.

2. Louis Richards, "Hon. James Wilson at Reading, Penna.," *Pennsylvania Magazine of History and Biography* 31 (1907): 49.

3. Smith, *James Wilson*, 38.

4. Smith, *James Wilson*, 38.

5. Smith, *James Wilson*, 39.

6. Smith, *James Wilson*, 39.

7. Smith, *James Wilson*, 40–41.

8. Smith, *James Wilson*, 41–42.

9. W. White Bronson, *A Memorial of the Rev. Bird Wilson . . .* (Philadelphia: J. B. Lippincott & Co., 1864), 42.

10. John K. Alexander, "The Fort Wilson Incident of 1779: A Case Study of the Revolutionary Crowd," *The William and Mary Quarterly*, 3rd Ser. (October 1974): 589–612; Smith, *James Wilson*, 133, 213; Lucien Hugh Alexander, *James Wilson—National Builder* (Boston: Boston Book Co., 1907), 99.

11. Smith, *James Wilson*, 205, 213.

12. Smith, *James Wilson*, 210.

13. Carla Mulford, ed., *Only for the Eye of a Friend: The Poems of Annis Boudinot Stockton* (Charlottesville: University Press of Virginia, 1995), 207.

14. Emily Hollingsworth is often quoted as "being the last" and so appears in court documents concerning the estate of James Wilson. There is at least one claimant on Ancestry.com, however, who says that William (Billy) Wilson married, had children, and has descendants, a claim not yet recognized by the Descendants of the Signers of the Declaration of Independence.

Bibliography

Much of the Wilson family correspondence is included in the collections of the Historical Society of Pennsylvania in Philadelphia. Some correspondence with Rachel Bird Wilson is published in Charles Page Smith's biography of James Wilson.

Marcus, Maeva, ed., *The Documentary History of the Supreme Court of the United States, 1789–1800* (New York: Columbia University Press, 1989).

McCloskey, Robert G., ed. *The Works of James Wilson*. 2 vols. Cambridge, Mass.: Belknap Press of Harvard University Press, 1967.

Montgomery, James Alan. "The Family of Judge James Wilson." *The Church Standard* 92 (24 November 1906): 124–25.

Richards, Lewis. "Hon. James Wilson at Reading, Penna." *Pennsylvania Magazine of History and Biography* 31 (1907): 48–52.

Seed, Geoffrey. *James Wilson*. Milwood, N.Y.: KTO Press, 1978.

Smith, Charles Page. *James Wilson, Founding Father: 1742–1798*. Chapel Hill: University of North Carolina Press, 1956.

Hannah Gray Wilson Bartlett

Birth: 1774, Boston, Massachusetts
Parents: Ellis Gray and Sarah Dolbeare
Marriages: 19 September 1793, James Wilson (1742–1798)
4 February 1802, Thomas Bartlett (1767–1856)
Children: Henry Wilson (1796–1797); Caroline Bartlett (1806–1838)
Death: March 1808, London, England

In April 1793 James Wilson was in Boston for the opening of the session of the Circuit Court for Massachusetts. He had heard that Dr. Peter Thacher was an eloquent and learned minister; therefore, on his first Sunday in Boston Wilson walked across the Common to Dr. Thacher's "meeting" at the Brattle Street Church. It was soon apparent that Wilson was highly impressed with one of the members of the congregation—a charming, dark-haired girl, sitting in a nearby pew. Nineteen years old, Hannah Gray was a niece of Harrison Gray, a Loyalist banished from Massachusetts, and a cousin of the rising young Federalist Harrison Gray Otis. James Wilson was fifty-one. It is reported that several sharp-eyed ladies noticed that Wilson seemed smitten, and soon the news that the distinguished Supreme Court justice was ardently courting Miss Gray was the subject of slightly scandalized gossip in Boston drawing rooms.[1] Hannah was at first somewhat embarrassed by the attention but was taken by his courtly manner. When Wilson had to go on to Newport to carry on the business of the circuit, he wrote Hannah asking her to marry him and begging for a speedy and favorable reply.[2]

Hannah accepted his proposal and spent the summer preparing for her wedding, along with her mother and sisters, Sarah and Lucy. Her father, a Boston merchant, had died in 1781 at the age of forty-one, when Hannah was seven. She also had two brothers, Thomas, a sea captain, and Ellis. A sister Harriet had died in childhood. James and Hannah were married on 19 September 1793 in the Brattle Street Church where they had so recently met. The minister, Dr. Thacher, who had been the unconscious agent of their meeting, married them. That day was the twenty-third anniversary of his ordination, and he wrote in his diary that he had preached "at home," adding that "in the evening I married Judge Wilson and Miss Gray."[3]

The Wilsons completed the eastern circuit though the fall months of September and October, and by early December they were in New York. Here alarming news awaited Wilson. When he had left his home in Philadelphia at the end of August to begin his tour of the eastern circuit, his business affairs seemed to be in order, but the precarious and irregular nature of his transactions forced him to constantly tread a razor's edge between affluence and bankruptcy. Now he had received notice that unless money to pay the expenses of surveys of his vast landholdings was forthcoming at once, some of his lands would be foreclosed. Wilson set out for Philadelphia at once, bringing his bride home to meet his six children. The new stepmother was, in fact, younger than Polly and Billy, the two oldest. Hannah settled into her new home, which Wilson had purchased that summer at Eighth and Market, a block from his old one.[4]

Shortly after the new year of 1794, Judge Wilson plunged once again into judicial matters, taking Hannah with him on his tour of the circuit in Newcastle, Annapolis, and Newport during the spring months. Then in September their circuit tour took them south to the Carolinas. Judge James Iredell and his wife gave them a warm welcome at their home in Edenton, North Carolina. The Wilsons found the Iredells' hospitality most pleasant and spent Christmas and New Year's there, joined by his son Bird before returning north to Philadelphia.[5]

On 12 May 1796 a son, Hannah's first child and Wilson's seventh, was born. He was baptized Henry at Christ Church in Philadelphia when Wilson returned from the southern circuit. Their joy was short-lived, however, for Henry died in infancy.[6]

The Panic of 1796–1797 gravely affected the land speculation and other business ventures of James Wilson, and by the spring of 1797 the Wilsons were in desperate straits. For a short while, James was imprisoned in New Jersey as a debtor. Hannah and the Wilson daughters managed to help Bird support the family by needlework. For a while, Hannah and James stayed in Bethlehem, Pennsylvania, and from there Hannah went to Boston to spend a few weeks with her family. James made his precarious way to Edenton to stay with his old friend, Judge Iredell. He was never able to return again to Philadelphia, except in death, as he was seized by a devastating illness.[7]

When her husband did not return, Hannah arranged to travel to North Carolina with Judge Iredell.[8] She found Wilson living at the Horniblow Tavern next to the courthouse in Edenton. Through the long hot summer Hannah became very homesick for her home in Philadelphia. Soon after her arrival in Edenton, she wrote Bird to give news of his father. She also wrote, "I think if I was once at home, I should be content never to leave it again."[9] Early in July 1798 Wilson suffered a violent attack of malaria. For days he lay unable to move, his powerful frame wracked and wasted by his illness, his brain tormented by his impending financial collapse. Hannah attended him faithfully in the exhausting heat of the little room at the inn.[10]

Wilson gradually recovered his strength and wrote Bird with new plans for satisfying his creditors. But suddenly James relapsed—he had had a stroke. After a three-day vigil, with little food and no sleep, Hannah was led away from her husband's bedside by Judge Iredell, and soon afterward James Wilson died on 21 August 1798. He was buried in a simple ceremony on the estate of Mrs. Iredell's brother, Governor Samuel Johnston. Many years later the state of Pennsylvania had his remains moved to the graveyard of Christ Church in Philadelphia, near the grave of his first wife, Rachel.[11]

Hannah recuperated at the Iredells' home in Edenton, after which she returned to her home in Boston by way of Philadelphia. In 1802 she married again, to widower Dr. Thomas Bartlett, an apothecary with two surviving daughters, as well as three stepchildren from his first marriage. After giving birth to a daughter Caroline (named for her husband's daughter who had died in 1801) in September 1806, Hannah and her husband sailed to London, leaving the baby behind with Bartlett's parents. Bartlett's two older daughters were sent to school, while a stepdaughter went to stay with the Wilson siblings in Philadelphia. Hannah never saw her daughter again, for she died in March 1808 in London at the age of thirty-four. Her daughter Caroline died unmarried in 1838.

Notes

1. Charles Page Smith, *James Wilson: Founding Father: 1742–1798* (Chapel Hill: University of North Carolina Press, 1956), 361; John Quincy Adams to Thomas Boylston Adams, 23 June 1793, and Henry Jackson to Henry Knox, 23 June 1793, cited in Maeva Marcus, ed., *The Documentary History of the Supreme Court of the United States, 1789–1800* (New York: Columbia University Press, 1989), 408–11.

2. James Wilson to Hannah Gray, 20 June 1793, cited in Marcus, *The Documentary History of the Supreme Court*, 408.

3. Smith, *James Wilson*, 366; *Boston Gazette* (23 September 1793).

4. Smith, *James Wilson*, 365–67.

5. Smith *James Wilson*, 370; *Daily Advertiser* (New York), 3 July 1794; James Iredell to Hannah Iredell, 8 August 1794; James Iredell to James Wilson, 24 November 1794, cited in Natalie Wexler, *A More Obedient Wife: A Novel of the Early Supreme Court* (Washington, D.C.: Kalorama Press, 2006), 213, 220, 222.

6. Smith, *James Wilson*, 380; James Iredell to Sarah Gray (Hannah's sister), 7 June 1796, quoted in Wexler, *A More Obedient Wife*, 264; also see 439.

7. Smith, *James Wilson*, 384; James Iredell to Hannah Iredell, 11 August 1797; "Writ of Simon Gratz in the New Jersey Superior Court," 23 August 1797; James Wilson to Bird Wilson, 3 September 1797; diary entry of Thomas Shippen, 3 September 1797; Hannah Wilson to Bird Wilson, 3 November 1797; John Rutledge to Edward Rutledge, 25 February 1798, quoted in Wexler, *A More Obedient Wife*, 301, 303–4, 309, 333.

8. Harrison Gray Otis to Sally Otis, 18 February 1798, quoted in Wexler, *A More Obedient Wife*, 326.

9. Hannah Wilson to Bird Wilson, 23 June 1798, quoted in Wexler, *A More Obedient Wife*, 376.

10. Smith, *James Wilson*, 387.

11. Smith, *James Wilson*, 388.

Bibliography

Much of the Wilson family correspondence is included in the collections of the Historical Society of Pennsylvania in Philadelphia. A few letters of Hannah Gray Wilson have been published in *The Documentary History of the Supreme Court . . .* , edited by Maeva Marcus, and also in the novel *A More Obedient Wife* by Natalie Wexler (see below).

Marcus, Maeva, ed., *The Documentary History of the Supreme Court of the United States, 1789–1800* (New York: Columbia University Press, 1989).

McCloskey, Robert G., ed. *The Works of James Wilson.* 2 vols. Cambridge, Mass.: Belknap Press of Harvard University Press, 1967.

Montgomery, James Alan. "The Family of Judge James Wilson." *The Church Standard* 92 (24 November 1906): 124–25.

Seed, Geoffrey. *James Wilson.* Milwood, N.Y.: KTO Press, 1978.

Smith, Charles Page. *James Wilson, Founding Father: 1742–1798.* Chapel Hill: University of North Carolina Press, 1956.

Wexler, Natalie. *A More Obedient Wife: A Novel of the Early Supreme Court.* Washington, D.C.: Kalorama Press, 2006.

Appendix
HISTORIC HOUSES ASSOCIATED
WITH THE WIVES OF THE SIGNERS

BASSETT

Bassett House, Dover, Delaware

The National Park Service has listed a house at 238 State Street as being acquired by Richard Bassett in 1804 at a foreclosure sale. It is unclear, however, as to whether or not the Bassetts ever actually lived there. The house is currently a private residence and not open to the public. See www.cr.nps.gov/history/online_books/constitution/site1.htm.

Bohemia Manor, Cecil County, Maryland

Lord Baltimore granted the original Bohemia Manor to Czech explorer and cartographer Augustine Herman in 1661 in return for his mapping the Chesapeake Bay. At least some of the property remained in the family until 2003. The original manor house, built about 1662, burned down soon after the deaths of Richard Bassett and his wife. The current manor house was built in 1920 by a Bayard descendant.

BEDFORD

Lombardy Hall, Wilmington, Delaware

The Bedfords purchased Lombardy Hall in 1786 and enlarged the existing house, moving there in 1793. After the death of Gunning Bedford Jr., his widow continued to live there until 1817, when the house was let. The heirs held the property until 1847. In 1889 part of the remaining twenty acres was converted into a cemetery, with the house becoming the caretaker's residence. Gunning Bedford was the first Grand Master of the Grand Lodge of Delaware, and in 1967 the Masonic fraternity bought the property, gradually restoring it. The house is open to the public by appointment. See granite-corinthian34.org/LH_History.html and www. cr.nps.gov/history/online_books/constitution/site4.htm.

BLAIR

John Blair House, Williamsburg, Virginia

The John Blair house, kitchen, and gardens are located within the colonial Williamsburg historic area. It is one of the oldest houses in the city, dating to the early eighteenth century. The house was restored in 1930. See www.history.org/ Foundation/journal/Spring06/blair.cfm.

BLOUNT

Blount Mansion, Knoxville, Tennessee

The mansion was built in 1792, one of the first frame houses west of the Alleghenies, for Mary Blount insisted on a "proper wooden house." It served as the territorial capital as well as the family home. The house remained in the family until 1827 and was later used as a residence for two mayors of Knoxville. During the Civil War, it became a hotel. In 1925 the house was slated for destruction as part of urban renewal, but the Blount Mansion Association was organized to save and restore the building. The house and its grounds are open to the public for an admission fee. See www.blountmansion.org.

Rocky Mount, Piney Flats, Tennessee

This is a large log cabin, built in 1772 by William Cobb, an early settler. It served as a temporary capital between 1790 and 1792 when the Blount family lived there. The house is currently a state-owned historical site. See www.rocky mountmuseum.com.

BROOM

Jacob Broom House (Hagley), Montchanin, Delaware

The four-and-one-half story, stone-stucco house, built about 1795, constitutes the north wing of a mansion known as Hagley. Broom sold the property in 1802 to E. I. DuPont, in whose family it still remains. The house is a private residence and is not open to the public. See www.nps.gov/history/history/online_books/constitution/site2.htm.

BUTLER

Although the Butler family owned extensive property in South Carolina, Georgia, and Philadelphia, it does not appear that any of the residences is extant.

CARROLL

The Carrolls were extensive landowners in Maryland and what eventually became the District of Columbia, but it does not appear that any of the residences has survived.

CLYMER

Summerseat, Morrisville, Pennsylvania

The house, built in the late eighteenth century, served as George Washington's headquarters in December 1776. It was owned from 1791 to 1798 by Robert Morris. George Clymer acquired the property in 1806 and resided there until his death in 1813. Restored in 1931 for use as a school administrative building, it is operated today as a museum and is open on the first Saturday of the month. Admission is free. See trees.ancestry.com/tree/12233591/person/121505144/media/1?pgnum=1&pg=0&pgpl=pid|pgNum and www.delawareandlehigh.org/index.php/visit/summerseat-historic-morrisville-society.

DAYTON

Boxwood Hall, Elizabeth, New Jersey

Built about 1750 for Elias Boudinot, president of the Continental Congress, the house was later sold to Jonathan Dayton, who made it his home from 1805 until his death in 1824. Extensively modified in 1870, the house was restored in the 1940s and turned into a museum that is open to the public. See en.wikipedia.org/wiki/Boxwood_Hall and www.getnj.com/historichouses/boxwoodelizabeth.shtml.

DICKINSON

Fair Hill, Philadelphia, Pennsylvania (no longer extant)

The mansion was built as a country estate by Isaac Norris in the early 1700s in the Northern Liberties section then north of Philadelphia. The British burned the house after the battle of Germantown, but it was restored by John and Mary Dickinson. The building was razed in the mid-nineteenth century when the property was developed for housing.

Poplar Hall, near Dover, Delaware

This house was the boyhood home and part-time residence of John Dickinson. Mary Dickinson never really cared for it and stayed there infrequently. The house was built in the mid-1700s by John Dickinson's father, Samuel. The British inflicted major damage on the house during the Revolutionary War, and it nearly burned down in 1804. The state of Delaware now owns the house, which is open to the public. See history.delaware.gov/museums/jdp/jdp_main.shtml.

Slate Roof House, Philadelphia, Pennsylvania (no longer extant)

The mansion was built around 1687 for merchant Samuel Carpenter and, after being used commercially starting in the eighteenth century, was demolished in 1867. In 1740, Mary (Polly) Norris Dickinson was born in the house, where her grandfather James Logan was then residing. During the Revolutionary War, it was the temporary residence of several prominent participants and members of the Continental Congress. In 1982 "Welcome Park," an urban courtyard, was erected on the site.

FEW

There do not appear to be any homes of the Nicholson or Few families extant.

FITZSIMONS

There do not appear to be any homes of the Meade or Fitzsimons families extant.

FRANKLIN

Franklin Court, Philadelphia, Pennsylvania

Franklin Court is the site of the home of Deborah and Benjamin Franklin. The house was demolished in 1812. The site contains a steel "ghost structure" outlining the house and includes a museum and other exhibits. See philadelphia.about .com/gi/o.htm?zi=1/XJ&zTi=1&sdn=philadelphia&cdn=citiestowns&tm=17& f=10&su=p554.21.342.ip_&tt=3&bt=1&bts=1&zu=http%3A//www.nps.gov/ inde/franklin-court.htm.

GORHAM

There do not appear to be any homes of the Call or Gorham families extant.

HAMILTON

The Grange, New York, New York

Now called Hamilton Grange, the house Alexander Hamilton built for his family (which was sold by his widow) is currently located in St. Nicholas Park at 141st Street, New York City. Completed in 1802, the house has been moved twice, most recently in 2008. It opened to the public at its new location in September 2011 and is open year-round, Wednesday through Sunday. See www.nps.gov/hagr/index.htm and en.wikipedia.org/wiki/Hamilton_Grange_ National_Memorial.

Hamilton-Holly House, New York, New York

The town house at 4 St. Marks Place was built in 1831 and in 1833 sold to Alexander Hamilton's son. For the next nine years, Elizabeth Schuyler Hamilton lived here with her son and his wife and her daughter Eliza and her husband, Sidney Holly. It is currently in use as a commercial building. See www.nyc.gov/html/lpc/downloads/pdf/reports/hamiltonholly.pdf.

Schuyler-Hamilton House, Morristown, New Jersey

In the winter of 1779–1780, Elizabeth Schuyler visited her aunt who lived in this house. It was here that Elizabeth met Alexander Hamilton. To save the house from demolition, the Morristown Chapter, Daughters of the American Revolution, purchased it in 1923 and opened it as a museum, which is open Sunday afternoons. See www.co.morris.nj.us/mchc/directory-museums.html#schuyler and rootsweb.ancestry.com/~njmcdar/SHHouse.htm.

Schuyler Mansion (The Pastures), Albany, New York

The house was built in 1761–1762 for Philip Schuyler, Elizabeth Hamilton's father. It was Elizabeth's childhood home and where she was married to Alexander Hamilton. After being used for an orphanage, the house was restored by the state of New York and dedicated as a historical site, which is open to the public. See nysparks.com/historic-sites/33/details.aspx and www.schuylerfriends.org/schuyler_mansion.html.

INGERSOLL

There do not appear to be any homes of the Pettit or Ingersoll families extant.

JOHNSON

William Samuel Johnson House, Stratford, Connecticut

The house, built in 1740 by Johnson's father, is on Main Street in Stratford. There is a historical marker in front of the house, which is currently being used as an office building. See www.hmdb.org/marker.asp?marker=25899.

KING

King Manor, Jamaica, New York

Rufus King bought the property in 1805 and the following year built a seventeen-room mansion, utilizing three existing structures. In 1897 the city of Jamaica acquired the property, which was later taken over by the city of New York. The King Manor Association of Long Island administers the mansion, which is open to the public. See kingmanor.org.

LANGDON

Governor John Langdon House, Portsmouth, New Hampshire

John Langdon built this house in 1784 while he was governor of New Hampshire, and the Langdons lived in it until their deaths. Other families then occupied the house until, at the end of the nineteenth century, Langdon descendants bought it and restored it to its eighteenth-century appearance. Now owned by Historic New England, the house is open to the public weekends from June to October for an admission fee. See www.historicnewengland.org/historic-properties/homes/gov.-john-langdon-house.

LIVINGSTON

Liberty Hall, Union, New Jersey

William Livingston built a fourteen-room house in 1772 on an estate he had acquired in 1760. During the family's first year of living in the house, Alexander Hamilton stayed with the family while a student at nearby Barber's Academy. The Livingstons' son Brockholst inherited the estate in 1790 and sold it eight years later. In 1811 a niece bought the estate, which remains in the family. Expanded in the nineteenth century, the house is now a fifty-room Italianate mansion. In 2007 the heir arranged with Kean University to give the school use and responsibility of Liberty Hall and to maintain it as a public museum and historic archive center. See www.kean.edu/libertyhall/home.asp.

MADISON

Dolley Madison House, Lafayette Square, Washington, D.C.

Dolley Madison's brother-in-law, Richard Cutts, then serving as comptroller of the Treasury, built the house in 1820. Eight years later, to clear his debts, Cutts sold the house to James Madison, who allowed the Cutts family to live in it until Anna Cutts, Dolley's sister, died in 1832. Dolley moved from Montpelier into the house in 1837 after the death of her husband. After Dolley's death in 1849, her son Payne sold the house, after which it had various owners. In the 1880s the Cosmos Club owned the house and made many changes to it. The federal government bought the house in 1940, leasing it back to the Cosmos Club until 1952. The Dolley Madison house is currently part of the U.S. Court of Appeals for the Federal Circuit.

Harewood, West Virginia

Harewood was built around 1770 for Samuel Washington, George Washington's half brother. Samuel's son, George Steptoe Washington, who married Dolley Madison's sister Lucy Payne, inherited the estate in 1781. Dolley married James Madison at the house in 1794. Still in the Washington family, the house is not open to the public.

Montpelier, Orange, Virginia

James Madison inherited the house, built about 1760, from his father in 1801. After earlier remodeling the house and upon completion of his second term as president in 1817, Dolley and James Madison moved into Montpelier. Madison died in 1836, and Dolley returned to Washington, D.C., to live. She sold Montpelier in 1844. Subsequently, various owners carried out extensive remodeling. In 1983 the house was bequeathed to the National Trust for Historic Preservation, and from 2003 to 2008 it underwent restoration. The mansion and grounds are open to the public. See www.montpelier.org.

Octagon House, Washington, D.C.

Colonel John Tayloe completed building this house on a triangular lot in 1800. Dr. William Thornton, first architect of the Capitol, designed it. After the British burned Washington during the War of 1812, Colonel Tayloe offered the

Octagon House to the Madisons as a temporary White House. They moved there in September 1814 and remained for about a year. It was here that James Madison signed the Treaty of Ghent, which ended the war. In the 1890s the American Institute of Architects acquired the building from the Tayloe family for its national headquarters and carefully restored it. The house is open to the public. See www.aia.org/conferences/green/AIAB082816?dvid=&recspec=AIAB082816 and www.cr.nps.gov/nr/travel/wash/dc22.htm.

Todd House, Philadelphia, Pennsylvania

John Todd and his wife, Dolley Payne Todd, lived in this house from 1791 to 1793. In the latter year, John Todd and his son William Temple both died during a yellow fever epidemic. Less than a year later, Dolley married James Madison. The house is open to the public; free tickets are available at the Independence Visitors Center. See www.nps.gov/inde/todd-house.htm and www.ushistory.org/tour/todd-house.htm.

The White House, Washington, D.C.

The cornerstone was laid in 1792 for the President's House, one of the first government buildings in the new capital. The Madisons moved here in 1809 but left in August 1814 when the British burned the house during the War of 1812. Restoration of the residence was completed in 1817 in time for James Madison's successor, James Monroe. The house was expanded and remodeled in 1824, 1829, the 1910s, and 1942. Tickets may be obtained in advance from one's congressman to tour the White House. See www.whitehouse.gov/ and www.cr.nps.gov/nr/travel/wash/dc31.htm.

MCHENRY

There do not appear to be any residences of the Allison, Caldwell, or McHenry families extant.

MIFFLIN

There do not appear to be any residences of the Mifflin or Morris families extant.

MORRIS, ANN CARY RANDOLPH

Tuckahoe Plantation, Virginia

The current house on Tuckahoe Plantation was built in two phases—1733 and 1740—by William Randolph. Before both he and his wife died, William named his friend Peter Jefferson and his wife, Jane Randolph (a cousin), as guardians to his children. The couple moved to Tuckahoe, along with their children, including young Thomas Jefferson, remaining until 1754. Thomas Mann Randolph, William's son, took over the plantation in 1757, and his daughter Ann Cary Randolph was born there in 1774. Still privately owned, Tuckahoe is open year-round for self-guided tours of the grounds and gardens. Tours of the house are by appointment. See www.tuckahoeplantation.com/ Tuckahoe_Plantation/Welcome.html.

MORRIS, MARY WHITE

There do not appear to be any Morris or White family homes extant. Also see Clymer.

PATERSON

White House Farm (Buccleuch Mansion), New Brunswick, New Jersey

Now known as Buccleuch Mansion, White House Farm was built in 1743 by Anthony White, Euphemia White Paterson's father, for his wife, Elizabeth Morris. Euphemia lived here until 1774. After having had several owners, the house and lands were deeded in 1911 to the city of New Brunswick as a park. The Jersey Blue Chapter, Daughters of the American Revolution, now takes care of the house, which is open Sundays, June through October, or by appointment. See www.rootsweb.ancestry.com/~njdar/Jerseyblue/mansion.html.

PINCKNEY, MARY ELEANOR LAURENS

Mepkin Plantation, Moncks Corner, South Carolina

Henry Laurens, father of Mary Eleanor Laurens, bought Mepkin Plantation in 1762, and it was the venue for her marriage to Charles Pinckney. The estate later passed through several hands, and in 1936 Henry R. and Clare Boothe Luce bought it. They created an extensive landscape garden. In 1949, the Luces donated a large part of the estate to Trappist monks, who now run Mepkin Abbey. The grounds are open to the public, but none of the original plantation houses exist. See south-carolina-plantations.com/berkeley/mepkin.html.

Snee Farm Plantation, Mount Pleasant, South Carolina

Charles Pinckney's father bought the property in 1754, and his son inherited it in 1782. Pinckney sold the house in 1817, and the house was demolished in 1824. Although there are no Pinckney-era buildings remaining, the National Park Service operates the site as the Charles Pinckney National Historical Site. See south-carolina-plantations.com/charleston/snee-farm.html and www.nps.gov/chpi/index.htm.

PINCKNEY, SARAH MIDDLETON

Hampton Plantation, Charleston County, South Carolina

Owned by relatives, Hampton Plantation was where Sarah and her children took refuge during the fall of Charleston. The family gave the plantation to the state of South Carolina in 1971, and it became a state historic site, which is open daily. See www.southcarolinaparks.com/hampton/introduction.aspx and south-carolina-plantations.com/charleston/hampton.html.

Middleton Place, Charleston, South Carolina

Henry Middleton, Sarah Middleton Pinckney's father, acquired the plantation through marriage in 1741, and it remained in the family for about 320 years. The house was built in 1755. During the Civil War, the plantation was ransacked. The main house and northern wing were burned beyond repair, and what remained was destroyed in the Charleston earthquake of 1886. The southern wing, less damaged, was restored after the war. In 1974 the heirs established the Middleton Place Foundation and the plantation became a living museum, which is open daily. See www.middletonplace.org.

Stenton, Philadelphia, Pennsylvania

Built between 1723 and 1730 by James Logan, secretary to William Penn, the home is currently operated as a museum by the National Society of the Colonial Dames. After the fall of Charleston, the Pinckneys took refuge here, sharing the house with the families of Thomas Pinckney and Edward Rutledge. The house remained in the Logan family until 1910 when it was acquired by the city of Philadelphia. It is open to the public. See stenton.org.

PINCKNEY, MARY STEAD

Charles Cotesworth Pinckney House, Charleston, South Carolina

Built in 1741, the house at 95 Bay Street is privately owned and not open to the public.

Pinckney Island, South Carolina

Charles Cotesworth Pinckney inherited the island, which then encompassed three plantations, from his father in 1758. From about 1804 until his death, Pinckney spent fall and spring on the island. Harriott Pinckney inherited the island upon the death of her father in 1825 and managed the plantations until about 1860. Union forces occupied the island during the Civil War and destroyed most of the buildings. After Harriott's death in 1866, the land was confiscated for back taxes but was regained by the heirs three years later, and the island remained in the family until 1937. After being used as a game preserve for a number of years, the island is now maintained as a wildlife refuge. It opened to the public in 1982. See www.fws.gov/pinckneyisland/.

READ

Stonum, New Castle, Delaware

This was the Reads' country home (now within the city limits), which George Read bought probably in the 1750s. Their principal residence in town burned down in 1824 and is now the site of the garden of their son George's house. Stonum began in 1730 with what is now the kitchen. The front was added prior to 1769 with later additions in 1850 and the 1920s. Flood damage prompted the Reads to sell the property in 1789. Now a private residence, Stonum is not open to the public. See www.cr.nps.gov/history/online_books/constitution/site5.htm and www.cityprofile.com/delaware/stonum.html.

RUTLEDGE

Grimke-Fraser House, 102 Tradd Street, Charleston, South Carolina

The site was acquired by Frederick Grimke in 1743 and became the childhood home of Elizabeth Grimke Rutledge. Following her father's death in 1778, Elizabeth's sister Mary Grimke Fraser inherited the property. Passing out of the family in 1847, the house was renovated and expanded in the mid-nineteenth century. It remains a private residence and is not open to the public.

John Rutledge House, 116 Broad Street, Charleston, South Carolina

John Rutledge built this house about 1763, when he married Elizabeth Grimke. He sold it in 1790. A third floor was added to the two-story house when it was remodeled in 1853. After passing through various owners, the house currently operates as an inn. See www.johnrutledgehouseinn.com/innoverview.aspx.

SHERMAN

There do not appear to be any residences relating to the Hartwell, Prescott, or Sherman families extant.

SPAIGHT

Clermont Estate, near New Bern, North Carolina

Built about 1735, the house was destroyed during the Civil War, but the family cemetery still remains.

Tryon Palace, New Bern, North Carolina

Royal governor William Tryon brought an English architect, John Hawks, from London to design the mansion, which was completed in 1770. It served as both the Tryon family home and as the first permanent capital of North Carolina. It served as the residence of North Carolina governors until 1794, and the Spaights lived there until fire destroyed the original building in 1798. An extensive thirty-year campaign to rebuild the palace and restore the grounds was undertaken by the citizens of New Bern, and the palace was reopened to the public in 1959. See www.tryonpalace.org.

WASHINGTON

The birthplace of Martha Dandridge, Chestnut Grove, burned down in 1926, and White House Plantation, where she lived with her first husband, Daniel Parke Custis, was destroyed during the Civil War.

Ford Mansion, Morristown, New Jersey

The house was built in 1774 by Jacob Ford, who died in January 1777, leaving his wife and four children. From December 1779 to June 1780, George Washington rented the house as his headquarters. Martha Washington spent the winter with him. Acquired by the Washington Association of New Jersey in 1873, the house is now operated by the National Park Service. See www.getnj .com/historichouses/fordmansionmorristown.shtml and www.nps.gov/morr/ planyourvisit/hours.htm.

Germantown White House (formerly the Deshler-Morris House), Philadelphia, Pennsylvania

The house was built in 1774. George Washington lived there during the yellow fever epidemic of 1793, conducting Cabinet meetings and other official business. The following summer Washington returned to live there with his family. Privately owned until 1948, the last family that lived there donated the house to the National Park Service. See www.nps.gov/demo/index.htm and www.ushistory .org/germantown/lower/deshler.htm.

Mount Vernon, Virginia

The house was begun in the first half of the eighteenth century by the Washington family. George Washington's brother Lawrence inherited it in 1740. After Lawrence died, George leased it from his widow, who had a lifetime right, and George inherited the estate after her death in 1761. In preparation for his marriage to Martha Custis, George enlarged and rebuilt the house. It was remodeled and enlarged again during the Revolutionary War and afterward. A nephew inherited the house upon the death of Martha Washington, and it remained in the family until 1858, when it was acquired by the Mount Vernon Ladies'

Association and restored. The house and grounds are open to the public for an admission fee. See www.mountvernon.org.

WILLIAMSON

There do not appear to be any homes relating to the Apthorp or Williamson families extant.

WILSON

Birdsboro Community Memorial Center, Birdsboro, Pennsylvania

The original house was built in 1751 (the central portion may have been built as early as 1737) by William Bird, Rachel Bird Wilson's father. He founded Hopewell Furnace, currently a historic site within the National Park system. The property was sold in 1796 to the owner of the Brooke Iron Company and Brooke Land Company. In 1921 the company deeded the Bird Mansion to the community for use as a youth center. Hurricane Agnes severely damaged the building in 1972, but the community rallied and restored it. The facility still operates as a center for the entire community. See bcmcbirdsboro.com.

James Iredell House, Edenton, North Carolina

James and Hannah Wilson took refuge in this house in 1798 after James Wilson was in danger of being imprisoned for debt and became ill. James Iredell was both a friend and a fellow Supreme Court justice. Hannah stayed with the Iredells to recuperate after her husband died in August. The earliest portion of the house was built in 1759 and was expanded in 1776 and 1810. Tours of the house are available through the Edenton Visitors Center. See www.ehcnc.org/history/iredellhouse.php.

Index

About the Author

Janice E. McKenney, a member of the District of Columbia Daughters of the American Revolution, is a military historian in Washington, D.C. Although most of her previous publications have been focused on artillery in the U.S. Army, she has been interested in early American history since childhood when her family used to visit historic sites in the Washington area and beyond. She took on this project, which had lain dormant for many years, as a special assignment.